Multilateral Development Banks

Ihsan Ugur Delikanli • Todor Dimitrov
Roena Agolli

Multilateral Development Banks

Governance and Finance

palgrave
macmillan

Ihsan Ugur Delikanli
Istanbul, Turkey

Todor Dimitrov
Thessaloniki, Greece

Roena Agolli
Thessaloniki, Greece

ISBN 978-3-030-08266-6 ISBN 978-3-319-91524-1 (eBook)
https://doi.org/10.1007/978-3-319-91524-1

Cover image: © RooM the Agency / Alamy Stock Photo
Cover design by Tjaša Krivec

Printed on acid-free paper

This Palgrave Macmillan imprint is published by the registered company Springer International Publishing AG part of Springer Nature.
The registered company address is: Gewerbestrasse 11, 6330 Cham, Switzerland

For our families and children as well as all children of the world.

Foreword

During several decades the benefits of multilateralism were taken for granted. This is no longer the case. In this context, *Multilateral Development Banks: Governance and Finance* is a very timely and valuable book that offers a rich description of Multilateral Development Banks (MDBs), an assessment of their roles, and a constructive critique with recommendations to enhance their contribution to the development agenda.

A useful taxonomy of 25 MDBs is proposed and applied for the analysis of these banks as a whole and by type of MDBs. Having worked for the three different types of MDBs considered in the book, I can attest that this classification makes sense.

This volume is an important contribution to the qualitative and quantitative knowledge about MDBs practices and standards. It addresses misconceptions concerning MDBs, provides a comprehensive review of governance and funding issues that constrain MDBs' effectiveness, and suggests means to overcome those constraints.

It is to be noted that Chap. 3 provides an adequate presentation of the important issue of additionality, whereas Chap. 5 presents a novel system of *MDB-specific governance principles,* which is used in an assessment and in identifying areas for improvement. It includes the standards developed for independent evaluation by the MDBs' Evaluation Cooperation Group (ECG), considering also other areas relevant for MDBs.

The book concludes with a discussion on the future of MDBs, providing ideas and suggestions for addressing complex problems, highlighting the importance of improving governance and strengthening independent evaluation, as well as the engagement with stakeholders and the promotion of synergies across MDBs. Thus it points out ways in which the MDBs can become more effective and efficient agents of change, playing a key role in shaping, implementing, and evaluating the development agenda.

Osvaldo Néstor Feinstein
Former manager and advisor at the World Bank, former senior evaluator and consultant for IFAD, former senior consultant with IADB, AfDB, CDB, and several UN and bilateral development agencies

Preface

Multilateral Development Banks: Governance and Finance is a novel, theory-inspired, and practice-based guide to the essence and prospects of Multilateral Development Banks (MDBs). It provides a comprehensive overview regarding virtually all MDBs, involved in lending for international socioeconomic development. With seven stand-alone chapters, the book represents insights on a wide range of often misconceived and unattended MDB aspects.

The analysis covers 25 MDBs worldwide to offer unprecedented understanding to a broad range of audiences who would be interested in the complexity and the prospects of these institutions. The MDBs are covered as a family and by groups, rather than presenting each one in detail. The grouping is based on geographical lending outreach and has three categories of MDBs: *Global, Regional, and Sub-regional.*

Unlike similar books and articles, which treat MDBs as banks, the authors offer a novel perspective by addressing the obscured specifics of multilateral lending institutions, revealing multiple aspects of their nature and operations, based on their unique self-regulation and governance. MDBs are addressed in a forward-looking manner, toward "knowledge banks", "change agents", and even "benchmark setters", diving into the very essence of the often elusive *additionality* (offering of a value that is additional to what is already available in the market). The variable elements of *additionality* make an MDB distinguished from any other institutions or banks.

The book's novelty and insight draw on relevant comparisons of the three regional groups of MDBs, with a focus on their governance and finance, to outline relative comparative advantages, among other key features. While criticism and reforms were addressed in the past, the book presents the importance of phased incremental elevations through an evidence-based advancement of values, human capital, and governance. This approach is in contrast with already known polar ad hoc pressures that led to various stop-and-go reform campaigns, associated with severe side effects such as "reform fatigue" and staff disengagement.

The book reflects on the key role of most MDBs in inspiring and advancing sustainable economic development through the transfer of knowledge and funding by addressing key global challenges. It provides a constructive elaboration on issues of recent criticism, such as opaque governance, domination by "donor" countries, controversial requirements and operations, and lack of inclusiveness. The bold calls for institutional reforms and the recent geopolitical and social turmoil in the world that have challenged multilateralism for development (among other post-war values) make the book timely and relevant, with a prospect to remain such for years ahead. Therefore, it is expected to constructively enhance the ongoing debate, involving a growing network of stakeholders, directly or indirectly, dealing with MDBs and their agenda (e.g. OECD and G20).

Originated by a team with experience at a relatively small MDB (the Black Sea Trade and Development Bank), the book presents a neutral position, backed by years of diverse experiences at/with numerous MDBs, providing a hands-on insider perspective. Utilizing their wide networks, as well as insight from working closely with peer MDBs, the authors offer analysis on a number of unexplored aspects, drawing from vast ex-post evaluation resources, reflecting the wealth of lessons learned at most MDBs. This makes the book a unique and hopefully inspiring source of knowledge on a wide range of standards and practices, for the benefit of practitioners, consultants, government officials, borrowers, and researchers.

The book is expected to be of particular interest and use to a very wide range of multilateral as well as bilateral organizations and stakeholders concerned with development. It should also become a key asset to academics and students with an interest in international finance and development. It may also be useful to members of the general public interested in the complex geopolitical context of international development and multilateralism, as they have never been more important, yet challenged. It is clear that rapid transformations are taking place toward political and social upheavals, driven by populism and nationalism, triggering unprecedented debate about the challenges of poverty, inequality, peace, and sustainability. This makes the MDBs particularly relevant and important, at a time when they are pressed to deliver deeper and wider, faster and better, with even more limited resources.

The opinions and positions expressed in the book belong to the authors and not to the institutions they are associated with. The authors take responsibility for all errors and omissions and acknowledge the importance of contributions by many other people.

The three authors worked jointly on the book upon the idea of Ihsan Ugur Delikanli. Their primary contribution is as follows:

Ihsan Ugur Delikanli: Chaps. 2, 3, 4, 6, 7.
Todor Dimitrov: Chaps. 1, 2, 3, 5, 6, 7, editing.
Roena Agolli: Chap. 2, index.

Credit for photograph of Todor Dimitrov (back flap): Kalina Dimitrova.

Istanbul, Turkey Ihsan Ugur Delikanli

Contents

List of Figures

List of Tables

1

Introduction

Rationale

Address Misconceptions, Clarify the Essence of MDBs

Despite existing publications and public discourse, the role, governance, and potential of Multilateral Development Banks (MDBs) remain obscured by fragmented and often inaccurate information. These institutions remain poorly understood, implying the need for an open, comprehensive, and balanced overview, going beyond history and data.

This book sheds light on a number of misconceptions regarding MDBs, widely spread not only among the public, but even among MDBs' stakeholders such as counterparts, shareholders, managers, and staff. These misconceptions include but are not limited to the following: (1) MDBs are UN agencies; (2) MDBs are aid/grant/subsidy funds; (3) all MDBs are subsidiaries of the World Bank; (4) MDBs are just international commercial/investment banks; and (5) MDBs provide a key share of financing in some countries but there are no tangible results.

Chapters 3, 4, and 5 (Financial Dynamics, Current Governance, and Governance Principles) constitute the core of the book, providing insight for the bumpy road ahead, outlined at the concluding Chap. 7 (The Future). These chapters provide a comprehensive review of multiple governance and funding issues that constrain MDBs' effectiveness, presenting seven novel governance principles (Chap. 5), followed by an assessment of reality against those principles.

I. U. Delikanli et al., *Multilateral Development Banks*,
https://doi.org/10.1007/978-3-319-91524-1_1

Compare Global, Regional, and Sub-regional MDBs

The book provides an overview of what the MDBs are often mistakenly assumed to be, in order to reveal and clarify their distinct nature and *modus operandi*, recent evolutions, toward future perspectives, covering all essential aspects, including the most recent challenges to institutional governance and finance. This is a timely and forward-looking response to the aggressive pressures on *multilateralism* and development, fuelled by contemporary tides of populism, nationalism, and protectionism, already affecting many MDBs and other international institutions.

Methodology

The book has a specific focus on recent waves of criticism and discontent with governance and results, both legitimate and ill-informed, that triggered ad hoc reforms, as well as a proliferation of "new", "green, lean, and clean" MDBs. The recent motion of creating "alternative" new MDBs is subject of a balanced assessment of pros and cons, with the ultimate objective of suggesting feasible improvements in both the "old" and the "new" generations of MDBs.

Approach

The book covers 25—virtually all—MDBs. While a reference to particular cases is used along with specific individual examples, the important institutional issues are approached in a forward-looking perspective, dealing with and comparing three groups of MDBs—*Global*, *Regional*, and *Sub-regional*—revealing their similarities, differences, strengths, and weaknesses. The goal of grouping and comparing is to perform "MDB family" mapping in order to suggest possible enhancements that are relevant for each respective group, as individual MDB approach would be less meaningful or efficient. Another goal is to make MDBs more aware of comparative advantages and potential to improve, toward becoming more synergetic and relevant to the pressing regional and global challenges of the future.

The methodology used in reviewing the 25 MDBs consists of an interdisciplinary process, integrating a number of interrelated components, outlined below. The issues covered by each chapter are addressed by extensive data reviews, as well as several rounds of peer-to-peer anonymous direct interviews with key MDB staff and management, focusing on the departments involved with institutional learning and memory—the *Independent Evaluation* departments. The analysis is also supplemented by interviews with key MDB borrowers, to reflect their perspective. Most interviews were conducted in the course of several years, within an ongoing MDB comparative research, covering 260 respondents from 19 MDBs.

The methodology, along with the main messages of each chapter, should remain informative and relevant in the years to come, as the focus is on how to improve MDBs' functioning, looking at the cross-cutting groups and issues. Hence, it is aimed at providing practice-based inspiration for further debate regarding the MDB evolution, with a particular attention on the need and obstacles to enhance old-fashion institutional governance, in the light of recent efforts of last generation MDBs to challenge the more traditional "old" development institutions (perceived as inefficient and donor-dominated).

Overall, the methodology constitutes an interdisciplinary mapping process, catalyzing insights from extensive reviews and discussions, involving the following key elements: (1) MDB categorization based on geographical outreach; (2) development and application of MDB-specific governance assessment framework (principles); (3) an assessment of the outreach and impact of MDBs, based on key ex-post evaluation results; (4) a financial assessment framework for MDBs, addressing inherent subsidies and privileges as unrecognized risk mitigation instrument; and (5) evaluating the accessibility of MDBs to borrowers through a borrower-based perspective. Details on the approach regarding these five elements are presented below.

Unlike existing research that treats MDBs as banks, hereby they are addressed by revealing the institutional aspects of their operations, going well beyond the *bank* concept—toward high-profile self-regulated *knowledge banks*, *change agents*, and franchise-based *standard setters*. These concepts involve relevant comparisons of the three regional groups of MDBs, with a focus on a feasible and sustainable governance-centered, rather than ad hoc, reform agenda. The goal is to improve all or most MDBs through an evidence-based advancement of values, management, staff, and governance, rather than already known polar pressures that resulted in various stop-and-go reform campaigns, triggering alarming staff disengagement and overall reform fatigue across most MDBs.

MDB Categorization

All MDBs are grouped by their regional coverage. This facilitates the process of understanding and improving different institutions, based on common denominators rather than extensive piecemeal approach. It is instrumental to demonstrate the similarities and differences among groups, as well as key issues and shortcomings without criticizing a particular individual institution. The ultimate goal is to offer feasible improvements that acknowledge MDBs as complex related institutions, providing *additional* value beyond mere finance, unlike conventional banks. This mainly refers to the provision of knowledge and *public goods*—hence arguing that MDBs are primarily knowledge banks and role models that should be treated very differently from any other financial institutions.

The categorization generally reflects the MDBs' size and ambition and is defined as follows:

1. *Global* MDBs lend to several continents, covering those almost entirely;
2. *Regional* MDBs lend to just one continent, covering it almost entirely;
3. *Sub-regional* MDBs focus on a specific region that is smaller than a continent.

Governance Assessment Framework

The very specific governance systems utilized by MDBs deserve central attention. For this reason, Chap. 4, dedicated to MDBs' Current Governance, followed by Chap. 5, which offers principles to elevate governance, are of specific importance. The latter chapter is based on a methodology involving a thorough process of reviewing and assessing respective governance systems against a set of principles, developed by the authors. This is done at group levels rather than at each MDB, but outlier cases are also addressed as a source of insight, from both negative (risk) and positive (potential) perspectives. Given the extensive experience and communication (including dedicated interviews over the past four years) of the authors in dealing with those governance systems within the MDBs, a particular attention is devoted to the less obvious but very important details and practices of implementing the governance rules, as they have substantial implications, rarely understood. The analysis is steered by a review of critical post evaluations at corporate/institutional levels, in order to derive common issues.

Chapter 5 (Governance Principles) presents the development and application of a unique governance assessment framework, specifically tailored to MDBs. This involves MDB-customized institutional matrices, addressing the role of two couples: formal/visible vs. informal/invisible practices at all levels measured against seven core principles. Hereby an outlier assessment is also instrumental in revealing and understanding borderline governance practices that could inspire improvements, with due respect of existing constraints and feasibility considerations such as the inherent complexity and inertia in multilateral dialogue.

Financial Assessments

The application of standard instruments of financial analysis (Chap. 3: Financial Dynamics) is enhanced by applying an assessment framework for the MDBs' financial performance, covering the complexity of their unique and poorly understood capital structure, risk mitigation, and institutional nature. This highlights the impact of important aspects such as *leverage*-based pricing and respective *additionality*-based premiums, inherent subsidies, and privileges, as well as linking financial resources with institutional safeguards and know-how, especially in a time when the latter is in the lead of providing a competitive edge. In this light, the financial resources, *leverage* and actual performance, are assessed in terms of their role and potential for multiplier effects, as the empirical evidence suggests that even the MDBs' combined financing is a tiny fraction of borrowing countries' GDP (under 1%). In other words, the concepts of *additionality* and *catalyzing* remain in the lead.

Borrower Perspective

The important perspective of the borrowers is covered by Chap. 6, revealing the various layers of the typical operational and approval cycle, often causing frustration among applicants. The ultimate goal is to help MDBs become more inclusive and user-friendly. The analysis is based on a mix of data sources, such as MDBs' policies, ex-post evaluation reports/studies, and interviews with actual and potential clients, as well as key front office staff—covering a period of 15 years and at least two MDBs in each group of institutions (*Global, Regional, Sub-regional*).

Structure of the Book

The book consists of seven chapters: 1. *Introduction*; 2. *The Nature of MDBs*; 3. *Financial Dynamics*; 4. *Current Governance*; 5. *Principles of Sound Governance*; 6. *Clients' Perspective*; 7. *The Future*. The chapters are related and naturally flow in that order. However, they also represent a stand-alone overview of the respective subjects. While the first two chapters are more descriptive, the other five are more analytical and forward-looking, balancing information with insight.

Chapter 2 contextualizes MDBs in terms of their institutional emergence, role, and evolution, starting with the broader issues of roots, categorization, and challenges. It groups the 25 MDBs into Global, Regional, and Subregional, to facilitate the scope of analysis. The nature of MDBs as complex public institutions is outlined, revealing common misconceptions. The review delves into a number of specific MDB conceptual features that are often poorly presented and understood—from the wider issues of multilateralism and development to the more specific political and extraterritorial dimensions, moving toward *knowledge bank* concepts.

Chapter 3 presents the complexity of MDB finance, revealing major differences with other institutions that may look similar, as well as across the three MDB groups. It covers capital formation, deployment and structure, borrowing and catalytic capacity, lending outreach and terms, as well as the importance of inherent subsidies, safeguards, *additionality*, credit ratings, and so on. While this chapter is inevitably more technical, it is written so that the wider public and policymakers can also grasp the key messages, if not all of the addressed financial metrics and concepts.

Chapter 4 goes beyond the mere description of typical MDB governance systems, as this issue is at the core of most MDB challenges and future evolution. It looks at multiple written and unwritten governance elements, identifying shortcomings and ill-based reforms that were often counterproductive, with the goal to highlight the way ahead.

Chapter 5 presents a set of novel MDB governance principles, developed by the authors. They cover virtually all aspects of governance, from the need to distinguish several Board roles and capacity, to the overshadowed importance of attracting, motivating, and nurturing the right mix of dedicated human capital. An assessment of governance against the new principles is also offered, to inspire possible improvements.

Chapter 6 is a reflection on the implications arising from key issues addressed so far from a very practical borrower perspective. In addition to an overview of the eligibility and application process, it also reveals issues of frustration and opacity that stem from an insufficient understanding of MDBs' complexity. Ultimately, the chapter aims at helping potential and actual clients, with a focus on private sector borrowers, to navigate the unchartered waters of MDB approval and project cycles.

The concluding Chap. 7 presents the actual and potential role of MDBs as agents of global change, as institutions with sustainable impact, beyond the mere objects of financing. This deals with their *raison d'être* and is built upon the main messages and conclusions of earlier chapters, suggesting how MDBs can better play this important role as a system of related institutions. Naturally, MDBs as knowledge institutions are addressed in relation to the independent evaluation function and the wealth of lessons registered, but not necessarily learned. The focus is on how MDBs may further excel in providing first-rank international leadership in high standards of norms and practices, across sectors and countries, beyond ideologies and politics—a worthwhile challenge. The chapter looks openly into the future of MDBs, in a global context, with direct reference to technological advancements and the *UN Sustainable Development Goals*, among other factors. It is a forward-looking reflection of all other chapters, suggesting a feasible and comprehensive reform agenda beyond the traps of the past. Key highlights include the need to elevate governance, improve the use of independent evaluation, enhance engagement with stakeholders, as well as ensure synergies across MDBs at a time of unprecedented technological and social shifts with high impact.

2

The Nature of MDBs

Introduction and Categorization

The chapter analyses the nature of Multilateral Development Banks (MDBs), revealing what makes these institutions specific and different from others. The important institutional issues are approached in a forward-looking perspective, dealing with and comparing three groups—*Global*, *Regional*, and *Sub-regional*—revealing similarities, differences, and some comparative advantages with the clear notion that regarding their categorization, they all belong to a complex system of public institutions. The categorization helps to perform *MDB family* mapping, allowing enhancements that are relevant for each respective group, as individual MDB approach would be less meaningful or efficient. A key goal is to reveal comparative advantages and potential to improve, toward becoming more synergetic and relevant to the pressing regional and global challenges of the future.

All MDBs are categorized in respect of their regional coverage. This facilitates the process of understanding similarities and differences among them, based on common denominators rather than extensive individual assessments. The regional classification generally reflects the MDBs' size and ambition and is defined as follows:

1. *Global* MDBs lend to several continents, covering those almost entirely;
2. *Regional* MDBs lend to just one continent, covering it almost entirely;
3. *Sub-regional* MDBs focus on a specific region that is smaller than a continent.

I. U. Delikanli et al., *Multilateral Development Banks*,
https://doi.org/10.1007/978-3-319-91524-1_2

This categorization is relative, as there are overlapping and border cases, arising from the dynamic nature of MDBs. While most MDBs naturally fall in those three categories, particularly those who directly target a continent such as the Asian Development Bank (AsDB) and African Development Bank (AfDB), there are some outlier institutions that are quite specific, targeting countries that are not necessarily belonging to one region/continent. The fluid nature of the classification means that its key role is to facilitate the analysis rather than push MDBs into watertight boundaries.

The MDBs' categorization, based on geographical lending outreach, is presented in Table 2.1.

Table 2.1 Classification of MDBs in terms of regional coverage by lending

Bank/Regional coverage	Established	Full name
Global		
World Bank		
IBRD	1945	International Bank for Reconstruction and Development
IFC	1956	International Finance Corporation
IDA	1960	International Development Association
IFAD	1977	International Fund for Agricultural Development
Regional		
CEDB	1956	Council of Europe Development Bank
EIB	1958	European Investment Bank
IDB	1959	Inter-American Development Bank
AfDB	1964	African Development Bank
AsDB	1966	Asian Development Bank
IsDB	1975	Islamic Development Bank
EBRD	1991	European Bank for Reconstruction and Development
NDB	2014	New Development Bank (formerly referred to as the BRICS Development Bank)
AIIB	2015	Asian Infrastructure Investment Bank
Sub-regional		
CABEI	1960	Central American Bank for Economic Integration
EADB	1967	East African Development Bank
CDB	1969	Caribbean Development Bank
CAF	1970	Development Bank of Latin America (formerly referred to as the Corporación Andina de Fomento)
IIB	1970	International Investment Bank
BADEA	1973	Arab Bank for Economic Development in Africa
WADB	1973	West African Development Bank
NIB	1976	Nordic Investment Bank
PTA	1985	Eastern and Southern African Trade and Development Bank or the Preferential Trade Area Bank
BSTDB	1997	Black Sea Trade and Development Bank
ETDB	2005	Economic Cooperation Organization Trade and Development Bank
EDB	2006	Eurasian Development Bank

Source: Authors' compilation

It is noteworthy that this classification is not absolute, as there are several overlapping and border cases, often arising from the dynamic nature of MDBs. While some MDBs such as the AsDB and AfDB directly fall into the regional group, some outlier institutions are not so easy to categorize. Good examples of outlier cases are the European Bank for Development and Reconstruction (EBRD), the European Investment Bank (EIB), the Islamic Development Bank (IsDB), and the New Development Bank (NDB):

1. EBRD's mandate focuses on the former communist countries but since recently it also covers Turkey, Greece, and even parts of Africa. Due to the wide scale/coverage that is deemed equivalent to a continent, EBRD falls in the *Regional* group.
2. Likewise, the EIB, the infrastructure finance arm of the EU, is focused on the EU member states but also invests elsewhere—in African, Pacific, and Caribbean countries. It is also noteworthy that the EIB, like a few other MDBs, is not exactly a "Development" Bank, except in the recently originated activities outside the EU. With all these in mind, the EIB also belongs to the *Regional* group, as its geographical scope is considered equivalent to a continental coverage.
3. The IsDB invests in many countries across the world and is therefore not focused on a specific region, but still comes short in having a global coverage in terms of two or more entire continents and therefore falls in the *Regional* group as well.
4. The NDB covers just a few countries (BRICS—Brazil, Russia, India, China, and South Africa) across different continents. However, as those countries are particularly large and do not fit a specific sub-region, it also falls in the *Regional* group.

These examples illustrate the overlapping and relative nature of the categorization, implying that it is utilized to facilitate the analysis rather than to assume absolute boundaries across the three groups.

The Bretton Woods Institutions

By the late 1930s and early 1940s, the concept of economic development in the contemporary sense began to emerge. The economic and social needs of the post-war world were primarily addressed by the prominent British economist John Maynard Keynes, inspiring policy makers. Harry Dexter White, an American economist, was a key figure in envisioning the set of institutions that had to be created over the visions of John Maynard Keynes. In 1942, White paved the path toward the fundamentals of a development policy as he prepared a proposal for a "United Nations Stabilization Fund and a Bank for Reconstruction and Development of the United and Associated Nations" which would provide the basis for post-war international monetary reform (Anderson-Gold 2011).

White considered the Keynes' principles from a more general perspective and used them in the US proposal to suggest national and international policies that would (1) foster economic growth by encouraging international economic and monetary cooperation through the stabilization and regulation of the national systems of exchange rates and (2) encourage economic and social security in war-torn areas of Europe through rebuilding economic and financial infrastructure throughout massive supply of capital that will be needed for reconstruction, relief, and economic recovery (Stiglitz 2003).

The proposal called for the creation of two related institutions with resources, powers, and structure adequate to meet the major post-war needs. For international currency matters, the International Monetary Fund (IMF) was to be established, which would recommend and enforce rules to install a system of convertibility of currencies and ensure a degree of exchange-rate stability—indispensable for a multilateral system of payments and trade. For assisting the economic development and reconstruction of post-war Europe, the International Bank for Reconstruction and Development (IBRD) was to be established—broadly recognized as the World Bank, with the purpose of providing funding and technical assistance for the economic reconstruction of war-ravaged areas of Europe, mainly by encouraging capital inflows into the region from surplus countries (Lipscy 2015).

In 1944, the United Nations Monetary and Financial Conference took place at the Mount Washington Hotel in Bretton Woods, New Hampshire. The broadly referred to as Bretton Woods Conference agreed to regulate the international monetary and financial problems after the conclusion of the World War II, and sealed the negotiation for the establishment of the World Bank and the IMF. The agreement is a milestone toward more orderly international relations and multilateralism on a global scale and toward having agencies predominantly adapted to maintain such relationships. The United States, of course, was and still is a dominant element.

With the Congress' approval of the Marshall Plan in 1948, the US preeminence was confirmed (Bordo and Eichengreen 2007). The organizational patterns of the IMF and the IBRD gave birth to a new track of thought—development diplomacy, where the American role was critical.

Proliferation: Global, Regional, and Sub-regional

The World Bank and the IFAD

Established in 1944, the World Bank is the world's largest provider of development finance, which lends worldwide to more than a hundred countries in several continents. Many of the features that were implemented and recognized in the context of the World Bank became a standard for most of the other MDBs set up later on.

From the outset, the World Bank was an institution which was to be owned and whose capital would be provided by governments. The commencing authorized capital ($10 million) comprised 20% paid-in capital or seed money and 80% callable or guaranteed capital. The callable capital worked as guarantee fund against which the World Bank could borrow commensurately large amounts in the international capital markets. Albeit, this was not as a matter of fact paid by the member countries, it still determined the credit rating of the Bank (Culpeper 1997).

The capital structure, which evolved under the aegis of the World Bank, became a cornerstone of the international financial system. It was considered as a mechanism to secure the obligations to the bondholders in the capital market to a guarantee by shareholders to pay off the needed amount to the full value of bonds outstanding. Thus, the bonds issued by the World Bank depended on the implicit guarantee of the shareholders, rather than on the loan repayments of the borrowing countries. Given the innovative side of this mechanism, during the 1950s, the World Bank managed to successfully raise money on the international capital markets, even though it was quite modest in size and lent to few countries that could afford the market interest rate (Harriss 2002).

With the increase in the scale and complexity, the World Bank established several affiliated institutions. The first addition was the International Financial Corporation (IFC) in 1956, which was created to supplement the IBRD's governmental orientation, by lending to private corporations, usually together with other investors. The second addition was the International Development Association (IDA)—created in 1960 to offer concessional or soft lending to government and private sector firms in low-income countries.

The establishment of IDA as one of the principal component of the World Bank Group[1] shifted the balance of power between shareholders and management in the World Bank. The IBRD was funding its lending operations primarily by selling low-interest, high-rated bonds, backed by prudent financial policies and strong financial support of their members. The accumulated funds were then on-lent at slightly higher interest rate with relatively long maturities (15–20 years) to creditworthy countries. However, concessional loans of IDA had an interest rate of zero or less than 1% and were made on terms up to 40 years, usually with a 10-year grace period. As the funds for concessional lending could not be obtained from private markets, member countries made direct contributions to fund IDA, causing the balance of power between shareholders and management to shift to donor members.

Along with the World Bank, the International Fund for Agriculture Development (IFAD) is a global international financial institution and specialized agency of the United Nations, providing development finance worldwide. Although IFAD is an outlier as noted in Chap. 1, it is included in the categorization of MDBs, as it has recently started to borrow from the international financial markets, essentially operating as an MDB. The agency was established in 1974 at the World Food Conference in Rome, in the wake of a global food shortage, which caused widespread famine, especially in the African countries. Three years after the Rome conference, IFAD was set up as an international financial institution. Since then, it has specialized in financing agricultural development projects aimed at food production in developing countries (Mosley and Hulme 2006).

The Regional MDBs

The members of regional MDBs are regional developing countries and donor countries, which can be both regional and non-regional. These institutions were modeled around the IBRD concept, to lend to one continent, covering it almost entirely. Two significant factors triggered the creation of these MDBs. The first one was the aspirations of developing and/or financially distressed countries for greater regional autonomy and economic stability, by addressing regional and national needs. The second one was the US geopolitical and geoeconomic strategic interest during the Cold War. The latter factor was crucial for overcoming the US defiance toward the establishment of the Inter-American Development Bank (IDB) and the AsDB. The respective response of the Soviet Bloc countries, who did not participate in IBRD or the follow-up regional MDBs, was to create in 1963 their own sub-regional MDB (The Moscow-based International Bank for Economic Cooperation, still operating today as the International Investment Bank [IIB]).

In Latin America, the proposal for a regional Inter-American Bank predated the idea for the World Bank. Latin American countries requested the

United States' help to improve the international cooperation in the region at the First International American Conference in Washington DC, in 1890. However, their demands for greater development financing were only answered in 1959, as a response to the US concerns about the spread of communism in the repercussions of the Cuban revolution (Santiso 2000).

The initiative for the IDB came from politicians who were advocating for cooperation and integration in regional forums, established by developing nations to discuss solutions for the marginalized nations in the post-war world order. The establishment of the IDB was ratified by 18 countries (the United States and 17 regional members). The United States was the largest shareholder of the IDB, controlling 42% of the voting power. In the 1970s, Canada and then non-regional countries, such as Japan and European countries, were admitted as non-borrowing or donor members. Unlike the World Bank where the voting share was heavily weighted in favor of developed nations, the IDB provided in its establishing articles that the voting share of regional developing countries could not be less than 50% of the total. The IDB was granted a built-in soft-loan facility, known as the Fund for Special Operations (FSO), and in 1986, the Inter-American Investment Cooperation (IIC) was established as a private sector affiliate, analogous to the IFC in the World Bank, focusing on financing of small- and medium-sized enterprises (Ocampo 2007).

In the interim, two regional MDBs emerged in Europe, the Council of Europe Development Bank (CEDB) in 1958 with an exclusively social mandate (dealing with problems of refugees and displaced people in Europe after the World War II) and the EIB, the European Union's long-term lending institution established in 1958, to facilitate the European integration and supplement the IBRD in offering market-based loans for infrastructure, sustainable development, and private sector development. Both MDBs were borrower-led and did not accommodate non-borrowing or donor shareholders, as a main difference to IBRD.

In contrast to the IDB, the initiative for the AsDB came from a relatively developed donor country—Japan, who had a prevalent influence by tradition. The AsDB came with an explicit mandate to foster economic growth and cooperation in Asia by investing in potentially viable projects in infrastructure. By 1974, a concessional loan facility was established—the Asian Development Fund (AsDF), the general purpose of which was to lend to low-income countries in the region.

The most distinguishing feature in the organizational dynamics of the AsDB is its strong Japanese influence. It was the only MDB at that time where the United States has been co-dominant with another shareholder (upon inception, the United States and Japan had each 17.1% of the votes; later declining to 12.7%). In order to preserve the Asian influence, the AsDB's charter requires at least a 60% voting majority for regional members, including non-borrowing nations—Australia, Japan, and New Zealand. As such, the AsDB has always been classified as a donor-dominated institution (Kilby 2006).

The AfDB was funded entirely by borrowing members. Its initiative came from Africa, and for the first 18 years, membership at AfDB was restricted only to African countries. The founders believed that the admission of non-regional donor members would endanger the ownership and governance, and also threaten the newly gained independence of the African countries. Such a view is still valid for some of the newer MDBs with a particular reference to sub-regional ones, addressed further.

The absence of a developed member in the region divested the AfDB of funds. South Africa was the only exception, but its membership was proscribed until 1995 on account of its apartheid policies. Soon after its foundation, it became a conundrum to raise the financing resources in the international capital markets based on the African callable capital subscription. Eventually, the AfDB fettered itself to lending only out of its paid-in capital. Originally its authorized capital was $250 million, nearly one half of which was expected to be paid-in capital—but only $52.6 million was actually paid in, which shrunk the lending potential and credibility even further.

In the early 1970s, having come to the conclusion, that it was better to gambit some measure of autonomy with the purpose of building a more influential institution, the AfDB started discussions to open membership to non-regional countries. In 1973, a concessional financing facility, known as the AfDF, was created to direct concessional resources from donor countries to the region. The AfDF was inaugurated with $82.6 million in grants from 13 non-regional members (mainly Japan and Canada). Despite intense polemics among the African members, the voting power in the AfDF was split 50–50 between regional and non-regional members.

By 1992, 25 non-regional countries, including the United States, had received the assent to membership in the AfDB and controlled 35.5% of the voting share, while regional members accounted for a majority of 64.5%. Developing member countries held a voting majority, but in fact, the developed country minority shareholders controlled access to resources and capital increases and replenishments.

In the early 1970s, substantial progress was made in the field of regional financial cooperation even in the Arab region with the establishment of the IsDB in 1974. The capital was subscribed in a new account currency, the Islamic Dinar (ID), and at its inception, the 22 member countries contributed a capital of ID 2 billion. Since then, the IsDB has increased its membership to 57 countries, spanning four continents (Europe, Asia, Africa, and Latin America). Consequently, the IsDB has upgraded its mandate to currently offer low-cost financing to Arab and non-Arab member countries with Muslim communities in the developing world that belong to the Organization of the Islamic Conference. It provides soft lending facilities through special programs, such as the Islamic Solidarity Fund for Development (ISDF) (Ocampo 2007).

At the beginning of the 1990s, the rationale for development finance evolved as many Eastern and Central European countries started a painful transition from centrally planned to market economies. The transition opened up a new development page for old and new MDBs. Almost immediately following the end of the Cold War, international development experts agreed to expand development to include activities and policies toward establishing and safeguarding political freedoms. Furthermore, increasing sentiments toward irreparable ecological damage as a by-product of economic development led to a vocal environmental movement that required another added aspect to development—the sustainable development, with respective environmental safeguards (Babb 2009).

In 1991, the EBRD was established, following an initiative of France to outspread its democratic values in Central and Eastern Europe that had already begun a transition to market-oriented economies. As the EBRD is financing development projects that serve the transition agenda, it introduced very novel features into the world of MDBs—by explicitly adopting a political mandate. More specifically, EBRD was established to foster democracy through economic development by providing resources that functioned as means toward change and reforms, while curtailing or cutting funding, if there was a lowering of democratic principles or retracing on reforms of a country. Resource distribution has a business-driven orientation, focusing on private and public sectors; hence EBRD did not open a concessional lending facility. In addition to its economic mandate, the EBRD's charter was distinctive in holding an environmental mandate, which required it to "promote in the full range of its activities environmentally sound and sustainable development".

Since its outset, EBRD has been a Western-European-led organization with the United States as the largest single shareholder (10% voting share). The members from the European Union, along with two institutional shareholders (the EU itself and the EIB), are collectively controlling 51% of the shares. Modifications in the articles of agreement require an 85% majority, meaning that no single country has a veto, unless it acts together with another country. EBRD is a donor-dominated institution, but as countries graduate and cease borrowing eligibility, the voting share between borrowing and non-borrowing countries changes frequently (Bastøe and Hanse 2015; Babb 2009).

In the recent years, China and four other large countries have established two new, somewhat alternative MDBs: (1) the NDB founded by Brazil, the Russian Federation, India, the People's Republic of China, and South Africa (collectively known as BRICS countries) in 2014 and (2) the Chinese-led Asian Infrastructure Investment Bank (AIIB) in 2015. Both MDBs aspire to introduce a new more efficient and inclusive model, described as "lean and clean" by AIIB. Although they are not fully operational yet, their initial focus is on providing sustainable development funds mainly in infrastructure, as well as in social sector projects, through non-concessional loans, in a simplified manner, friendly to borrowers. However, despite this claim, even China continuous to borrow more from the IBRD, rather than from the AIIB.

For several years, China had contended that international financial institutions have failed to acknowledge China's stature in the international economic affairs, as the second largest global economy in terms of nominal GDP. Some observers have linked the creation of the AIIB to the inefficiency of the current Bretton Woods international finance infrastructure, especially to the long delay in US approval of the IMF reforms (it took five years to finally approve, among others, in 2015, an increase of China's capital contributions and voting power in the IMF). Others associate the emergence of AIIB with China's aspiration to take over strategic and economic influence in the continent from Japan—the Asia's established power, at the helm of AsDB. Despite opponent and ambivalent voices, Japan and United States joining the AIIB in the future would help expand and improve the process of economic development of countries in the region, given the extensive experience of these countries in the field, as they do already with the AsDB, where the United States and Japan are co-dominant shareholders (Yu 2017).

Like the AIIB and in contrast to the rest of MDBs, the NDB was designed as an alternative to the World Bank and the IMF, two institutions in which the BRICS countries have long pushed for more influence. The BRICS countries constitute a fundamental part of the global economy, which in the last two decades have represented the cutting edge of emerging economies with regard to capital market development and economic growth. Their total nominal GDP by 2050 (excluding South Africa) is anticipated to surpass $128 trillion, parallel to the $66 trillion of the G7 countries. Over the next 15 years, these countries are expected to account for 43% of the world's market capitalization (Mensi et al. 2014). However, their controlling shares, in the IMF and the World Bank, reflect more the realities in the aftermath of World War II than the present time. The BRICS could increase their voting shares by appropriating financial contributions in these two institutions, but the veto power of the United States blocks this possibility. Consequently, BRICS have chosen to pursue influence in the global economy through the NDB.

NDB has announced distinctive features which join together the tasks of both the IMF and the World Bank into one institution. On the one hand, it provides infrastructure financing to its five BRICS members and other developing countries. On the other, it offers emergency reserves to its member countries, similar to the IMF's emergency lending.

Each of the five founding member countries holds 20% voting share. The Articles of Agreement specify that all members of the United Nations could join. However, the share of the BRICS nations can never be less than 55% of voting power, shared equally among them, while any prospective members will equally split the remaining 45%.

The Sub-regional MDBs

While regional MDBs have a specific focus on continents, not sufficiently covered by global institutions, their sub-regional peers offer flexible financial and technical support to local development efforts and operate on a considerably smaller scale and scope. They assist a group of borrowers that have in common geographical or other characteristics. Sub-regional MDBs focus on the growth, cooperation, and development of their member countries. While being modeled around the experience and concept of the other MDBs, the sub-regional institutions provide financing and knowledge for tangible investment projects in public and private sectors and are generally not involved in policy lending and conditionality. Furthermore, they typically have a strong sub-regional ownership, with some cases not having any non-borrowing country as a member, aiming to avoid external political influence.

There are three arguments which support the creation of sub-regional MDBs. The first relates to the virtue of complementarity that these institutions provide to the global and regional MDBs. Due to smaller information asymmetries in sub-regions, given proximity and close economic links, the sub-regional MDBs are better placed to capture the idiosyncrasies of their member countries and respond to their specific needs and context. Hence, they play a significant role in the adoption of international practices and norms to sub-regional conditions, through significantly reduced costs. The second argument is of a "federalist" nature. These siblings of the major MDBs are particularly appreciated for small- and medium-sized countries, which are unlikely to gain enough influence and negotiation power in global and regional institutions. The final argument is efficiency—the aimed advantage of more flexible and timely disbursements of loans to member countries. Such a comparative advantage is based on the generally softer aspects of otherwise MDB-inherent conditionality. With the advent of policy-based lending in the 1980s, after the years the debt-crisis, both the World Bank and regional MDBs (where the United States is an important donor, except at the AfDB), conditioned project loans on sound economic reforms. Such lending conditionality turned unduly harsh for small, low and middle-income countries.

Latin America and the Caribbean indisputably offer the best illustration of a well-developed network of sub-regional institutions: the Central American Bank for Economic Integration (CABEI), the Development Bank of Latin America, formerly referred to as the Corporación Andina de Fomento (CAF), and the Caribbean Development Bank (CDB). These institutions were established in the 1960s with the purpose of facilitating financial integration and cooperation in their respective sub-regions by promoting economic growth and sustainable development. They adopted the same organizational dynamics as the global and regional MDBs, and incorporated both borrowing and non-borrowing members. Nonetheless, their membership composition generally maintains a strong sub-regional identity: member countries of geopolitical importance in the sub-region obtained the large majority of shares and voting power.

Integration efforts in Africa have also led to the design of an African network of sub-regional MDBs, consisting of four major institutions, the East African Development Bank (EADB), the Arab Bank for Economic Development in Africa (BADEA), the West African Development Bank (WADB), and the Eastern and Southern African Trade and Development Bank, commonly referred to as the Preferential Trade Area Bank (PTA). In their formal structure, they have similar stated functions which vary little, reflecting the similar characteristics of their respective sub-regions. The environment within which these MDBs had to evolve has similar identity in terms of development needs, requiring cooperation across institutions and countries to facilitate regional economic integration among member states and other parts of Africa. In particular, they engage in financing the construction of roads, power plants, dams, airports, hospitals, telecommunication infrastructure, and embryonic industries, such as micro, small, and medium enterprises in support of industrialization.

The last wave of sub-regional MDBs operates in the Euro-Asian area. The IIB is among the first, established in 1970 to finance cooperation among Soviet Bloc countries, recently transformed into an institution without such reference. It was previously recognized as the International Bank for Economic Cooperation and started as the investment bank of the Eastern Bloc. Its member states include either ex-socialist or socialist countries. Its current existence is a proof that once established MDBs do not disappear, but rather transform and evolve. Other sub-regional MDBs in the Euro-Asian area include the Nordic Investment Bank (NIB, 1976), the Black Sea Trade and Development Bank (BSTDB, 1997), the Economic Cooperation Organization (ECO) Trade and Development Bank (ETDB, 2005), and the Eurasian Development Bank (EDB, 2006).

Unique Institutions

Unlike other institutions or banks, MDBs follow a unique process of establishment and functioning. They are typically set up by a *multilateral agreement* among several (founding) member states. This creates a collective principal (shareholder governments) and agent (MDBs) relationship. *International development* is the other intrinsic aspect of these institutions and is therefore addressed from different angles by this and other chapters, highlighting key stakeholder perspectives that were often neglected by the public discourse, as well as conflicting perceptions of development, aid vs. lending, inclusiveness and transparency, and so on.

In contrast to any other banks, MDBs have a specific public development mandate—their *raison d'être*. This makes them intrinsically different from any other financial institutions. The MDBs are driven by their mandates to engage in complex programs of activities focusing on the development of regions and sectors of importance.

The *modus operandi* of MDBs is generally similar across them, with some variations. It defines these institutions by their unique role and approach, governance and decision-making, product mix, and special supranational extraterritorial status. This implies a complex process of *target activities* and *internal policies* that address the respective public mandates. Although MDBs may articulate their mandates in different ways, their roles and instruments are quite similar. Mandate compliance and execution are done through a wide range of products and operations, constituting a variety of financial, knowledge, coordinating, convening, and catalytic services.

The specific *modus operandi* includes a preferential treatment status of MDBs, usually justified by the obligation to ensure additionality (to what other lenders already offer), in order to address market failures and asymmetric supply of public goods. The special status involves explicit and implicit subsidies, self-regulatory framework, preferential access to foreign exchange reserves, preferred creditor treatment, legal ex-territoriality, immunity, and so on. To this end, the rather common reference to MDBs as ordinary financial institutions is very misleading and should be avoided, despite that their names include the word “bank”. It is more appropriate to think these complex institutions as *knowledge banks*, or highly complex lending institutions, whose operations extend well beyond finance, and whose main asset, so critical for delivering their mandates, is a very rare mix of human capital and institutional values.

Rationale for Membership

An important aspect of the unique nature of MDBs is the very rationale for their establishment. Simply speaking, it is based on the need for a multilateral approach to resolve complex issues that cannot find a solution by conventional means such as bilateral and national efforts. A key driver for the creation of MDBs is that *borrowing member countries* benefit from membership by obtaining access to financing on better terms than they could from commercial lenders (or, for some countries, when they have no access to commercial lenders). In addition, in times of financial stress, MDBs often lend when commercial lenders hesitate. The poorest and least creditworthy members, who cannot borrow from MDBs, typically access the soft-loan windows of some of these institutions. Since loans from soft-loan windows are at concessional rates, countries that are eligible and borrow from them benefit from an inherent subsidy directly. Furthermore, MDBs are typically an important source of impartial financial and technical advice and often play the catalytic role of standard setting and risk sharing, to lead the way of private investors in regions of certain hardship.

The benefit to donor countries (non-borrowing members) is primarily political. MDBs serve as a vehicle to promote their interest and influence in the area, by propagating “appropriate” socioeconomic policies for sustainable development, based on a system of values translated into conditionality and safeguard frameworks, requiring borrowers to comply with standards and practices on a wide range of issues, from economic policy to environment and corporate governance. The financial rationale for donor countries is the MDBs’ ability to fund themselves in the capital markets, ensuring leverage to the allocated financial resources by means of capital contributions or grants.

Why Multilateral?

To address complex issues, sovereign states share and delegate their authorities to the institutions they set up. Hence MDBs act as agents (Hawkins et al. 2006; Vaubel 2006), similar to firms in economics and bureaucracies in public administration and politics. Member countries, in their capacity of shareholders, establish an MDB-specific supranational jurisdiction and delegate authority to MDBs as special status agents in order to solve specific problems reflecting their own interests. This principal-agent relationship is at the core of the multilateral supranational nature of MDBs (a relationship often used by the theory of international relations, creating international organizations as independent authorities with own jurisdiction that supersedes national norms).

The essence of *Delegation involves* an actor A, who (conditionally) designates another actor (the MDB agent or body) to make a decision or take an action on behalf of A (Hawkins et al. 2006). This implies a set of rules that determine both the property and authority rights, known as rights of ownership in economics. In the complexity of public policy, these rules are *constitutions or statutes* that determine delegation of authority. In a similar manner, legislators obtain the authority to make laws while courts to resolve disputes. The sovereignty of countries implies that states are the primary decision-making authority. In this capacity, they are the actors that delegate authority internationally, including to MDBs who act as semi-autonomous agents. Member countries, acting as the *principal* (unilateral or multilateral), delegate authority to MDB (the agent), as illustrated by Fig. 2.1.

The countries, acting as principals, typically represented by the MDB Board of Governors, have a hierarchical relationship with the MDB (agent) and possess the ultimate authority. Consequently, the agents (*MDBs*) are the

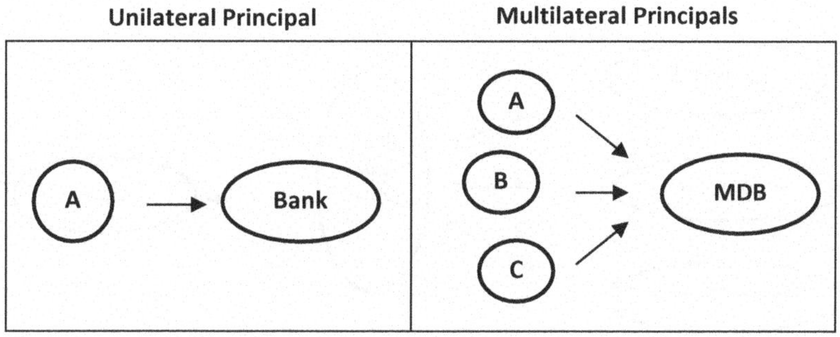

Fig. 2.1 Unilateral and multilateral principles

actors who are hired and subordinated to the principals, to perform tasks in their name and expense. This naturally involves a delegation contract, implying certain conditions of control, asymmetry, conflicts of interest, and so on (Moe 1984). The case of MDBs is complex as there are *multiple principals* who delegate to an agent of special status (Kiewiet and McCubbins 1991). In this case, the MDB as an agent has a single contract with a principal composed of more than one actor as *multilateral (known as collective) principal*, represented by the Board of Governors and further delegated to Board of Directors (BoD and BoG), as illustrated by Fig. 2.2. This multilateral principle takes decisions jointly—within the BoG of an MDB.

Members of a *multilateral principal* cannot act independently as they need an agreement before issuing authoritative directions to their agent (MDB). Members collectively hold a single contract with the agent, and no individual member is able to alter the contract unilaterally. In order to alter their contract (establishing agreement of an MDB) with the agent, members of a collective principal must act as a group, typically by a majority vote, forming a *voting coalition.*

The complexity of multilateral principals implies principal-agent problems of obscured information or activity. This represents various challenges for members to coordinate and monitor contracts, screen, select, and sanction management, as well as redesign administrative policies and procedures.

Analysts often presume that a multilateral principal such as electorate can act as one. This assumption is flawed because collective bodies often are constrained by coordination dilemmas. Collective-action problems in delegation settings are typical for MDBs, due to the very complexity of the combination of multilateral, as well as the principal-agency relationships. This is the core reason for BoG and BoD of MDBs to over-delegate authority, as a measure of minimizing coordination and information issues, among others such as capacity (as addressed by Chaps. 4 and 5).

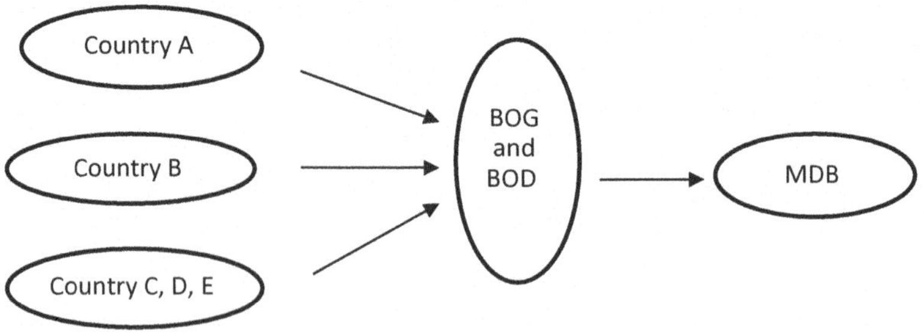

Fig. 2.2 Multilateral delegation

The case of hybrid principals (Auerswald et al. 2006) combines the collective and multiple principal forms, as there are at least two principals, each with its own delegation contract to the agent. At least one of the principals is a collective entity, for example, when one MDB is a member shareholder of another.

MDBs are institutions with a multilateral principal-agent relationship, as they are established with a contract among three or more sovereign states—referred to as *Multilateral Agreement* or *Treaty*, giving the first word of the MDB acronym.

While many authors compare the voting power of member states (required for key decisions of an MDB such as loan approval) with the decision process within a joint stock company, these are fundamentally different. First, member countries negotiate shares and voting rights in MDBs upon entry, usually to be proportional to the respective contributions of *paid-in capital*. Second, some countries often have their own representatives on the BoD, while others have to share a director (see Chap. 4).

The staff and management of an MDB typically develop projects in consultation with potential borrowers (public or private), to be approved by the BoD. In theory, the Board takes a decision by majority but in practice, it formally approves all presented projects without actual voting, with some very rare exceptions. This constitutes another layer of de facto delegation, driven by the complexity of the multilateral principal-agent relationship.

Why Banks?

Most MDBs bear the word "bank" in their title and are therefore often treated, both within as well as outside, as banks. This is quite misleading, however. To understand why, it would be useful to define a "bank" and see to what extent MDBs match the definition.

The primary feature of a licensed bank is deposit taking from the public, as stated by the Principle 4: Permissible Activities of Core Principles for Effective Banking Supervision[2] by the Basel Committee. While the list of permissible activities of banks is not part of the Basel Core Principles, a key requirement is to clearly define them, as well as control the use of the word "bank" in names of entities. The EU Directive 2013/575 uses the term Credit Institutions (instead of banks), defining their main business as *receiving deposits or other repayable funds from the public* and granting credits for their own accounts in line with the Basel Core Principle. The list of permissible activities is given in the Directive's Annex I, as presented below. Accordingly, each EU member state has a freedom to decide whether one or more of these activities requires banking license, *with the exception of activity number 1 (deposit taking)*, which can be practiced only by authorized credit institutions. This re-confirms that the key feature of a Bank is *deposit taking*.

List of Banking Activities Subject to Mutual Recognition

1. *Taking deposits and other repayable funds.*
2. *Lending including,* inter alia*: consumer credit, credit agreements relating to immovable property, factoring, with or without recourse, financing of commercial transactions (including forfeiting).*
3. *Financial leasing.*
4. *Payment services as defined in Article 4(3) of Directive 2007/64/EC.*
5. *Issuing and administering other means of payment* (e.g. *travelers' checks and bankers' drafts) insofar as such activity is not covered by point 4.*
6. *Guarantees and commitments.*
7. *Trading for own account or for account of customers in any of: (a) money market instruments (checks, bills, certificates of deposit,* etc.*); (b) foreign exchange; (c) financial futures and options; (d) exchange and interest rate instruments; (e) transferable securities.*
8. *Participation in securities issues and the provision of services relating to such issues.*
9. *Advice to undertakings on capital structure, industrial strategy and related questions and advice as well as services relating to mergers and the purchase of undertakings.*
10. *Money broking.*
11. *Portfolio management and advice.*
12. *Safekeeping and administration of securities.*
13. *Credit reference services.*
14. *Safe custody services.*
15. *Issuing electronic money.*

According to these standards, two main criteria define a bank*: (1) being licensed and subject to the supervision of the banking authority and (2) regularly taking repayable funds from the public in order to extend credits.*

MDBs are not licensed and supervised entities by any regulatory banking authorities—neither at their headquarters nor at any of their member states. They operate according to the policies and rules approved by either their BoG or BoD, as a matter of supranational *self-regulation*. Their activities may be grouped into four main categories: finance, knowledge, co-ordination, and standard setting—where only the first category has something in common with what banks usually do.

The financial services of MDBs typically include the provision of loans to private and public sector projects, equity and quasi-equity investments, management of trust funds and grants, risk management services, underwriting of security shares of enterprises, as well as guarantees. These services have to match the development mandate, long list of development safeguards, and not compete with other banks (to be additional).

MDBs' main asset is knowledge and therefore they offer a wide range of relevant services, for example, country-level analytic work, technical assistance, and capacity-building; cross-country development and benchmarking data; international studies and research; and multidisciplinary design and implementation of complex development projects in different contexts.

The *coordinating, convening, and catalytic services* focus on overcoming institutional coordination failures, mobilizing and managing aid from donors, vehicles for co-financing, chairing consultative group meetings, and international public goods.

The standard-setting role is both explicit and implicit (within project requirements), aiming at sustainable demonstration effects in multiple areas, for example, environment, social/employment norms, procurement, corporate governance, and public consultations. Recently the MDBs have significantly increased their standard-setting role mostly by upgrading their wide range of safeguard policies, offering standards in many areas such as business integrity, governance, labor and human rights, and many industry sectors (see Chap. 7).

As licensing and deposit-taking are not applicable to MDBs, these institutions are wrongly referred to and named as banks. Furthermore, their financial activities are complemented by even more important services that are not conducted by banks. MDBs have the "bank" word in their titles to denote their financing role, as well as resemble the title of the World Bank (the pioneering institution, that recently made substantial efforts to present itself as a *knowledge bank*).

There are also other characteristics (outlined by Chaps. 3 and 4) that distinguish MDBs from financial institutions: (1) their multilateral shareholding structure and preferred creditor status and (2) a subsidized capital base and access to other subsidies. In conclusion, it is noteworthy that MDBs deserve better generic and individual titles, such as Multilateral Development Institutions (MDIs) (Table 2.2).

Table 2.2 Why MDBs are different from banks

Key features	Deposit taking	Licensing/ supervision	Profit focus	Special status	Additional	Subsidy	Safeguards
Banks	Yes	Yes	Yes	No	No	No	No
MDBs	No	No	No	Yes	Yes	Yes	Yes

Why Development?

While varying in scope and nature, all MDBs have developmental mandates, specified in their *constitutions* (*establishing agreements*), and generally aiming at socioeconomic advancement, through focusing on various aspects, regions, and instruments, typically combining hard lending with some grant assistance and/or soft lending.

This implies a constant challenge of combining the Bank with the Development Institution elements. The financial aspect deals with the fact that MDBs lend money. However, it is always hard for the MDBs to incorporate the development element—to lend only to projects that meet the respective development (mandate) criteria, in addition to the rest (financial, economic, technical, and legal). A further challenge is to lend money that may enhance but not crowd out private sector lending, because in practice it is very difficult to determine whether or not a project would have existed without MDB involvement (*additionality*).

As development institutions, MDBs follow mandates from shareholder countries to promote a wide range of activities that often go well beyond the traditional infrastructure. The development elements are normally delivered by loans conditionality and elaborate safeguard requirements, often setting up respective international standards. In turn, borrowing countries and companies have to change their policies in ways that cannot be required by a private bank. Naturally, MDBs have higher policy leverage in countries with more restricted access to finance.

In practice, MDBs always make difficult choices about the extent and form of delivering their development mandate, ranging from the extreme cases of stringent conditionality to financing every project application under the (wrong) assumption that every investment automatically contributes to development (Semuels 2018). The MDBs emphasizing their financial institution characteristics (typically most sub-regional MDBs, and often all who lend to the private sector) are often driven by borrower (*client* or *market*) demands and less interested or able to design and promote particular developmental projects to borrowers. This represents a clear existential (mandate) risk. For example, a *bank-focused* MDB generally has fewer incentives to design environmental activities (relative to a more *development* MDB) and also has less staff, often with commercial rather than developmental skills and capability (claiming "efficiency"). Thus, the EIB, who was not set as a development institution, lends more than the World Bank but has just about 10% of the staff, respectively.

While their name suggests that MDBs should provide finance for investments in human and physical capital that promote development, clearly the actual variations are many. The ill-based argument that any investment is good for development is further flawed by the recent rapid development of international capital markets, triggering many borrower countries to challenge the nature of MDBs. The spread of global private capital flows and the advancement of domestic financial systems have improved the access to commercial finance by governments and private entities. As most borrowing countries liberalized markets and trade and abandoned state-led strategies of economic development, MDBs are facing a key challenge. To redefine their mandate interpretation they have to reflect the contemporary development agenda (UN Sustainable Development Goals, addressed by Chap. 7) and improve their role and governance accordingly (Chap. 5).

It is clear that the MDB mechanisms for the selection, monitoring, and enforcement of loans, as well as the way they select and nurture human capital need to be reshaped accordingly. The unique features of the MDBs imply a certain comparative advantage in providing finance that is geared to specific development goals. The commitment of governments to the policy reforms and changes toward accommodating the MDB safeguards is fundamental.

As many of the policy reforms supported by the MDBs aim at catalyzing of private investment and innovation, the MDB approach should seek new avenues to crowd in the private sector more effectively (e.g. by better mitigating political and other risks that discourage private initiatives, as well as address the challenges of the ongoing technological revolution, see Chap. 7). This would require a deepening but not necessarily a broadening of the roles and networking of the MDBs—in line with their special status comparative advantage.

Concluding Remarks

In many ways, the MDBs are very different from banks, as well as relative to what they were in the early years of their emergence, as designed at Bretton Woods. From a conditional government financing, they evolved toward a diversified but related family of development institutions that are engaged

Table 2.3 MDBs—weighting the M, D, and B

MDBs	Multilateral	Development	Bank	Total (max 30)
Global	10 (10–10)	8 (8–8)	2 (2–2)	20
Regional	7 (6–8)	7 (5–9)	4 (2–8)	18
Sub-regional	3 (2–4)	2 (1–3)	7 (6–8)	12
Total (max 30)	20	17	13	

Note: 1 denotes lowest, while 10 highest emphasis on M, D, and B, respectively, as assessed by the authors via data gathering and interviews with 19 MDBs. The scores in brackets show lowest and highest score within the respective group. Wider variations were observed in the Regional group, as it is least homogeneous

with the market and private sector, acting quite independently from the political frameworks who originated them. A term that would better reflect their nature would be Multilateral Development Institutions. The overview of the three groups of MDBs indicates that some are more developmental than banks, and vice versa, as illustrated by Table 2.3.

Notes

1. The term "World Bank" typically refers to IBRD and IDA specifically. In addition to IBRD and IDA, the bank also includes the International Finance Cooperation (IFC), the Multilateral Investment Guarantee Agency (MIGA), and the International Center for Settlement of Investment Disputes (ICSID). This affiliated group of the institutions is referred to as the World Bank Group (WBG). MIGA and ICSID are not covered in this report. Even though they play a significant role in the economic development, they do not provide loans and financial guarantees to developing countries. MIGA provides guarantees against non-commercial risks (e.g. political risk insurance coverage) to foreign investors in developing member countries. The ICSID provides facilities to resolve investment disputes in developing countries between governments and foreign investors through international arbitration.
2. The Core Principles establish a level of sound supervisory practice that can be used as a benchmark by supervisors to assess the quality of their supervisory systems. They are also used by the IMF and the World Bank, in the context of the Financial Sector Assessment Programme (FSAP), to assess the effectiveness of countries' banking supervisory systems and practices.

References

Anderson-Gold, S. 2011. Bretton Woods Institutions. In *Encyclopedia of Global Justice*, 87–89. Netherlands: Springer.

Auerswald, D., S. Saideman, and M. Tierney. 2006. *How to Kill a Military Career: Problems of Delegation in Multilateral and Unilateral Interventions*. Paper presented for the American Political Science Association's Annual Meeting, Philadelphia, PA, August 31–September 3, 2006.

Babb, S. 2009. *Behind the Development Banks: Washington Politics, World Poverty, and the Wealth of Nations*. London: University Of Chicago Press.

Bastøe, P.Ø., and S. Hanse. 2015. *New Challenges and New Roles: Development Financing in the 21st Century*. Oslo: Z-forlag Publishers.

Bordo, M.D., and B. Eichengreen. 2007. *A Retrospective on the Bretton Woods System: Lessons for International Monetary Reform*. Chicago: University of Chicago Press.

Culpeper, R. 1997. *Titans or Behemoths?* Vol. 5. Boulder, CO: Lynne Rienner Publishers.

English, E.P., and H.M. Mule. 1996. *The African Development Bank*. Boulder, CO: Lynne Rienner Publishers.

Harriss, J. 2002. *Depoliticizing Development: The World Bank and Social Capital*. London: Anthem Press.

Hawkins, D., D. Lake, D. Nielson, and M.J. Tierney. 2006. *Delegation and Agency in International Organizations*. Cambridge: Cambridge University Press.

Kiewiet, D., and M. McCubbins. 1991. *The Logic of Delegation: Congressional Parties and the Appropriations Process*. Chicago, IL: University of Chicago Press.

Kilby, C. 2006. Donor Influence in Multilateral Development Banks: The Case of the Asian Development Bank. *The Review of International Organizations* 1 (2): 173–195.

Lipscy, P.Y. 2015. Explaining Institutional Change: Policy Areas, Outside Options, and the Bretton Woods Institutions. *American Journal of Political Science* 59 (2): 341–356.

Mensi, W., S. Hammoudeh, J.C. Reboredo, and D.C. Nguyen. 2014. Do Global Factors Impact BRICS Stock Markets? A Quantile Regression Approach. *Emerging Markets Review* 19: 1–17.

Moe, T. 1984. Political Institutions: The Neglected Side of the Story. *Journal of Law, Economics and Organization* 6: 213–260.

Mosley, P., and D. Hulme. 2006. *Finance Against Poverty: Country Case Studies*. Vol. 2. London: Routledge.

Ocampo, J.A., ed. 2007. *Regional Financial Cooperation*. Washington, DC: Brookings Institution Press.

Sanford, J.E. 2002. World Bank: IDA Loans or IDA Grants? *World Development* 30 (5): 741–762.

Santiso, C. 2000. Towards Democratic Governance: The Contribution of the Multilateral Development Banks in Latin America. In *Democracy Assistance: International Co-operation for Democratization*, 150–190. London: Frank Cass.

Semuels. 2018. What Amazon Does to Poor Cities. *The Atlantic*, February 1. https://www.theatlantic.com/business/archive/2018/02/amazon-warehouses-poor-cities/552020/.

Stiglitz, J. 2003. *Globalization and the Logic of International Collective Action: Re-examining the Bretton Woods Institutions*, 238–253. Oxford: Oxford University Press.

Vaubel, R. 2006. Principal-Agent Problems in International Organizations. *Review of International Organizations* 1 (2): 125–138.

Yu, H. 2017. Motivation Behind China's 'One Belt, One Road' Initiatives and Establishment of the Asian Infrastructure Investment Bank. *Journal of Contemporary China* 26 (105): 353–368.

3
Financial Dynamics

Introduction

This chapter offers a comprehensive analysis of the complexity of Multilateral Development Banks' (MDBs) finance. It provides a wealth of data, covering a ten-year period, revealing substantial disparities among the *global*, *regional*, and *sub-regional* institutions. The starting point is the design of capital structure (e.g. *paid-in* vs. *callable* capital) and its rationale. It expands into several aspects of the capital structure, including the relative shrinking of paid-in-capital, the relation between callable capital and liquidity, the increasing role of financial *leverage*, credit rating controversies, and so on. Shareholder value aspects are also addressed, such as the role of *implicit subsidies* and *catalyzing of private investments.*

While MDBs' capital structure is designed to mobilize resources primarily from international capital markets, it is evident that different groups of MDBs do not enjoy a similar access to these markets, which affects their efficiency and overall resilience. The chapter analyzes how MDBs' borrowing policies are closely linked to their *liquidity* and efficiency, looking at net *disbursement* trends and *credit ratings*. Several funding issues, such as underutilization of leverage and the limited ability of rating agencies to adequately address MDBs (as further elaborated in Chap. 4), are also covered.

The terms of the loans, including their gross pricing (interest and fees), are reviewed to outline the financial conditions offered, as well as illustrate some aspects of subsidy and *financial additionality (value added)*, across groups of MDBs. These comparisons shed light on the relationship between novelty, risk appetite, governance, and shareholder-composition, on one hand, and

I. U. Delikanli et al., *Multilateral Development Banks*,
https://doi.org/10.1007/978-3-319-91524-1_3

loan terms and outreach, on the other, illustrating substantial disparities. This analysis demonstrates, inter alia, various levels of affordability of MDB loans, as well as other critical differences across groups. A key goal is to suggest an insight to better understand the relative comparative advantages of MDBs, as well as to enhance their profile and impact over time.

As MDBs are complex institutions, rather than banks, their common financial model is quite specific. They use their capital resources to invest in mandate-relevant operations, as well as borrow from the capital markets in order to attract external funding. Their operations include lending to sovereign governments and private companies. As supranational institutions, MDBs typically pay neither dividends to their shareholders, nor taxes. This is part of their self-regulatory nature and extraterritorial jurisdiction, allowing implementation of development mandate by specific selection, monitoring, and evaluation of loans and investments, in sharp contrast to banks in general. In turn, MDBs have a wide range of specific mandate-based compliance requirements (*conditionality*). The elements of implicit subsidy allow for various soft-lending schemes as well as grants in the form of technical cooperation that may fall within or outside a specific loan program. Hence, most MDBs provide both financial and non-financial service (know-how) to their clients, geared to their development mandate.

Unlike conventional banks, MDBs have ambitious public mandates rather than a goal to maximize profits. This does not imply neglect of *sound banking principles* in structuring and pricing of financing operations, or lack of prudent financial and risk reporting. On the contrary—given their high-profile mandates and public nature—MDBs observe prudent and conservative banking principles, requiring sound security and collateral in the assets of investment projects. These institutions also self-impose the highest requirements for financial transparency and risk mitigation, well beyond the regulatory requirements observed by commercial banks. While MDBs are highly self-regulated, they publish audited financial reports at least annually in accordance with the International Financial Reporting Standards (IFRS). These reports are the main source of information assessed in this chapter. To ensure validity and comparability, the data sets are aggregated into large time series (available at annexes). They are sourced from the financial reports of the reviewed 25 MDBs, covering ten years (2007–2016) and are aggregated and analyzed in three groups—*global*, *regional*, and *sub-regional* MDBs.[1]

The review of the capital structure moves toward the MDBs' operations with an asset-liability perspective. Various cross-cutting comparisons among groups of MDBs are utilized to draw conclusions in order to suggest enhancement of MDBs' financial effectiveness and efficiency—toward delivering more with less.

Funding Framework

MDBs are autonomous international financial institutions, very different from banks in general. Their shareholders, typically countries but often also other entities, set and oversee operating policies through participation in the Boards of Governors (BoGs; or similar bodies). Generally, MDBs were established by articles of agreement that specify the MDB's purpose, operations, capital structure, and various financial policies. The articles outline conditions for borrowing and lending activities. They describe the voting shares of members, typically based on a member's *subscribed capital*, as well as the status, immunity, and privileges of the institution. MDBs are not subject to supervision or oversight by national financial regulators as they are self-regulated supranational organizations. Their own Boards of Directors determine the regulations to be observed.

Key financial differences relative to commercial banks are that MDBs were not established to maximize profits, do not use customer deposits, do not pay taxes, do not distribute dividends, and have their own self-regulation, outside the scope of central banks and other authorities. Based on their mandates the MDBs provide loans, equity investments, guarantees, and technical cooperation. The primary vehicle of development operations is direct lending to sovereign and private borrowers. While most loans are offered at market-based interest rates, some MDBs offer concessional (below market) rates to the poorest developing countries.

Financial Resources

MDBs use two main sources of funding. The first one is when they invest their own *paid-in* capital and *retained earnings* in mandate-relevant assets, mostly in loans. The *paid-in* capital and *retained earnings* are often referred to as *free funds*, as MDBs do not pay interest or fees on them. The second one is when the MDBs borrow on world capital markets to invest in additional mandate-relevant assets. As these borrowed funds are not free, MDBs on-lend them at higher rates, to earn a net interest income. MDBs are not required to get credit ratings but do so in order to access capital markets at better terms (maturity, interest, etc.) than their borrowers could obtain. This is how MDBs enable borrowing countries (with lower credit ratings) to access financial resources on better terms than what would be available to them otherwise.

The combination of own free funds and borrowing implies that the lending price of an MDB increases when the share of the borrowed funds moves upward, ceteris paribus. The issue is more complex as the cost of funds depends on the MDBs' credit rating, which in turn is positively affected by a relative increase in the share of own capital. This is because the increase in own capital not only reduces repayment risks but also manifests a stronger support from shareholder countries. This is why MDBs often increase their capital which, in turn, diminishes the cost of borrowing for both the MDB and its borrowers.

Capital Structure

Despite the common funding principles, the actual capital formation procedures vary across MDBs. Typically, a member country's authorities (usually ministry of finance) negotiate and parliaments ratify initial and further financial contributions to MDBs. Country shareholders regularly assess the adequacy of an MDB's financial resources. This often results in agreeing to commit a *capital increase*, subsequently approved by Boards of Directors and governors, typically by a qualified majority vote of over 75%. In most countries, a participation in a capital increase requires parliamentary ratification.

Prior to discussing the capital structure, it is important to clarify the rather specific terms used by MDBs, regarding their capital:

- ***Authorized capital:*** the total capital approved to be available for *subscriptions.*
- ***Capital increase:*** a new funding plan, to which member countries "subscribe" when they make their contributions (in some cases such as concessional MDB programs, the term is "replenishment"). This includes subscription to the *initial* capital, *voluntary capital increases, special capital increases* (e.g. *when adopting new members)*, and *general capital increases.*
- ***Subscribed capital:*** a portion of the authorized capital that is actually allocated (*subscribed*) to shareholders, based on their commitment to contribute it as *paid-in* and *callable* capital.
- ***Callable capital:*** To assure the MDBs' more advantageous access to the international markets, their shareholder countries subscribe most of their contributions in the form of *callable capital*, a commitment by each shareholder to make additional capital available, only if and when it is required (called) to avoid default on the MDB's borrowing or guarantee. Its use is limited to pay off bondholders if the institution has no liquidity. The MDB is obliged to liquidate all its reserves and other resources before calling its members to pay in a portion of their callable capital to cover the remaining

claims of its bondholders. Calls apply on a pro rata basis—each country has to pay in proportion to its ownership share. While the outstanding debt of MDBs is sizable, it is payable over many years and the amount due each year to bondholders is relatively modest. The repayment of such debt is not accelerated regardless of the MDB's financial condition, unless the institution misses an interest payment. As a rule, MDBs are extremely capitalized, particularly relative to the credit risk on their balance sheets. Therefore the role of the *callable capital* is to ensure comfort, as a matter of demonstrated shareholders' support, aiming at a better credit rating. A call is a measure of last resort. It is generally avoided as it might trigger an international financial crisis. A shareholder country is obliged to respect a capital call even if another shareholder country defaults on that obligation. However, no country can be required to provide more than the amount of callable capital it has subscribed to. Credit rating agencies, discussed further, come short in recognizing the role of callable capital sufficiently. This is because they are unable to measure the risk of countries not meeting their commitments to provide callable capital (due to the distinct nature of callable capital at MDBs, not having actual cases of calls). It is also associated with the fact that most MDBs include shareholder countries with limited financial strength. The underlying argument is that a global financial stress that may require a capital call is likely to make many shareholders unable to comply. Rating agencies therefore calculate capital-based ratios in two ways: by using balance sheet capital (adjusted as appropriate), assuming that there is no callable capital; and by using balance sheet capital plus "AAA"-rated callable capital, assuming that all "AAA"-rated countries (but no others) would in fact meet a capital call. It is also acknowledged that for some countries, responding to a capital call may require legislative action. To mitigate such delays MDBs maintain strong liquidity, allowing time for member countries to meet the capital call.[2] Since recently, many MDBs opted to increase the callable-capital share of capital increases, especially when they have more AAA-rated shareholders. However, rating agencies consider such increasing use of callable capital as eroding the support that capital increase otherwise implies. Therefore, as shown further, the lower the share of AAA-rated countries in the callable capital, the higher the share of the paid-in capital is, to satisfy the requirements of the credit rating process.

- ***Paid-up and paid-in capital:*** The MDBs' shareholders subscribe some of their capital contributions as *paid-in capital*, in a fixed ratio (often ranging from 5% to 50%) with the callable share. The difference between the *paid-up* and *paid-in* shares reflects the shares to be issued on payment of subsequent installments. Thus the paid-up includes the commitment to pay-in, while the paid-in is what is actually paid already, according to the agreed payment schedule.

- ***Shareholders' equity:*** Equity is composed of capital, retained earnings, and fair value gains on available-for-sale equity investments. While most MDBs' financial statements comply with generally accepted accounting principles, there are differences in the treatment of certain items and therefore comparisons of shareholders' equity are presented only in aggregate form, to denote divergence among MDB groups, rather than absolute values. To this end, rating agencies often adjust shareholders' equity of some institutions to improve comparability, typically by deducting receivables related to capital, even when they are of very high credibility.[3] For instance, some MDBs (e.g. European Bank for Reconstruction and Development—EBRD) report "paid-in capital" inclusive of "members' promissory notes", "payments due but not yet received", and "payments committed but not yet due". In contrast, other MDBs (e.g. Corporación Andina de Fomento—CAF) include in shareholders' equity only amounts that have *actually been received.*

In summary, the MDBs' total capital committed by the shareholders, is known as *subscribed capital.* A small portion of it is the *paid-in capital,* which, together with *reserves* and *retained earnings,* constitutes the directly disposable capital that MDBs operate with.

The difference between the *subscribed* and *paid-in* capital is the *callable capital*—as shareholders are committed to pay it in portions or entirely in case of need to meet bond or other borrowing obligation of the MDB. The *subscribed capital* (total committed capital, including *paid-in* and *callable capital*) has a primary institutional role relative to the actual *paid-in* capital, as it represents the total unconditional capital commitment of the sovereign shareholders. While the large unpaid (*callable*) component of the *subscribed capital* is not immediately available, it constitutes a sound financial commitment of sovereign shareholders—equivalent to a sovereign guarantee regarding the MDBs' financial sustainability, providing assurance to all MDB bondholders.

Subscribed Versus Paid-In Capital

The total amount of all MDBs' combined *subscribed* capital has grown by a yearly average of 5.7%, to USD 1.4 trillion at the end of 2016 (from USD 845.7 billion at the end of 2007, see Annex 1). It represents 1.8% of the world's GDP at the end of 2016. More than 55% of the subscribed capital belongs to the regional MDBs.

As can be seen from Fig. 3.1, 97% of the total subscribed capital of the *global* MDBs belongs to IBRD and IDA, amounting to USD 521.7 billion as of the end of 2016. Also, 45% of the subscribed capital of the *global* MDBs has been paid (Fig. 3.1; Annex 2). Within this group, IBRD has a strikingly low share (6%) of *paid-in* capital relative to its *subscribed* capital. In contrast, IFC, IFAD (International Fund for Agriculture Development), and IDA have large shares of paid-in capital—100%, 85%, and 75.4% of their subscribed capital amounts, respectively.

Unlike *global* MDBs, the *regional* ones maintain substantially lower share of *paid-in* capital—10.2% as of the end of 2016 (as can be seen from Fig. 3.2). However, these institutions demonstrated a strong financial response to the global economic crisis by increasing their subscribed capital by USD 178 billion in total, between 2008 and 2010.

While EIB (European Investment Bank), IDB (Inter-American Development Bank), and AsDB (Asian Development Bank) have the highest amounts of subscribed capital within the *regional* group, their average paid-in capital is below the rest of institutions—7%, 4%, and 4.9% of their subscribed capital in the last ten years, respectively. AfDB (African Development Bank), IsDB, and EBRD are operating with highest shares of paid-in capital, with a 10-year average of 94.1%, 19.7%, and 23.5%, respectively.

As can be seen from Fig. 3.3, *sub-regional* MDBs have higher *paid-in* capital shares (43.6% at the end of 2016)—close to the levels of the *global* MDBs, and well above the levels of the *regional* ones. NIB (Nordic Investment Bank) is among the institutions with the highest subscribed capital within

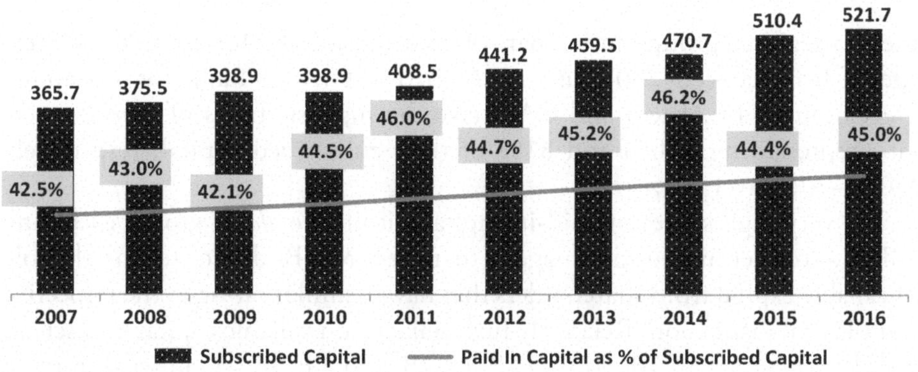

Fig. 3.1 Subscribed and paid in capital, global MDBs (USD, billion). Source: Authors' compilation from MDBs' annual reports

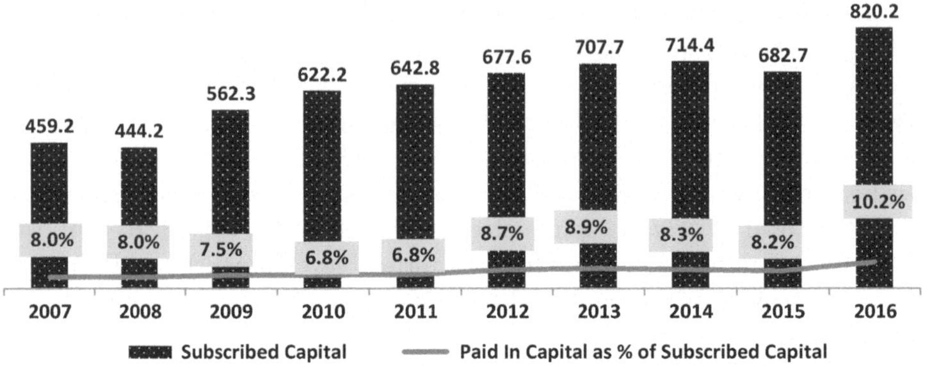

Fig. 3.2 Subscribed and paid in capital, regional MDBs (USD, billion). Source: Authors' compilation from MDBs' annual reports

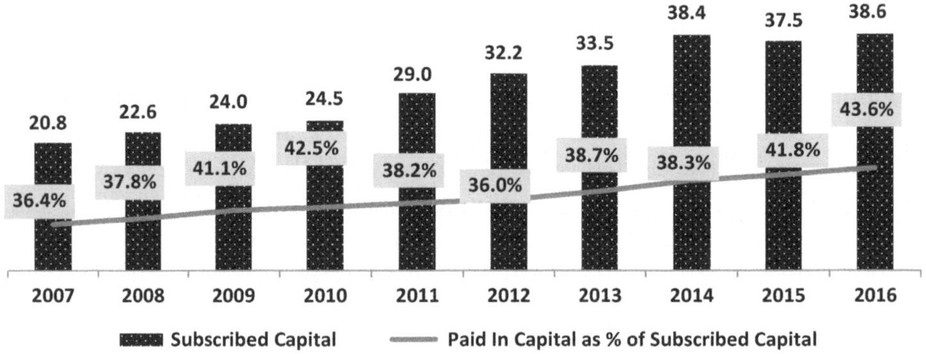

Fig. 3.3 Subscribed and paid in capital, sub-regional MDBs (USD, billion). Source: Authors' compilation from MDBs' annual reports

the sub-regional group but its share of paid-in capital is lowest, with an average of 8% between 2007 and 2016. BADEA (Arab Bank for Economic Development in Africa) and CAF have the highest shares of *paid-in* capital—representing 100% and 81% of their subscribed capital, respectively (2007–2016 average).

The very high shares of paid-in capital within the *global* group, excluding IBRD as outlier institution, suggests that these MDBs do not rely on the role of callable capital from shareholders that have a similar rating as the respective multilateral institution. Relatively high reliance on callable capital is observed mostly at regional MDBs (IDB, EIB, AsDB, and CEDB—Council of Europe Development Bank), as well as at NIB from the sub-regional group (with a paid-in capital of less than 15% of their subscribed capital).

Paid-In Capital Versus Equity

Another distinctive financial aspect of the MDBs is their high level of retained earnings, allowed by the absent (or very low in the case of a few exceptions, as approved by BoGs) distribution of dividends or equivalent payments to shareholders. This results in (intended) substantial internal capital accumulation, increasing total equity and respective ability to withstand financial stress and grow the capital base. The total amount of the MDBs' equity has grown by an annual average of 3.6%, to USD 423.7 billion at the end of 2016 (from USD 309.8 billion at the end of 2007, see Annex 3), reaching 30.7% of total subscribed capital. Over 50% of the total equity belongs to the *global* MDBs.

As can be seen from Fig. 3.4, the total equity of the *global* MDBs consists of over 95% of the paid-in capital (2007–2016 average). IFC is a special case since its total equity has reached a level of more than eight times of its paid-in capital amount due to sizable increases in retained earnings and reserves. Consequently, the very high increase in IFC's equity explains why the institution, unlike other MDBs, does not need an increase in its subscribed and callable capital.

The total equity of the *regional* MDBs has been consistently increasing primarily by *retained earnings and reserves*, rather than *paid-in* capital. The share of paid-in capital in total equity has been limited to 35.8% as an average of the last ten-year period. In other words, total equity amount has reached a level of 2.8 times the paid-in capital (ten-year average). IDB and CEDB have highest equity/paid in capital ratio—4.5 times on average. *Regional* MDBs have also higher ratio of total equity to subscribed capital (in addition to equity to paid-in capital). This high share of equity could be explained by the

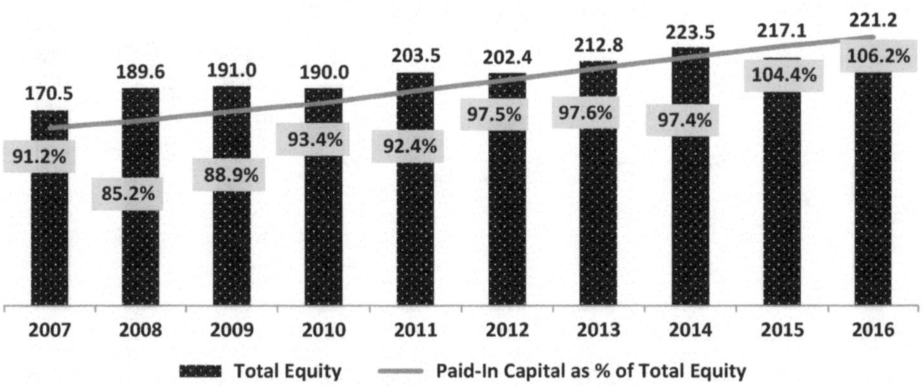

Fig. 3.4 Equity and paid in capital, global MDBs (USD, billion). Source: Authors' compilation from MDBs' annual reports

deliberate efforts of *regional* institutions to enhance their financial strength vis-à-vis relevant stakeholders with a particular reference to credit rating agencies and bond investors in order to meet the expectations of shareholders regarding affordable access to international capital markets (given the relatively lower credit rating of many of their sovereign shareholders) (Fig. 3.5).

Sub-regional MDBs have increased their total equity more than both *global* and *regional* institutions—by an average of 6.7% in the last ten years. As can be seen from Fig. 3.6, this increase is primarily due to additional contributions of *paid-in capital.* NIB, CABEI (Central American Bank for Economic Integration), and CDB (Caribbean Development Bank) have the lowest share of paid-in capital in their equity with an average of 17%, 27%, and 33%, respectively. At the other end, the paid-in capital represents over 80% of the

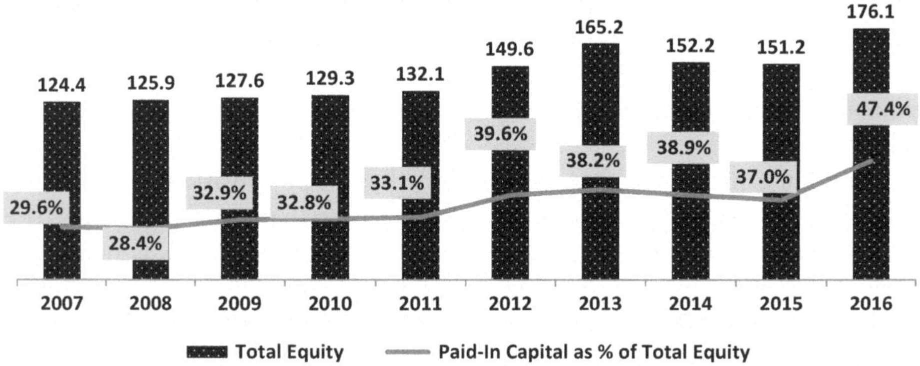

Fig. 3.5 Equity and paid in capital, regional MDBs (USD, billion). Source: Authors' compilation from MDBs' annual reports

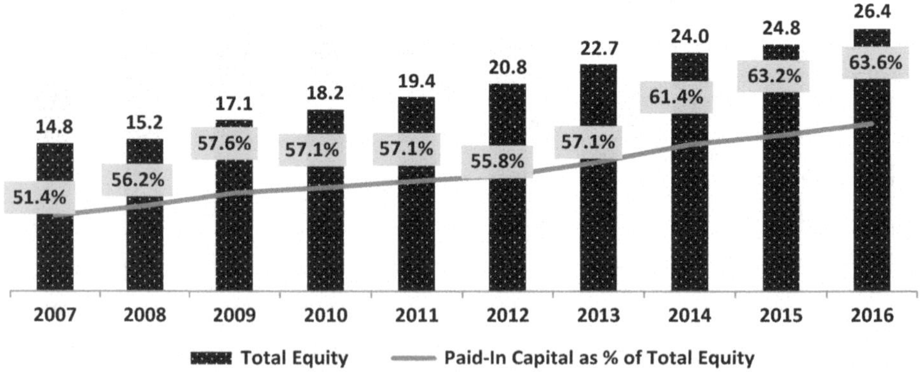

Fig. 3.6 Equity and paid-in capital, sub-regional MDBs (USD, billion). Source: Authors' compilation from MDBs' annual reports

total equity at BADEA and BSTDB (Black Sea Trade and Development Bank), and over 90% at EADB (East African Development Bank), ETDB (Economic Cooperation Organization Trade and Development Bank), and EDB (Eurasian Development Bank).

Sub-regional MDBs are also ahead of *global* and *regional* institutions in terms of having rather high share of equity, relative to their subscribed capital—68% on average for the last ten years, with CAF and BADEA being in the lead with an average equity of 127% of their subscribed capital.

Resource Mobilization

The rationale of financing of MDBs' operations is based on the combined use of own equity, as well as resources they *mobilize* (borrow) from the financial markets. Many MDBs have very explicit goals of resource mobilization—for example EBRD,[4] among several other institutions, has in its mandate the goal to attract additional domestic and foreign resources—as a catalytic effect of their own financing, including crowding-in private sector investments.

The direct resource mobilization (borrowing) originates either from financial (lending) institutions or by issuing bonds in the international capital markets. In both cases, MDBs rely on high credit ratings, allowing them to borrow at better terms than most of their *borrowing members* would achieve if they borrow themselves.

Though MDBs formulate their borrowing policies in slightly different ways, they have in principle three basic objectives: ensure the availability of funds for development lending purposes; minimize the cost of funds for on-lending; and predict such costs in future periods.

Total borrowings of the MDBs increased to USD 1.14 trillion as of 2014 from USD 674.5 billion in 2007 but later decreased to USD 1.12 trillion at the end of 2016 due to decreasing borrowings of the regional MDBs, affected by downward pressure on their credit ratings (see Annex 4 and Fig. 3.7). Although *global* and *sub-regional* institutions have consistently increased their borrowing every year by 9.0% and 6.7%, respectively (on average for last ten years), *regional* MDBs are in the lead in terms of resource mobilization since 76.3% of the total borrowings belong to them, on average in the last decade. In view of their high share of total equity (boosted by retained earnings), *regional* institutions have achieved the highest level of resource mobilization (with relatively low paid-in capital). They are way ahead of both *global* and *sub-regional* ones in this respect as their average annual borrowing from the international capital markets exceeds by 5.3 times their total paid-in capital, reserves and retained earnings, on average. Borrowing level for CEDB and

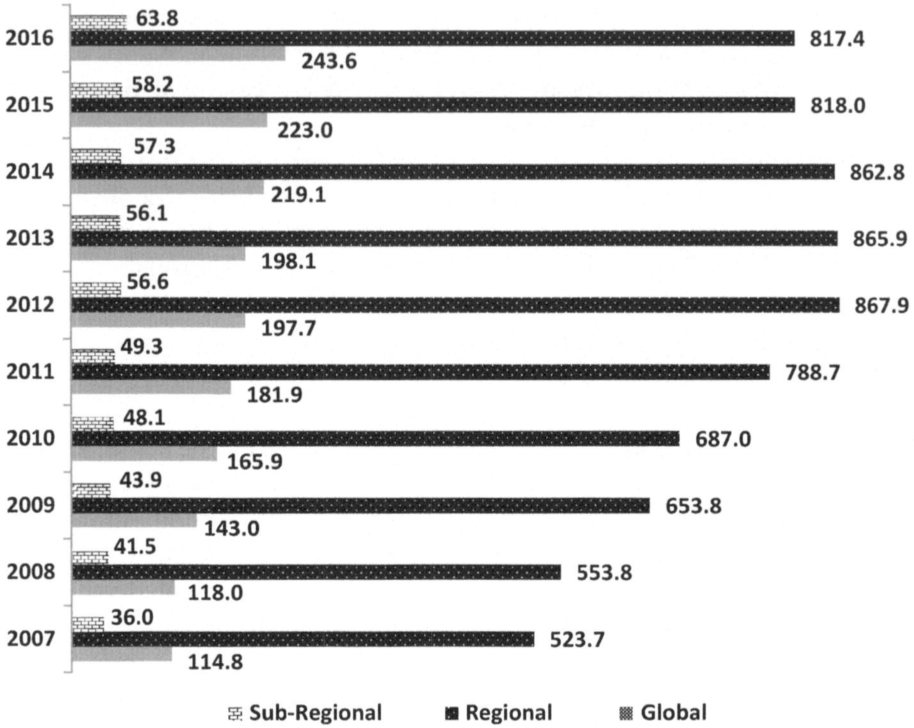

Fig. 3.7 Total borrowings (USD, billion). Source: Authors' compilation from MDBs' annual reports

EIB has risen to 9.1 and 8.4 times, respectively. It represents 2.5 times the total equity of sub-regional MDBs on average (although NIB became the outlier of the sub-regional group with a borrowing of 8.2 times its equity).

Figure 3.8 presents the relationship between the MDBs' mobilized funds (borrowings) and total equity, on one hand, and the disbursed and undisbursed lending, equity, and guarantee commitments, on the other. The figure shows a ten-year time series of the ratio of total borrowings (Annex 4) plus total equities (Annex 3) to total loans, equities, and debt securities (Annex 5) plus guarantees (Annex 7) plus undisbursed commitments (Annex 8). The horizontal line represents a ratio of 1, indicating a balanced asset-liability structure. Therefore, all data above this line illustrate a higher borrowing amount, relative to the actual investment portfolio of outstanding amounts and undisbursed commitments of loans, guarantees, and other products. The average ratio for the last ten years is 0.95, 0.93, and 1.18 for the *global*, *regional*, and *sub-regional* MDBs, respectively. *Global* and *regional* institutions demonstrate a lower ratio as their borrowing (liquidity) covers only current

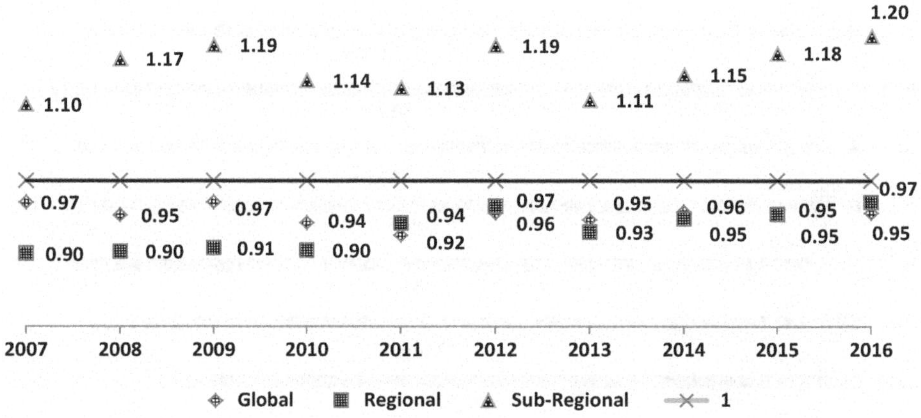

Fig. 3.8 Gearing ratio *(Borrowings + Total equity)/(Loans + Guarantees + Undisbursed commitments)*. Source: Authors' compilation from MDBs' annual reports

investment obligation (excluding some undisbursed commitments). This indicates that these MDBs enjoy relatively better access to funding, as they add-up further liquidity when needed to cover new disbursements. In contrast, *sub-regional* MDBs maintain a higher level of borrowing (liquidity), exceeding their disbursed and undisbursed commitments and guarantees. This implies that these institutions have a more restricted access to the capital markets and therefore maintain higher liquidity as they have to borrow whenever better market terms are available, building some liquidity for future commitments. This maintenance of substantially higher liquidity on average (about 20 percentage points), combined with the relatively higher cost of borrowing due to lower credit ratings, represents a key efficiency challenge for the sub-regional MDBs. In other words, the relatively higher cost of capital, as well as the need to keep idle financial resources, makes the sub-regional MDBs less competitive in financial terms, relative to their larger peers. This puts a pressure on them to be more innovative toward their mainstream (mandate-based), as well as short-term treasury investments, often implying the need to cope with higher uncertainty and risks, *ceteris paribus*.

Assets Growth

Similar to commercial banks, MDBs generally have two groups of operations: the main one is lending and other investments devoted to their mandates, and the auxiliary group includes *treasury operations*, focused on attracting external resources and liquidity management. As MDBs are neither profit-maximizing

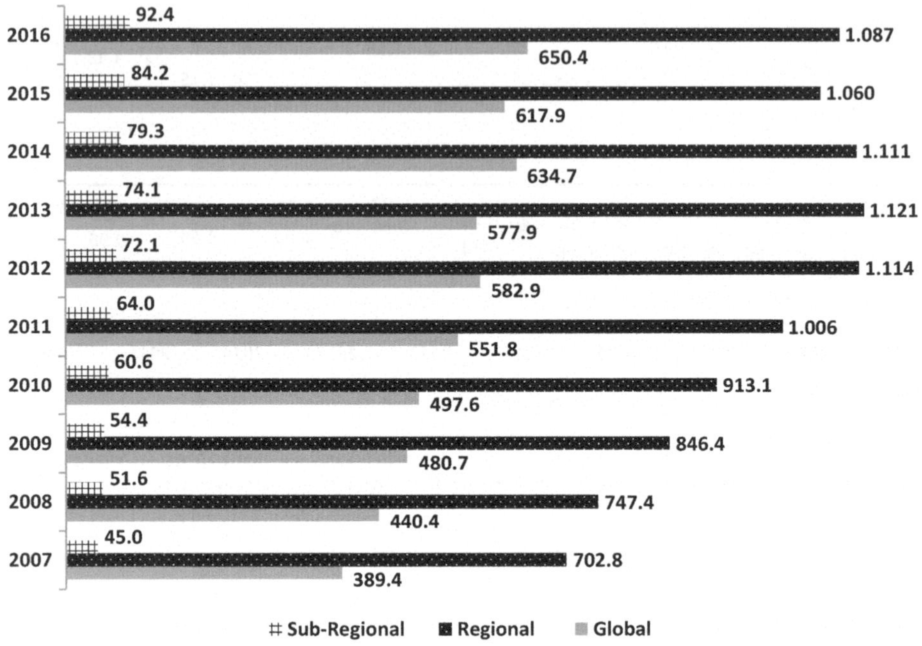

Fig. 3.9 Total assets (USD, billion). Source: Authors' compilation from MDBs' annual reports

nor distributing shareholder dividends by definition and exist to fulfill their development mandates through the first group, the second one (treasury) is devoted to ensuring the success of the former.

The total assets of the MDBs have grown to 1.83 USD trillion as of the end of 2016 from 1.14 USD trillion at the end of 2007 (Annex 9). Due to the decreasing portfolio of the *regional* MDBs after 2013 (in line with the dynamics of borrowings), the average growth rate for the last ten years was limited to 5.5%. While naturally, the assets of the *sub-regional* MDBs are small relative to the other two groups, they have increased their total shares from 3.9% in 2007 to 5.0% in 2016, based on a higher average growth rate of 8.4% (Fig. 3.9).

Treasury Operations

As illustrated by the structure of assets and liabilities, presented in Fig. 3.8, MDBs have to manage their liquidity in a balanced manner—by investing it to generate returns on idle resources while making sure that expected loan disbursements will be matched with sufficient and timely resources. MDBs need substantial time to develop and finance their operations in line with their complex mandate requirements and approval cycles. This implies the need for adequate treasury management—to maintain certain cash liquidity in order to fund forthcoming disbursements, as well as invest in a mix of instruments and securities with appropriate balance of return and maturity, to match timing and size of future disbursements.

The analysis of the ratio of cash and funds due from banks to the total assets (Annex 10/Annex 9) and borrowings (Annex 10/Annex 4) reveals that *sub-regional* MDBs maintain 12% of their assets in cash (representing 15.7% of their borrowings on average). In deep contrast, both *global* and *regional* MDBs maintain very low average cash equivalent of just 1% of their assets (or 1.7% of their borrowings). Meanwhile, treasury assets of the *global* and *regional* MDBs comprise 17.4% and 10.4% of their total assets, respectively (ten-year average). Figure 3.10 illustrates that cash and due from banks together with treasury assets (Annexes 10 and 11) constitute over one-third of the assets of *sub-regional* MDBs, in line with their higher level of borrowings (liquidity) relative to their disbursed and undisbursed commitments and guarantees. In contrast, *global* and *regional* MDBs maintain a half of that ratio—just 17.9% and 11.7% of their assets are cash and due from banks, accordingly (ten-year average, Fig. 3.10).

The liquidity/borrowing ratio presented in Fig. 3.11 illustrates another divergence among groups. Liquidity and treasury investments represent just 15.3% of *regional* MDBs' borrowings on average. On the other hand, at the *global* and *sub-regional* groups these ratios are much higher—54.9% and

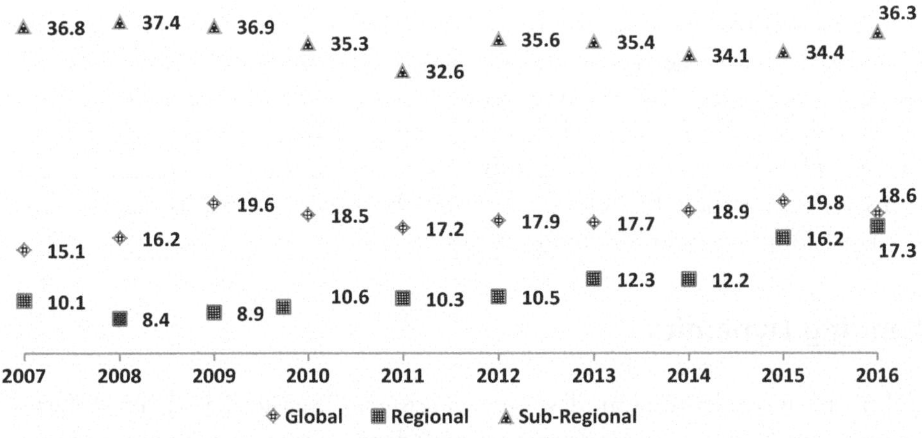

Fig. 3.10 Liquidity asset ratio *(Cash and due from banks + Treasury assets)/Total assets (%)*. Source: Authors' compilation from MDBs' annual reports

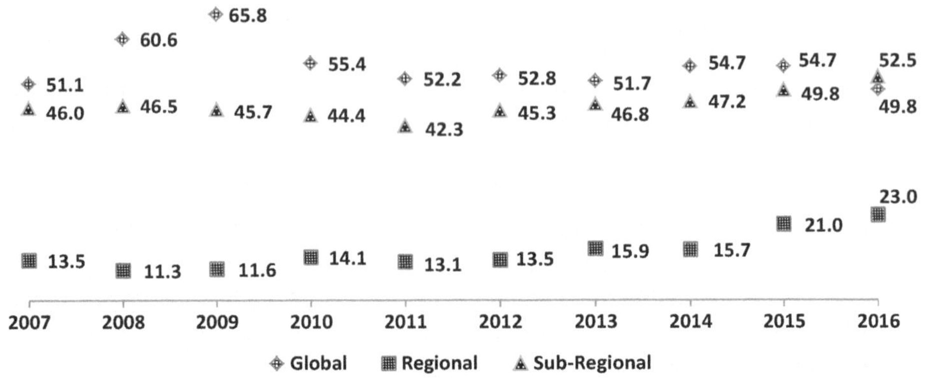

Fig. 3.11 Liquidity borrowing ratio *(Cash and due from banks + Treasury assets)/Borrowings (%)*. Source: Authors' compilation from MDBs' annual reports

46.6%, respectively. For the *global* MDBs, the high ratio could be explained mainly by the relatively lower levels of borrowing as a share of their assets. For the *sub-regional* ones, it is generally triggered by the pressure from credit rating institutions to maintain higher liquidity in order to achieve higher ratings, given that these MDBs and many of their shareholders have lower rating profile/perspectives, in relative terms. Another intervening factor in this direction, regarding the sub-regional group, is the apparently limited financial competitiveness, implying more efforts and time in the search for appropriate lending transactions, in contrast to larger and better-rated peer institutions. Regardless of the actual cause, the relatively high level of treasury assets at sub-regional MDBs highlights the importance of enhancing their treasury departments.

Across MDBs, treasury divisions typically generated modest revenues (1.4–1.6% on average as gross income from cash, banks, and treasury assets in the last seven years). This seems acceptable for *global* and *regional* institutions as their borrowing rates are close to this range, based on their higher credit ratings. However, *sub-regional* MDBs need to enhance their treasury operations reflecting their higher liquidity and borrowing costs, associated with their predominantly lower credit ratings.

Lending Dynamics

MDBs have two lending modes: *non-concessional* (market-based, also referred to as *sound banking*) and *concessional* (soft loans with below market interest rates and fees, available only at some *global* and *regional* MDBs, with only least developed countries being eligible). *Non-concessional* lending is funded by issuing low-interest, high-rated bonds into the international financial market, while *concessional* flows are typically funded by multilateral clubs of donors, who collaborate in providing grant resources. In some respect, the difference between *non-concessional* and concessional lending is very blurred by a number of intrinsic subsidies, addressed further.

The total amount of loans, equity investments, and debt securities (before provisioning for expected losses) extended by all MDBs peaked to USD 1.25 trillion in 2013 (from USD 832 billion at the end of 2007) but later decreased to USD 1.19 trillion as of the end of 2016. It has shown a very similar trend to the dynamics of total assets, reaching 1.6% of the world GDP. The pace of the lending growth has peaked twice: in 2009 by 15.1% relative to the pre-crisis level of 2007 and again in 2013 by 30.4%, relative to 2009. This illustrates that overall the MDBs were able to play the intended countercyclical role, in order to mitigate the scarcity of investments at a time of global turmoil (2008). In line with the share of assets, *regional* MDBs are in the lead in terms of operations, having a ten-year average share of 69.2% of all MDBs (Fig. 3.12).

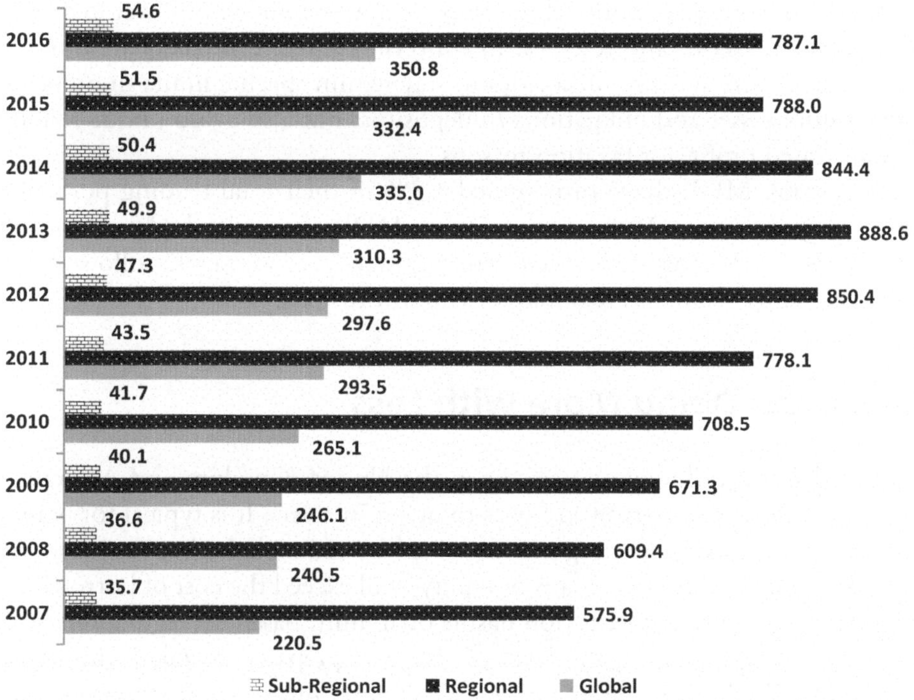

Fig. 3.12 Total loans, debt securities and equity investments (USD, billion). Source: Authors' compilation from MDBs' annual reports

Generally, the off-balance sheet lending operations (e.g. guarantee issuance, also known as unfunded risk participation) represent a negligible part of the MDBs' portfolio. While their total volume has doubled in the last ten years (reaching USD 22.4 billion at the end of 2016, from USD 11.1 billion at the end of 2007; see Annex 7), the share of such operations remains small. It has increased to just 1.9% of the total loans in 2016 from 1.3% as of the end of 2007 (Annex 7/Annex 5). The regional MDBs have the largest share of guarantees (ten-year average of 61.5%), in line with their relatively high share of operations. The issue of off-balance sheet operations deserves a particular attention as they have a substantial potential to do more with less, in both financial and impact terms, in the context of the financial architecture of MDBs (e.g. the role of *callable capital*).

Like commercial banks, MDBs set aside provisions (loss allowances), based on assessments and impairment tests for identified specific risks, non-performing loans, as well as general risks of loss in future periods. While MDBs follow similar provision practices as those applicable to commercial banks, they enjoy a substantial relative flexibility. This is due to the specifics of MDBs as highly capitalized self-regulated institutions that are exempt from tax and dividend obligations. This allows them to set higher or lower loan loss and other provisions and reserves. In contrast, commercial banks are limited by the regulators and tax authorities to stay within specific limits in order to meet future losses and obligations to depositors but also avoid undue reduction of stated profit, for taxation reasons.

In general, MDBs have provisioned 1.3% of their total lending portfolio on average (Annex 12/Annex 5). Global MDBs have the highest level of provisions—3.9% of their total lending (ten-year average), followed by sub-regional (1.6%), and regional (0.3%) institutions.

Leverage: Doing More with Less

Financial *leverage* (known as *gearing* in the United Kingdom and Australia) represents the use of borrowed funds to invest in assets. It is typical for banking and non-banking lending institutions. The rationale is that the after-tax income from the asset (e.g. loans or equity) will exceed the cost of borrowing. Normally, the lending institution has its own limit, based on regulations and internal policy, regarding the level of risk it is prepared to take. The latter determines the limit on leverage, as well as other measures such as type and value of the collateral (security) for the borrowing and lending.

Leveraging attracts external resources, in addition to own capital. In this regard it is essential for the MDBs' functioning, to provide funding at a lower cost relative to the cost of borrowing of many of the shareholders. The rationale of the cost differential is that the MDB would have higher credit rating than the sovereign credit rating of some of the shareholder countries (in the case of particular sub-regional MDBs, the institutional rating is higher than the ratings of all shareholder countries).

Banking institutions are subject to many regulatory requirements, including leverage limits, as set by the Basel Committee on Banking Supervision (BCBS) and respective national central banks. This is because leverage involves substantial individual and systemic risk as it enables both gains and losses to be multiplied. Leveraging may result in a loss in two ways: when borrowing costs exceed the income from lending, or when the lending becomes impaired and non-collectible. The latter case can trigger an inability to pay back the funds borrowed by the MDB and is therefore mitigated by stringent loss provisions, reserves, and ultimately a large amount of own *paid-in* and *callable capital* (keeping leverage levels within limits). However, it is noteworthy that leverage per se does not necessarily imply more risk because there are many other factors such as asset liability and maturity management, as well as adequate provisions and reserves.

While, ceteris paribus, higher leverage generally implies higher risk, it does not necessarily mean that any levered investment is always riskier than an unlevered one. For example, many highly levered hedge funds exhibit lower return volatility than unlevered bond funds. Likewise, many levered public utilities are often less risky stocks than unlevered technology companies. Hence, leverage at MDBs should be seen in the context of the institutional safeguards and mandates that mitigate substantially the otherwise risky nature of debt.

Leverage is an inherent and essential element of MDBs *modus operandi*, as their mandate is to catalyze and attract resources toward a respective development agenda, rather than just re-invest the capital contributed by shareholder countries. This is at the core of the rationale for high leverage. The underlying assumption is to attract capital from international markets and invest it in countries which do not have access to such capital at same or lower cost.

The BCBS introduced a leverage ratio standard in the 2010 *Basel III* package of reforms, detailed in 2014 and updated in 2017 with a rare MDB reference regarding their risk treatment as borrowers (BCBS 2011, 2014, 2017).

As the 2008 financial crisis was triggered by excessive on- and off-balance sheet leverage in the banking system, the natural BCBS response was to address this issue in depth. A particular concern was that many banks built up excessive leverage while reporting apparently strong risk-based capital ratios. Consequently, the deleveraging process at the peak of the crisis resulted in a vicious circle of losses and severe credit (and credibility) crunch in the real economy. In response, BCBS introduced a leverage ratio in *Basel III* to reduce the risk during similar times of deleveraging in the future, as they cause substantial shocks on the global financial system and economy. The introduced leverage ratio framework aims to reinforce the risk-based capital requirements with a simple, non-risk-based ceiling. It applies to all internationally active banks. While this standard, like all other BCBS standards, does not directly apply to MDBs in view of their own self-regulatory legal status, it is a relevant reference, used further to assess the MDBs' leverage dynamics.

In contrast to other measures such as previous capital adequacy requirements, the BCBS framework is addressing leverage arising from both on- and off-balance sheet exposures. It also reveals two underlying concerns. First, that differing accounting frameworks across jurisdictions cause level playing field risks; and second that safeguards comprised of accounting measures alone may not capture all risks.

BCBS defines the leverage ratio as the *capital measure* (see below) divided by the *exposure measure* (loans and other investments, see below), expressed as a percentage (BCBS 2014: 1). Unlike other capital ratios, the leverage is straightforward as it does not involve any risk weighting. Since 2014 its minimum level[5] is set at 3%. It may be re-set by BCBS after 2018 based on expected calibrations and adjustments to the definition of the *exposure measure*,[6] reflecting the *Pillar 1* treatment[7] introduced on January 1, 2018.

The *capital measure* is *Tier 1 capital*[8] as defined by the *Basel III* risk-based capital framework (BCBS 2011, 2014, 2017). The *exposure measure* includes both *on-balance sheet*[9] and *off-balance sheet*[10] exposures (investments, loans, etc.).

Reflecting the BCBS standards outlined above, the MDBs' leverage has been assessed and presented in Fig. 3.13, for a ten-year period, for each institutional group. The leverage was calculated as a ratio between total equity to the gross amount of investments (loans, equity investments, debt securities and guarantees issued, and undisbursed commitments—for details see Annex 3, 5, 7 and 8).

Figure 3.13 reveals two major findings. First, all MDBs are very conservative in terms of leverage as even the lowest ratio figures are well above the BCBS minimum requirement—at least over six times higher than the 3% threshold. The second observation is that there is a substantial difference (threefold in magnitude) in the leverage levels among the three institutional groups. On one hand, *regional* MDBs are highly leveraged institutions as their

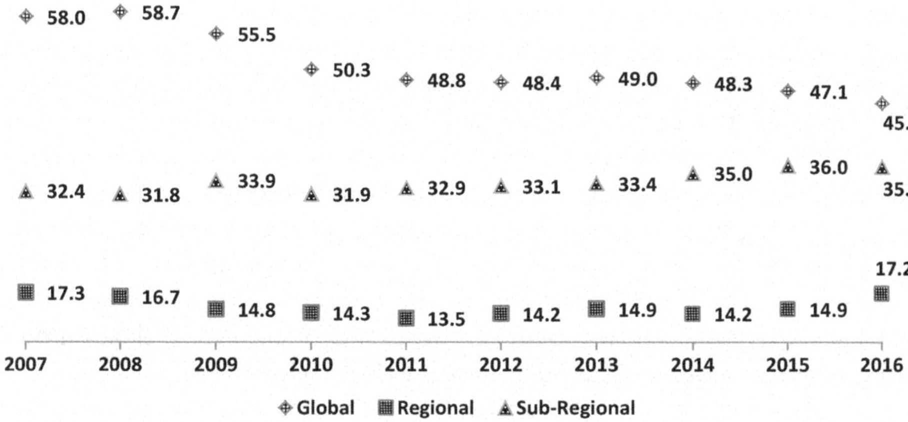

Fig. 3.13 Leverage ratio (%). Source: Authors' compilation from MDBs' annual reports

lending commitments are on average 6.6 times their equities. In sharp contrast, *global* and *sub-regional* MDBs' exposure portfolio is just two and three times their equity, respectively. The data indicate that *regional* MDBs are clearly ahead of the other two groups in terms of meeting the key mandate requirement of mobilizing external resources toward the development agenda. In other words, these MDBs utilize better their own equity toward doing more with less, relative to *sub-regional* and *global* MDBs. It is clear that even the best performing regional group, has a large further potential to increase leverage ratios and funds mobilization a lot further, and still staying within the BCBS standards.

As further elaborated in Chaps. 4 and 5, the necessary increase in MDB's effectiveness and efficiency, including the use of higher levels of leverage and balance sheet optimization, requires revisiting of the legacy of institutional and regulatory deficiencies. This refers mainly to the roles of BCBS, on one hand, and the credit rating agencies, on the other.

Impact of Basel Requirements

While BCBS does not cover MDBs directly, given the self-regulatory nature of these institutions, the Basel standards have an indirect impact of high importance. Here a main reference is made to the BCBS standards on banks and other entities, dealing with the quantification and mitigation of their risk exposures arising from lending to other entities. In this regard, for many years MDBs were treated as supranational borrowers with a high magnitude of risk weight, unless rated as AAA. As per the BCBS standards, an exposure to an MDB could have a *risk weight* of between 0% and as high as 50%, depending on the *credit rating*[11] of the institution (BCBS, Basel III, 2017). Meanwhile, the exact same Basel rules treat sovereign debt (even regarding countries in financial distress such as Greece and Italy) at a zero risk weight. This implies that holding sovereign debt bonds provides banks and other investors with interest-earning investments that do not require them to raise any additional capital. In contrast, holding of bonds of B-rated MDBs is substantially different, as it implies a 50% discount on the respective exposure asset. This illustrates a very uneven treatment of sovereign debt and MDB debt on one hand, as well as a disparity of 50% among MDBs' bonds as well.

BCBS has partially recognized this issue (reflecting the specific nature of MDBs) for the first time in December 2017, by issuing the Basel III requirements whereby the risk weight of exposures to A-rated MDBs was reduced from 50% to 30%. While this is a bold step in the right direction, there is a lot more to be done in this regard. It is obvious that Basel III should not have assigned to all sovereign debt a zero *risk weighting* while treating MDB bonds as higher risk, as these institutions are by no means riskier than their sovereign shareholders.

The *Basel III* capital requirements for banks, finalized in December 2017, updated the risk weight of exposures to MDBs, as shown in Table 3.1.

This update established a more detailed *risk-weighting* treatment of exposures to MDBs. As already noted, it dramatically reduced the *risk weight* of A-rated MDBs (CABEI and BSTDB) from 50% to 30%. This reduction will enable the A-rated MDBs to improve their access to international capital markets and substantially reduce their cost of borrowing. However, for all other MDBs, the risk weights remain unchanged—for example the zero *risk weight*[12] for virtually all global and regional MDBs provides them with a substantial

Table 3.1 MDBs' credit ratings and risk weights

Credit rating	Risk weights	Global MDBs	Regional MDBs	Sub-regional MDBs
AAA	0%	IBRD, IFC, IDA	CEDB, EIB, IDB, AfDB, AsDB, IsDB, EBRD, AIIB	CDB, NIB
AA-	20%			CAF
A	30% (50% prior to December 2017)			CABEI, BSTDB
BBB	50%			WADB, IIB, EDB, PTA, EADB
Unrated	50%	IFAD	NDB	BADEA, ETDB

Source: Authors' compilation from BCBS (Basel III) and MDB's annual reports

cost advantage relative to all others. The lowered funding costs for A-rated MDBs have a critical potential in the future, when global interest rates are expected to rise from the currently near-zero levels.

What is even more important than the lowered funding cost of A-rated MDBs is the unprecedented positive message, associated with the reduced risk weight. This is a long-awaited message that MDBs should not be treated just as banks. This has a particularly strong meaning regarding relatively smaller and newer *sub-regional* institutions, as market participants are unaware of their specific nature, in contrast to better known larger MDBs. This will help to ensure deserved visibility and recognition of smaller institutions in the financial markets, bringing them a step closer to larger peers. Large MDBs have historically enjoyed a favorable market access, especially in times of financial crisis when their bonds were considered a safe harbor. This allowed them to fulfill the intended countercyclical developmental role, but deprived their smaller peers of doing the same.

Impact of Credit Rating Agencies

Both the Basel rules outlined above and other market regulations and perceptions assign an important role to the credit ratings of MDBs. This gives an implicit regulatory power to the respective *credit rating agencies* as their ratings affect not only the MDBs' access to leverage, but also a variety of governance aspects within the institutions, as a result of particular rating methods and requirements. The essence of the problem is that *rating agencies* continue to address MDBs just as banks, without comprehending their very specific nature of resilient self-regulating institutions. While BCBS made a bold step in 2017 (Basel III) toward recognizing the MDBs' specifics by lowering of the risk profile of A-rated institutions, *rating agencies* do not seem to take similar steps. In its response to the Basel III update, in early 2018 Moody's stated that they do not anticipate MDB rating updates because while improved access to financial markets and the cost of funding are part of their assessments, this is only one of many measures of liquidity assessment. Furthermore, Moody's stresses on the prevailing importance, as rating factors, of the size of an MDB's capital buffer relative to the riskiness of its operations and the balance sheet leverage, on one hand, and the shareholders' support, on the other[13] (Moody's 2018). These rating factors are no doubt relevant. However, their assessment requires a deep comprehension of the very nature of MDBs in general and the particular institution under review, rather than a simplistic treatment.

The controversial role of *credit rating agencies* is further revealed in Chap. 4 (*Current Governance*), as it has implications on multiple governance issues.

Naturally, this role affects the financial dynamics of MDBs as well. While MDBs do not have a formal requirement to obtain ratings, they do this to facilitate their borrowing from the international capital markets.

The *credit rating agencies* assess the MDBs' capacity and willingness to pay their obligations. The credit ratings of both non-borrowing (*donor*) and borrowing (*regional*) countries are also reflected in MDBs' ratings. The institutions' shareholders are assessed as capital contributors, as well as borrowers affecting the respective loan portfolios. Hence, the *rating agencies* assess not just the MDBs, but numerous relevant stakeholders, including the shareholder and borrower countries.

The *credit rating* of an MDB also depends on the robustness of its governance, as well as the evidence of shareholders commitment. Key indicators of shareholder support *by borrowing countries* include repaying the loans to the MDB, even in a time of financial distress (proof of respect of the MDB's *preferred creditor status*), as well as participation in the periodic capital increases. The latter reflects both the willingness and ability to pay (certain beneficiary countries in financial distress have either not subscribed to capital increases or are in arrears regarding payments for the capital increases of some MDBs—both situations signal compromised commitment, negatively affecting credit rating reviews).

A key indicator of shareholder support for non-borrowing (donor) shareholder countries is the willingness to increase contributions of *paid-in capital* and, secondarily, *callable capital.* The willingness to increase *paid-in* capital strengthens shareholders' equity and is a main criterion for commitment, for all types of shareholders. The willingness to contribute callable capital is an untested, less tangible, and harder-to-assess form of support, but it also matters.[14]

While *rating agencies inherently play an implicit regulatory and oversight role over MDBs*, this process is controversial. The challenge stems from the very nature of MDBs as unique supranational institutions with *preferred creditor status* and multiple implicit subsidies such as tax and dividend exemptions. This complexity is often poorly understood and reflected by the actual rating process that generally treats the MDBs as a simple mixture of banks (lenders and borrowers) and sovereigns (shareholders)—and not as complex self-regulated public institutions with highly conservative approaches and systems regarding risk, leverage, prudence, and ownership support, as well as a mandate to catalyze vast resources. It is noteworthy that all MDBs maintain capital ratios much stronger than those of commercial institutions, in most cases supplemented by huge *callable capital* that essentially rules out a default, as confirmed by the long history of these institutions. Furthermore, MDBs' liquidity is typically robust. MDBs' generally low returns on equity (relative to commercial financial institutions) reflect strong capital positions and the *raison d'etre* as development rather than profit-maximizing. That is further mitigated by not paying dividends, as well as by the inherent tax and other privileges of MDBs.

In the past, the rating was a rather simple process as most MDBs had a large number of AAA-rated shareholder countries and, with some exceptions, routinely got AAA or similar high credit rating. With the proliferation of MDBs, particularly sub-regional ones, as well as the need to increase leverage in light of the recent global crisis developments, rating agencies adopted a more stringent approach, limiting the easy access to AAA and similar ratings. Even large regional MDBs are currently likely to lose their AAA rating, which was once taken for granted.

These rating challenges result in higher cost of funding that in turn puts a pressure on the MDB's efficiency and competitiveness. This triggers an increasing attention on the importance and peculiarity of the rating process. It also affects the MDBs' governance and even their strategies. To issue high credit ratings, the agencies routinely put certain requirements on the banks, such as portfolio risk reduction, sector and country diversification, and so on. While this may be meaningful in the case of banks in general, it has a controversial rationale and relevance vis-à-vis MDBs as they are special public mandate institutions, intrinsically different from banks and the associated risk mitigation needs.

While some rating agencies have recently started to issue regular reviews on MDBs under a specific category of "supranationals", the applied methodology is still short of reflecting the very distinct nature of MDBs and challenges the credibility of the ratings. On the positive side, these rating reviews just started to cover not only the financial features of MDBs, but also the "business profile", reflecting some institutional governance aspects. They also start to acknowledge the distinct essence of MDBs (rightly referred as Multilateral Lending Institutions—MLI, noting their institutional nature; see *S&P Global Ratings* 2017).

The insufficient reflection by rating agencies of the very specific institutional features of MDBs has already drawn the attention of MDBs and shareholders (including G20) who are considering how to mitigate it. Some of the BRICS (Brazil, Russia, India, China, and South Africa) countries already announced the establishment of alternative rating agencies, calling for reconsideration of the rating system as such. Likewise, some MDBs took a course toward "sweating" or "optimizing" their balance sheets, meaning a regrouping of assets in order to boost the actual capital adequacy and thus make more resources available for lending. The balance sheet optimization initiative was started in 2013 by a few MDBs but is now gaining further momentum (The World Bank 2015). It started by an exchange of sovereign exposures among MDBs, to collectively optimize balance sheets for better development effectiveness.

Commercial financial institutions diversify their loan portfolio across thousands of borrowers. In contrast, MDBs lend to their sovereign shareholders and in some cases the private sector on a rather targeted mode. This creates an asset concentration, based on a strong relationship between MDBs and their borrowers. However, from a credit rating simplistic perspective, such concentration calls for additional capital.

Beyond the issue of how adequate the credit ratings are, there is a concern that the rating agencies are impacting on the strategies and governance of MDBs, effectively undertaking the implicit role of strategy makers and even regulators, who however have very little depth of comprehension regarding the MDBs' complexity.

Additionality and Subsidies

Additionality is a core principle at virtually all MDBs, although it remains rather elusive in real terms. In essence, it stipulates that the MDBs' operations should be additional to what is already available in the market. In other words, as tax-payer-financed public institutions, MDBs should not compete with (or crowd out) market participants as their role is to offset market and institutional deficiencies by offering unavailable products and services. While *additionality* is a broad concept, it generally has two aspects: (1) financial, for example offering of products with certain financial terms that are not available (e.g. longer loan maturity, broader risk coverage, etc.); and (2) non-financial, such as know-how, advice, honest brokerage, and enhanced social, environmental, and other development features of the financed operations.

Through their *additionality*, MDBs have the challenging task to detect and mitigate both *market and institutional failures* and inefficiencies. While certain elements of their operations may be subsidized (e.g. concessional lending or free technical cooperation), *additionality* does not imply any deviation from *sound banking principles* (e.g. that all operations should be financially sustainable and priced in line with the market). In other words, an MDB is additional when it offers products, services, terms, and conditions not offered by other institutions and the private sector. Obviously, this is easily said than done, as the market is very dynamic and the private sector has demonstrated its ability to adapt and deliver development elements such as *corporate social responsibility*, green businesses, and so on.

The terms and structure of MDBs' financing (including not only pricing but also other key aspects such as *tenor*, *grace period*, and currency), along with risk mitigation and *resource mobilization*, constitute the core of the *financial additionality*. Ideally, these should be supplemented by a strong element of *non-financial additionality* that adds value to each project by incorporating strong development and other mandate-relevant features such as sound social and environmental measures, fair income distribution, inclusiveness, and gender balance. While commercial banks' performance is measured by the market in terms of profitability, MDBs' performance is utterly complex. This is why MDBs have institutionalized a distinct own function—the independent evaluation that has the task of providing a rigorous impartial assessment of all aspects of mandate fulfillment—including the relevance, efficiency, impact, and *additionality* of all operations. This ensures an important combination of public accountability and institutional learning, as MDBs have to be at the helm of development innovation and risk mitigation, to inspire and encourage other institutions and the private sector.

While measuring all aspects of *additionality* is outside the scope of this review, some indications could be revealed by a closer look at the pricing dynamics over the last ten years. Figure 3.14 presents the distribution of gross income from lending operations. While the commonly shared concept of sound banking principles implies that MDB returns should be close, in line with market rates, the data illustrate yet another substantial differentiation among the three groups of institutions.

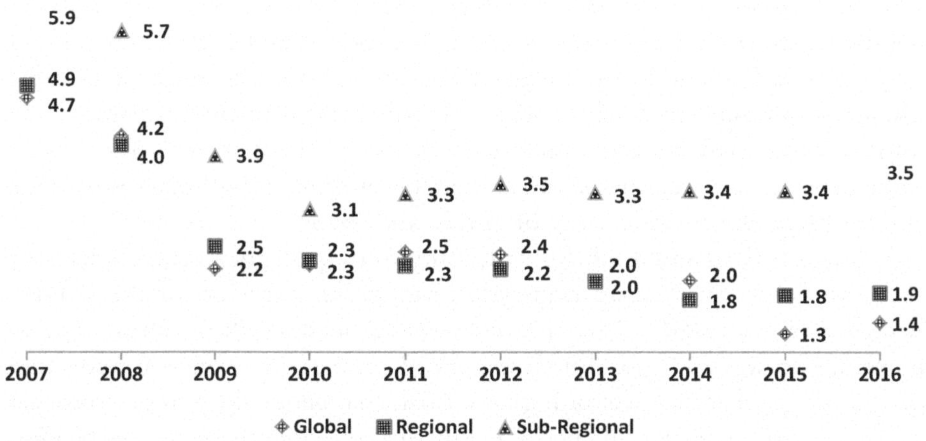

Fig. 3.14 Gross income from lending (%). Source: Authors' compilation from MDBs' annual reports

The common feature is that there has been a sharp reduction in the lending interest rates (Annex 13/Annex 6) of MDBs in 2009, associated with the global crisis and respective loosening of monetary policies worldwide. In contrast to the common trends, the rates of sub-regional MDBs have been consistently higher relative to the rest of peers—on average 130 to 140 basis points above the rates of *global* and *regional* MDBs. This differential stems mainly from the large gap between the borrowing (leverage) costs of the differently rated groups of institutions (generally smaller sub-regional MDBs having lower credit ratings such as A and below, while almost all regional and global MDBs maintain AAA ratings).

Further to their public nature, development mandates, and the outlined role of demonstrating *additionality*, MDBs are backed by multiple layers of inherent and often very implicit subsidies. The core source of subsidy is the opportunity cost of the *paid-in* capital and accumulated reserves: as MDBs by definition are not profit-driven and therefore do not pay dividends to their shareholders, they consistently enhance their equity by all retained earnings, thus increasing their cost-free paid-in capital. The scale of the capital subsidy can be estimated by the respective market price (interest) of engaged capital and retained earnings, as well as the potential shareholders' ultimate claim on this equity. The latter claim is rather theoretical as MDBs typically are set and do stay for good, rather than be wound up upon mandate completion when equity plus accumulated reserves would be returned to the shareholders (Buiter and Fries 2002).

An important additional cost-free element of their capital base is the large portion of unpaid but callable capital that is equivalent to a cost-free sovereign guarantee of large magnitude, subject to regular upgrades. Last but not least, MDBs are extraterritorial international institutions that benefit from a broad range of privileges and immunities that represent another form of subsidy. These include but are not limited to a tax-free status of the institution and most of its human capital, a preferred creditor status that mitigates risks of capital and currency controls, jurisdictional immunity of both the institutions and staff regarding a wide range of duties, and so on.

While it is hard and doubtfully meaningful to quantify all these subsidies, they can be revealed in an aggregate form by an overview of the MDBs' *Return on Equity (RoE)*. This ratio is used as a benchmark of subsidy assessment in two ways: (1) absolute level of RoE, subject to average interest rate discounting indicates lower or higher returns that generally increase the overall equity and financial resilience of the institution, if levels are relatively high;

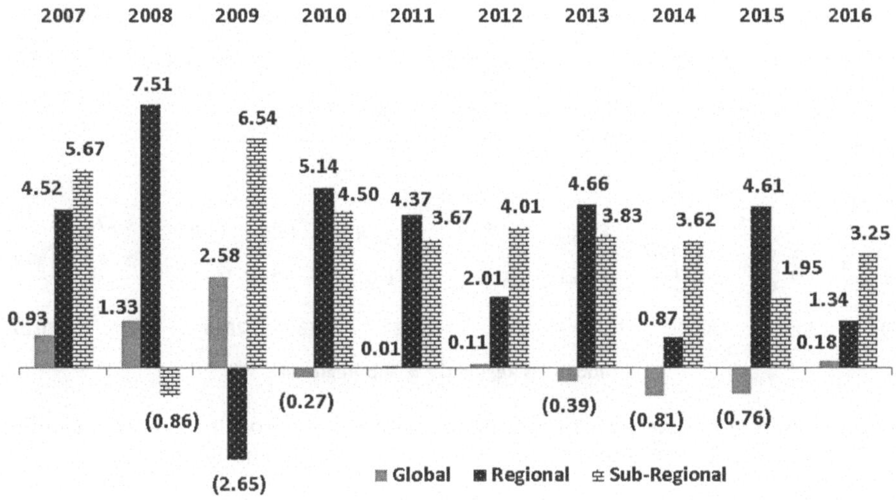

Fig. 3.15 Return on equity (RoE, %). Source: Authors' compilation from MDBs' annual reports

(2) comparisons among groups of institutions suggest a disparity in terms of returns and hence actual overall subsidy. Both assessments relate to shareholders' indirect contribution, in the absence of dividend returns (for details see Annex 14/Annex 3). Figure 3.15 illustrates the group dynamics of RoE, revealing a large gap between global MDBs, on one hand, and *regional* and *sub-regional*, on the other.

The impact of the global crisis on the MDBs caused negative returns in 2008 (sub-regional), 2009 (regional), and 2010 (global). The time lag reflects the size of the MDBs as the smaller MDBs were affected first. It is also apparent that while the global MDBs experienced a minor negative return in 2010, these institutions show consistently weaker returns overall. This can be attributed mainly to the relatively high administrative expenses of global MDBs. Figure 3.16 illustrates the ratio of administrative expenses to gross income from lending and treasury operations (Annex 15/Annex 16) before interest expenses peaked to over 50% for the *global* MDBs in the last four years. In contrast, *regional* MDBs have the lowest administrative expenses ratio—approximately six times lower on average compared to *global* MDBs. Sub-regional MDBs demonstrate slightly better ratio relative to the global group. Given their relatively small size, the inefficiency of the sub-regional group is mostly attributed to lack of economy of scale and scope.

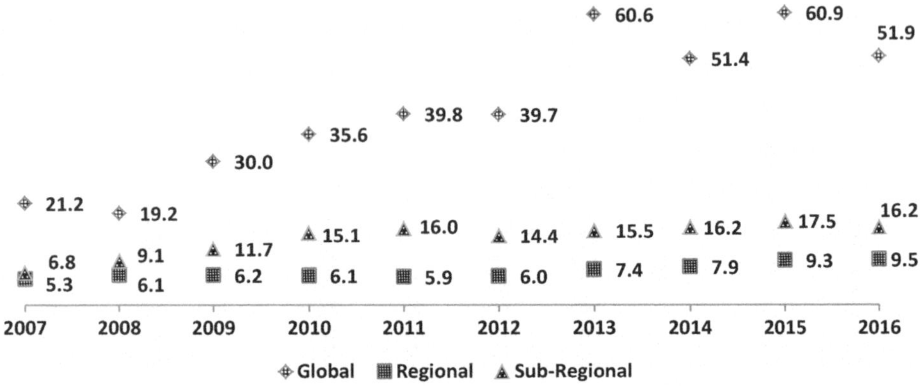

Fig. 3.16 Administrative costs ratio (Administrative Costs/Gross Income from Lending and Treasury, %). Source: Authors' compilation from MDBs' annual reports

Beyond Leverage: Crowding-In Private Investments

As already noted, for most MDBs, an important element of *additionality* is their catalytic role regarding the crowding-in of private financing toward relevant investments, for example in infrastructure, private businesses, climate change initiatives, and so on[15] (*Development Committee* 2015). Recently, MDBs have started coordinating their assessment of the relationships between private investment flows and MDB activities, covering both sovereign and non-sovereign financing. The most challenging element of such assessment is the private investment flow (beyond mobilization and co-financing) catalyzed by the MDBs. This includes but is not limited to the social and physical infrastructure that was established with MDB financing, as well as the other positive benefits created by the MDB operations, and by the impact of relevant policy changes and technical cooperation (*Development Committee* 2015).

Currently, MDBs distinguish three major types of crowding-in:

- *Mobilization*—a private financing on commercial terms due to the direct involvement of an MDB (e.g. a mandate letter or other evidence of direct involvement; it does not include sponsor financing but includes guarantees on the loan or equity).
- *Private co-financing*—financing from private sources (including sponsor and third parties) committed along a specific MDB financing, including *mobilization.*

- *Catalyzing*—private financing triggered by the development impact of an MDB operation or other activity (e.g. an improved investment climate, risk sharing, better infrastructure, new skills, etc.). It includes co-financing and mobilization.

As the concerted effort to measure and report catalytic effects is a recent initiative, MDBs need time to adjust their information systems to produce reliable data.

Concluding Remarks

Both the governance and the financial dynamics of MDBs are very distinct relative to other financial institutions. This calls for a dedicated approach, with particular reference to issuers of credit ratings and standards. While self-regulated, MDBs maintain high-profile mandates and observe prudent and conservative banking principles, require sound security and collateral in the assets of investment projects, and self-impose the highest requirements for financial transparency and risk mitigation, well beyond the regulatory requirements set for commercial banks. MDBs are intrinsically different from commercial banks as they were not established to maximize profits, do not use customer deposits, do not pay taxes, do not distribute dividends, and have their very own self-regulation, outside the scope of central banks and other authorities.

A key goal of MDBs is to enable borrowing countries to access financial resources on better terms than what would be available to them otherwise. Therefore, it is essential to enhance borrowing from the international markets while maintaining the highest credit rating. This requires a new dialogue with policymakers and all involved actors, to develop and articulate the intrinsically strong risk mitigation of MDBs. Unlike any other financial institutions, MDBs are extremely capitalized, relative to their credit risk. Therefore the role of the *callable capital* as a reliable measure of shareholders' support should be adequately appreciated and reflected by all market agents. While total borrowings of the MDBs have doubled between 2007 and 2014 to over one trillion USD, later on they decreased because regional MDBs were affected by downward pressure on their credit ratings. As *regional* institutions demonstrate the highest level of resource mobilization (with relatively low paid-in capital), other MDBs should make an effort to catch up.

An improved borrowing capacity should also positively affect liquidity management, with a particular reference to sub-regional MDBs who currently maintain higher shares of cash (over 11% vs. just 1% at regional MDBs) in order to meet future obligations, which erodes further their price competitiveness. This implies the need to enhance MDBs' treasury functions, reflecting the outlined challenges. This should also involve efforts to raise awareness at credit rating agencies as the latter press sub-regional MDBs to maintain higher liquidity. The apparently limited financial competitiveness of sub-regional MDBs has forced them to innovate and look for other aspects of *additionality*—a source of potential learning for the other two groups.

The MDBs' combined *subscribed* capital grew by 5.7% p.a. on average, reaching USD 1.4 trillion at the end of 2016, or 1.8% of the world's GDP. While this is an important trend and resource, the overwhelming development agenda requires a more efficient use of that capital. This implies increased leverage, as well as catalyzing further investments from the private sector. It also implies addressing the MDB group disparities and taking a course toward boosting overall efficiency. Looking at the examples of the regional group, as well as IBRD, it is clear that MDBs could operate successfully with generally lower levels of paid-in capital (around 5%), while increasing the share of callable capital.

The inherently high levels of retained earnings, which are a key engine of capitalization of MDBs, consistently increase their equity (3.6% p.a. on average, reaching over 30–60% of subscribed and over 300–700% of paid-in capital, depending on the group of MDB) and financial resilience. As the equity/capital ratio of sub-regional MDBs is particularly high, this factor should be used, along with others, to close the many gaps between this group and the other two, with reference to ratings and Basel risk treatment in particular.

The total of MDBs' loans, equity investments, and debt securities (almost equivalent to the MDBs' borrowed funds) reached USD 1.2 trillion, or 1.6% of the world GDP. The pace of the lending growth illustrates that overall the MDBs are countercyclical, as intended, mitigating the scarcity of investments at a time of turmoil. Once again, *regional* MDBs demonstrate highest relative portfolio. For all groups, the amount of off-balance sheet lending operations (guarantees) is negligible but deserves attention as it could enhance resource efficiency, provided that MDB-mandated goals could be effectively embedded in the process.

MDBs are very conservative in terms of leverage as even the lowest ratio figures are over six times above the Basel minimum requirement of 3%. As with many other aspects, MDB groups differ substantially in terms of leverage—threefold in magnitude. While *regional* MDBs are highly leveraged (lending is 6.6 times their equities), *global* and *sub-regional* MDBs are on the lower end. This puts the regional group in the lead in meeting the mandate requirement of mobilizing external resources. Other MDBs should, respectively, try to better utilize their own equity toward doing more with less, noting that there is a large potential to increase leverage ratios, relative to the Basel standards. The necessary increase in MDBs' effectiveness and efficiency, including the use of higher levels of leverage and balance sheet optimization, requires revisiting of the legacy of institutional and regulatory deficiencies (namely Basel standards and credit rating process).

Through their *additionality*, MDBs mitigate both *market and institutional failures* and inefficiencies. This requires further balancing and articulating the two aspects of *additionality*—financial and non-financial, based on comparative advantages across institutions. A review of the MDBs' returns reveals strong divergence, implying varying levels of subsidy and *additionality*. Another factor that deserves attention is the relatively high level of administrative expenses, particularly at global MDBs (over six times above the regional group). Given their relatively small size, the inefficiency of the sub-regional group is mostly attributed to lack of economy of scale and scope.

To improve their impact and efficiency, MDBs should complement higher levels of borrowing (leverage) with more effective crowding-in of strategic private investments, with a particular focus on specific measures that enhance catalyzing. These may include closer cooperation with potential investors already in the early project phases, to outline and implement factors that are essential in delivering follow-up investments.

Overall, the ***regional*** MDBs demonstrate leadership in many domains, over the last decade. Their share in total assets, lending operations, and borrowings exceeds 60% of all MDBs, respectively. As they have been operating with relatively modest ***paid-in*** capital (as share of subscribed capital), these institutions achieved higher mobilization and efficiency, relative to other peers. While performance varies across MDBs, the regional group leads in many aspects because of their stronger local presence, their size (not too big or small), as well as sound track record.

List of Abbreviations

Global

IBRD	International Bank for Reconstruction and Development
IDA	International Development Association
IFAD	International Fund for Agricultural Development
IFC	International Finance Corporation

Regional

AfDB	African Development Bank
AIIB	Asian Infrastructure Investment Bank
AsDB	Asian Development Bank
CEDB	Council of Europe Development Bank
EBRD	European Bank for Reconstruction and Development
EIB	European Investment Bank
IDB	Inter-American Development Bank
IsDB	Islamic Development Bank
NDB	New Development Bank (formerly referred to as the BRICS Development Bank)

Sub-regional

BADEA	Arab Bank for Economic Development in Africa
BSTDB	Black Sea Trade and Development Bank
CABEI	Central American Bank for Economic Integration
CAF	Development Bank of Latin America (formerly referred to as the Corporación Andina de Fomento)
CDB	Caribbean Development Bank
EADB	East African Development Bank
EDB	Eurasian Development Bank
ETDB	ECO Trade and Development Bank (also referred to as ECO Bank, where ECO stands for Economic Cooperation Organization)
IIB	International Investment Bank
NIB	Nordic Investment Bank
PTA	Eastern and Southern African Trade and Development Bank or the Preferential Trade Area Bank
WADB	West African Development Bank

Annexes

Annex 1: Subscribed Capital (Million USD)

	2007	2008	2009	2010	2011	2012	2013	2014	2015	2016
IBRD	189,801.00	189,801.00	189,918.00	189,943.00	193,732.00	205,394.00	223,181.00	232,791.00	252,821.00	263,329.00
IDA	167,926.00	177,038.00	199,423.00	199,131.00	204,332.00	224,412.00	224,303.00	225,800.00	244,694.00	245,103.00
IFC	2366.00	2366.00	2369.00	2369.00	2369.00	2372.00	2403.00	2502.00	2566.00	2566.00
IFAD	5658.00	6344.00	7158.00	7538.00	8109.00	9062.00	9627.00	9626.00	10,327.00	10,681.00
Global	**365,751.00**	**375,549.00**	**398,868.00**	**398,981.00**	**408,542.00**	**441,240.00**	**459,514.00**	**470,719.00**	**510,408.00**	**521,679.00**
CEDB	4862.35	4596.79	4758.30	4413.47	6407.39	7211.84	7546.44	6643.56	5957.37	5768.04
EIB	242,613.86	229,363.29	334,785.36	310,523.53	300,693.30	319,813.32	335,512.96	295,371.10	264,863.29	256,445.66
IDB	100,953.00	100,938.00	104,980.00	104,980.00	104,980.00	116,880.00	128,781.00	144,258.00	156,939.00	170,940.00
AfDB	3691.46	3613.47	3684.07	3628.31	3847.39	4363.32	4846.38	4981.01	5166.00	5404.21
AsDB	55,978.00	54,890.00	60,751.00	143,950.00	162,486.00	163,129.00	162,809.00	153,056.00	147,052.00	142,699.00
IsDB	21,918.07	23,221.42	24,869.05	26,899.06	27,674.08	27,140.95	27,261.38	74,055.05	70,465.25	67,346.90
EBRD	29,138.75	27,547.31	28,515.24	27,783.61	36,720.88	39,055.56	40,922.03	36,027.20	32,306.08	31,309.93
NDB	–	–	–	–	–	–	–	–	–	50,000.00
AIIB	–	–	–	–	–	–	–	–	–	90,327.00
Regional	**459,155.48**	**444,170.28**	**562,343.02**	**622,177.97**	**642,809.05**	**677,593.99**	**707,679.19**	**714,391.92**	**682,748.99**	**820,240.74**
CABEI	1723.00	1723.00	1723.00	1723.00	1723.00	3834.00	3959.00	3959.00	3959.00	4186.00
EADB	448.00	459.00	529.00	529.00	529.00	529.00	807.00	932.00	1008.00	1302.70
CDB	713.00	713.00	713.00	937.00	1502.00	1549.00	1635.00	1699.00	1764.00	1764.00
CAF	3157.00	3732.00	4084.00	4956.00	5452.00	6291.00	6461.00	6494.00	6511.00	7219.00
IIB	1913.73	1809.21	1872.78	1737.06	1682.07	1715.22	1792.83	1578.33	1415.31	1370.33
BADEA	2200.00	2200.00	2800.00	2800.00	2800.00	2800.00	2800.00	3575.00	3696.00	3798.00
NIB	6097.44	5764.42	5966.97	5534.54	7947.13	8103.75	8470.43	7457.00	6686.80	6474.28
PTA	1079.00	1180.40	1180.40	1180.40	1301.40	1301.40	1307.30	1395.30	1466.70	1602.60
BSTDB	1531.13	3080.54	3135.38	3106.13	3039.76	3056.65	3156.07	2778.47	2491.49	2412.31
ETDB	473.55	464.34	468.57	462.00	1535.30	1536.90	1590.05	1568.33	1509.03	1463.98
EDB	1500.00	1500.00	1515.70	1515.70	1515.70	1515.70	1515.70	7000.00	7000.00	7000.00
Sub-regional	**20,835.84**	**22,625.91**	**23,988.80**	**24,480.83**	**29,027.36**	**32,232.63**	**33,494.38**	**38,436.43**	**37,507.32**	**38,593.20**
Total	**845,742.33**	**842,345.19**	**985,199.81**	**1,045,639.80**	**1,080,378.41**	**1,151,066.62**	**1,200,687.57**	**1,223,547.35**	**1,230,664.31**	**1,380,512.93**

Annex 2: Paid in Capital (Million USD)

	2007	2008	2009	2010	2011	2012	2013	2014	2015	2016
IBRD	11,486.00	11,486.00	11,491.00	11,492.00	11,720.00	12,418.00	13,434.00	14,005.00	15,192.00	15,805.00
IDA	136,456.00	142,416.00	150,085.00	157,413.00	167,610.00	175,587.00	184,511.00	193,747.00	201,045.00	208,430.00
IFC	2365.00	2366.00	2369.00	2369.00	2369.00	2372.00	2403.00	2502.00	2566.00	2566.00
IFAD	5280.00	5302.00	5844.00	6158.00	6261.00	6987.00	7250.00	7273.00	7897.00	8049.00
Global	**155,587.00**	**161,570.00**	**169,789.00**	**177,432.00**	**187,960.00**	**197,364.00**	**207,598.00**	**217,527.00**	**226,700.00**	**234,850.00**
CEDB	544.68	514.93	533.02	494.39	716.82	807.47	844.01	743.03	666.28	645.11
EIB	12,130.10	11,467.61	16,739.77	15,526.64	15,035.12	28,525.43	29,925.09	26,344.76	23,623.70	22,872.92
IDB	4340.00	4339.00	4339.00	4339.00	4339.00	4640.00	4941.00	5357.00	5699.00	6039.00
AfDB	3438.62	3365.49	3430.11	3377.29	3600.21	4108.19	4579.96	4730.36	4931.81	5187.77
AsDB	3842.00	3777.00	3818.00	4256.00	5237.00	6010.00	6843.00	7313.00	7293.00	7154.00
IsDB	4843.47	5081.35	5706.39	6204.52	6806.86	7005.40	7350.14	7208.63	6973.40	6913.89
EBRD	7651.98	7234.06	7488.24	8280.43	8020.89	8182.92	8553.18	7529.85	6752.12	6542.80
NDB	–	–	–	–	–	–	–	–	–	10,000.00
AIIB	–	–	–	–	–	–	–	–	–	18,065.00
Regional	**36,790.85**	**35,779.43**	**42,054.53**	**42,478.27**	**43,755.90**	**59,279.40**	**63,036.38**	**59,226.62**	**55,939.32**	**83,420.48**
CABEI	420.00	427.00	447.00	451.00	451.00	487.00	620.00	731.00	865.00	1002.00
EADB	86.00	97.00	100.00	100.00	100.00	100.00	152.00	173.00	186.00	189.80
CDB	157.00	157.00	157.00	157.00	186.00	219.00	259.00	299.00	343.00	382.00
CAF	2249.00	2457.00	3025.00	3430.00	3969.00	4419.00	5284.00	6162.00	6845.00	7673.00
IIB	315.03	297.82	308.29	285.95	276.89	217.70	332.36	331.45	329.88	329.93
BADEA	2200.00	2200.00	2800.00	2800.00	2800.00	2800.00	2800.00	3575.00	3696.00	3798.00
NIB	616.81	583.12	603.61	559.87	542.14	552.83	577.84	508.71	456.17	441.67
PTA	117.50	127.90	133.60	145.20	179.00	193.70	259.70	327.80	366.90	407.10
BSTDB	459.34	462.08	472.66	573.23	604.51	652.31	714.37	659.01	627.53	647.01
ETDB	170.48	241.46	318.63	388.08	460.59	461.07	465.08	444.06	430.68	423.60
EDB	804.80	1500.00	1500.60	1515.70	1515.70	1515.70	1515.70	1515.70	1515.70	1515.70
Sub-regional	**7595.95**	**8550.38**	**9866.39**	**10,406.02**	**11,084.84**	**11,618.31**	**12,980.06**	**14,726.73**	**15,661.84**	**16,809.81**
Total	**199,973.80**	**205,899.82**	**221,709.92**	**230,316.29**	**242,800.73**	**268,261.71**	**283,614.44**	**291,480.35**	**298,301.16**	**335,080.29**

Annex 3: Total Equity (Million USD)

	2007	2008	2009	2010	2011	2012	2013	2014	2015	2016
IBRD	39,796.00	41,548.00	40,037.00	36,261.00	39,683.00	36,685.00	39,523.00	38,895.00	38,637.00	37,063.00
IDA	110,212.00	123,619.00	127,950.00	128,275.00	136,416.00	137,546.00	143,462.00	153,749.00	147,149.00	154,700.00
IFC	14,130.00	18,261.00	16,122.00	18,359.00	20,279.00	20,580.00	22,275.00	23,990.00	24,426.00	22,766.00
IFAD	6411.00	6209.00	6939.00	7140.00	7086.00	7587.00	7538.00	6845.00	6925.00	6639.00
Global	**170,549.00**	**189,637.00**	**191,048.00**	**190,035.00**	**203,464.00**	**202,398.00**	**212,798.00**	**223,479.00**	**217,137.00**	**221,168.00**
CEDB	2688.05	2484.18	2822.14	2751.24	2732.72	2984.48	3392.59	3089.88	2951.47	2964.13
EIB	50,893.44	56,763.27	55,527.93	55,012.69	58,230.68	72,181.74	80,487.03	71,038.21	69,576.64	65,847.52
IDB	20,353.00	19,444.00	20,674.00	20,960.00	19,794.00	20,681.00	23,550.00	23,697.00	25,253.00	26,460.00
AfDB	7439.82	7177.66	7432.42	7422.94	7493.65	8207.15	8979.74	8808.76	8979.53	8880.64
AsDB	14,255.00	15,269.00	15,318.00	15,878.00	16,533.00	16,420.00	17,138.00	16,938.00	17,446.00	17,214.00
IsDB	8395.87	8406.79	9233.69	9895.52	10,317.67	10,703.45	11,094.12	11,466.38	11,079.81	11,077.28
EBRD	20,423.92	16,352.48	16,588.51	17,339.87	17,044.54	18,405.63	20,515.49	17,178.30	15,879.78	16,265.82
NDB	–	–	–	–	–	–	–	–	–	9605.00
AIIB	–	–	–	–	–	–	–	–	–	17,790.00
Regional	**124,449.10**	**125,897.38**	**127,596.68**	**129,260.25**	**132,146.26**	**149,583.45**	**165,156.98**	**152,216.54**	**151,166.22**	**176,104.39**
CABEI	1635.00	1708.00	1812.00	1929.00	2028.00	2142.00	2268.00	2396.00	2573.00	2723.00
EADB	79.00	82.00	87.00	96.00	111.00	159.00	182.00	219.00	239.00	251.20
CDB	506.00	543.00	565.00	604.00	674.00	694.00	744.00	822.00	874.00	896.50
CAF	4127.00	4554.00	5287.00	5753.00	6351.00	6865.00	7816.00	8763.00	9524.00	10,474.00
IIB	500.51	304.78	422.10	455.64	445.10	468.39	485.44	472.28	433.30	411.10
BADEA	3257.00	3150.00	3298.00	3419.00	3480.00	3650.00	3843.00	4087.00	4204.00	4428.00
NIB	2998.67	2407.64	2953.66	3022.48	3178.47	3517.52	3904.23	3625.30	3425.05	3452.18
PTA	132.00	154.60	178.40	210.20	278.40	344.30	477.00	622.00	736.30	856.50
BSTDB	517.27	532.47	569.70	676.25	720.70	793.09	884.14	843.92	785.50	793.42
ETDB	175.84	251.21	334.56	401.32	482.08	492.88	502.81	488.39	481.39	483.02
EDB	853.90	1531.50	1634.00	1663.50	1680.00	1709.10	1632.20	1638.30	1499.30	1667.00
Sub-regional	**14,782.19**	**15,219.20**	**17,141.42**	**18,230.40**	**19,428.75**	**20,835.28**	**22,738.83**	**23,977.20**	**24,774.84**	**26,435.92**
Total	**309,780.29**	**330,753.58**	**335,786.10**	**337,525.66**	**355,039.02**	**372,816.73**	**400,693.80**	**399,672.73**	**393,078.06**	**423,708.30**

Annex 4: Borrowings (Million USD)

	2007	2008	2009	2010	2011	2012	2013	2014	2015	2016
IBRD	87,759.00	87,690.00	112,363.00	129,575.00	137,426.00	149,039.00	149,434.00	164,416.00	164,555.00	183,408.00
IDA	10,819.00	9722.00	4684.00	4970.00	6013.00	3824.00	3622.00	5012.00	7054.00	4874.00
IFC	15,879.00	20,261.00	25,711.00	31,106.00	38,211.00	44,665.00	44,869.00	49,481.00	51,265.00	55,142.00
IFAD	325.00	327.00	222.00	269.00	281.00	175.00	169.00	177.00	162.00	191.00
Global	**114,782.00**	**118,000.00**	**142,980.00**	**165,920.00**	**181,931.00**	**197,703.00**	**198,094.00**	**219,086.00**	**223,036.00**	**243,615.00**
CEDB	23,590.40	26,005.31	28,803.36	28,235.24	27,877.08	29,009.65	28,606.67	25,071.17	21,396.22	21,416.15
EIB	383,502.66	403,984.07	472,989.32	488,119.20	571,936.15	635,747.61	634,493.57	622,561.34	577,058.90	559,746.07
IDB	47,049.00	49,394.00	60,307.00	62,953.00	63,923.00	65,565.00	68,701.00	77,309.00	79,137.00	80,326.00
AfDB	9795.97	10,330.59	16,587.73	18,451.10	19,809.59	20,407.22	19,938.38	21,449.63	22,793.87	27,752.35
AsDB	31,570.00	35,640.00	42,089.00	51,846.00	58,278.00	64,297.00	61,630.00	62,701.00	66,054.00	74,476.00
IsDB	2220.25	2821.77	4444.40	4064.14	5712.74	6814.70	9524.90	10,661.79	11,429.50	13,197.29
EBRD	26,013.48	25,657.38	28,587.27	33,334.18	41,152.49	46,060.25	43,030.68	43,047.13	40,140.37	40,065.29
NDB	–	–	–	–	–	–	–	–	–	403.00
AIIB	–	–	–	–	–	–	–	–	–	–
Regional	**523,741.76**	**553,833.12**	**653,808.07**	**687,002.87**	**788,689.04**	**867,901.44**	**865,925.20**	**862,801.06**	**818,009.87**	**817,382.15**
CABEI	3181.00	3531.00	3799.00	4402.00	4659.00	5118.00	5026.00	5297.00	5756.00	6404.00
EADB	172.00	138.00	113.00	104.00	62.00	54.00	52.00	58.00	125.00	123.70
CDB	477.00	609.00	718.00	653.00	858.00	920.00	675.00	530.00	503.00	654.00
CAF	8246.00	9406.00	10,404.00	12,474.00	14,859.00	17,431.00	19,021.00	20,887.00	21,781.00	23,778.00
IIB	–	108.55	–	–	–	5.28	68.96	259.82	402.82	489.10
BADEA	–	–	–	–	–	–	–	–	–	–
NIB	22,919.12	26,118.59	26,868.63	28,353.23	25,916.82	28,948.56	25,916.60	24,668.08	24,459.82	26,601.27
PTA	200.50	414.80	451.10	740.20	978.70	1329.50	1796.60	2768.70	3053.30	3163.50
BSTDB	365.89	707.45	565.00	398.59	346.89	492.66	394.84	414.25	588.99	909.16
ETDB	–	–	141.35	151.38	194.68	190.11	191.88	168.21	159.01	146.67
EDB	450.30	464.30	849.60	867.20	1380.90	2129.70	2912.60	2249.60	1357.80	1564.00
Sub-regional	**36,011.82**	**41,497.69**	**43,909.68**	**48,143.60**	**49,255.99**	**56,618.82**	**56,055.47**	**57,300.66**	**58,186.74**	**63,833.40**
Total	**674,535.58**	**713,330.81**	**840,697.75**	**901,066.47**	**1,019,876.03**	**1,122,223.26**	**1,120,074.67**	**1,139,187.72**	**1,099,232.60**	**1,124,830.54**

Annex 5: Loans, Debt Securities, Equities (Million USD)

	2007	2008	2009	2010	2011	2012	2013	2014	2015	2016
IBRD	97,805.00	99,050.00	105,698.00	120,103.00	132,459.00	136,325.00	143,776.00	154,021.00	157,012.00	169,655.00
IDA	102,457.00	113,542.00	112,894.00	113,474.00	125,287.00	123,576.00	125,135.00	136,011.00	130,878.00	136,735.00
IFC	16,644.00	24,167.00	23,452.00	27,293.00	31,241.00	32,819.00	36,305.00	39,862.00	39,321.00	39,131.00
IFAD	3581.00	3778.00	4007.00	4257.00	4533.00	4859.00	5107.00	5077.00	5165.00	5318.00
Global	**220,487.00**	**240,537.00**	**246,051.00**	**265,127.00**	**293,520.00**	**297,579.00**	**310,323.00**	**334,971.00**	**332,376.00**	**350,839.00**
CEDB	21,832.72	23,040.99	22,662.08	20,951.62	24,934.75	24,998.67	25,109.27	21,978.85	20,010.31	19,996.28
EIB	435,086.52	451,676.24	492,418.69	524,879.40	577,445.57	636,981.25	668,684.22	624,116.60	560,503.04	546,668.91
IDB	47,954.00	51,173.00	58,049.00	63,007.00	66,130.00	68,640.00	70,679.00	74,585.00	78,745.00	81,952.00
AfDB	9203.38	9384.87	12,296.96	13,313.56	15,065.60	17,852.86	18,828.04	19,489.39	19,260.26	21,780.83
AsDB	31,426.00	36,850.00	42,787.00	47,277.00	50,946.00	54,031.00	54,092.00	56,869.00	63,027.00	68,894.00
IsDB	7405.68	7838.13	9457.40	10,672.87	12,010.57	13,251.94	15,080.76	16,006.45	16,827.47	18,047.76
EBRD	23,001.56	29,430.28	33,627.93	28,410.28	31,524.58	34,690.98	36,179.31	31,356.56	29,669.25	29,751.97
NDB	–	–	–	–	–	–	–	–	–	–
AIIB	–	–	–	–	–	–	–	–	–	33.00
Regional	**575,909.85**	**609,393.49**	**671,299.06**	**708,511.73**	**778,057.08**	**850,446.71**	**888,652.60**	**844,401.86**	**788,042.34**	**787,124.76**
CABEI										
EADB	3962.00	4328.00	4384.00	4864.00	5205.00	5526.00	5426.00	5743.00	6112.00	6504.00
CDB	240.00	171.00	137.00	132.00	79.00	89.00	107.00	114.00	166.00	190.00
CAF	750.00	770.00	820.00	995.00	1012.00	980.00	973.00	989.00	999.00	1023.00
IIB	9575.00	10,208.00	11,716.00	13,808.00	15,016.00	16,425.00	18,151.00	19,347.00	20,759.00	22,363.00
BADEA	–	222.67	259.31	236.51	209.61	225.62	133.77	296.24	342.94	400.56
NIB	965.20	1033.80	1075.30	1137.10	1184.10	1251.40	1328.30	1384.00	1464.50	1561.20
PTA	19,124.49	18,289.72	19,972.91	18,603.91	18,476.89	20,172.70	20,443.23	18,621.50	17,222.47	17,687.17
BSTDB	309.20	586.80	655.50	860.60	1094.30	1326.40	2013.20	2511.00	2902.40	3234.30
ETDB	747.57	949.58	912.24	890.71	922.29	1028.08	1065.49	1158.13	1203.23	1247.74
EDB	–	4.95	215.70	184.34	265.91	244.06	287.36	259.19	325.64	359.88
Sub-regional	**35,673.46**	**36,564.52**	**40,147.96**	**41,712.17**	**43,465.11**	**47,268.26**	**49,928.36**	**50,423.06**	**51,497.18**	**54,570.84**
Total	**832,070.31**	**886,495.01**	**957,498.01**	**1,015,350.90**	**1,115,042.19**	**1,195,293.97**	**1,248,903.95**	**1,229,795.92**	**1,171,915.52**	**1,192,534.60**

Annex 6: Loans, Debt Securities, Equities (Net, Million USD)

	2007	2008	2009	2010	2011	2012	2013	2014	2015	2016
IBRD	95,433.00	97,268.00	103,657.00	118,104.00	130,470.00	134,209.00	141,692.00	151,978.00	155,040.00	167,643.00
IDA	90,241.00	100,474.00	102,347.00	104,556.00	118,368.00	116,880.00	121,157.00	132,010.00	126,760.00	132,825.00
IFC	15,812.00	23,319.00	22,214.00	25,944.00	29,934.00	31,438.00	34,677.00	38,176.00	37,578.00	37,356.00
IFAD	3426.00	3597.00	3889.00	4152.00	4456.00	4782.00	5053.00	5047.00	5141.00	5301.00
Global	**204,912.00**	**224,658.00**	**232,107.00**	**252,756.00**	**283,228.00**	**287,309.00**	**302,579.00**	**327,211.00**	**324,519.00**	**343,125.00**
CEDB	21,832.72	23,040.99	22,662.08	20,951.62	24,934.75	24,998.67	25,109.27	21,978.85	20,010.31	19,996.28
EIB	435,032.05	451,652.58	492,265.99	524,756.47	577,195.85	636,577.52	668,236.01	623,610.32	559,970.67	546,166.10
IDB	47,903.00	51,037.00	57,933.00	62,862.00	65,980.00	68,460.00	70,435.00	74,215.00	78,301.00	81,420.00
AfDB	8892.07	9226.22	12,137.06	13,138.00	14,884.44	17,656.14	18,604.74	19,269.17	18,981.73	21,443.41
AsDB	31,411.00	36,841.00	42,684.00	47,235.00	50,911.00	53,988.00	54,056.00	56,834.00	62,993.00	68,849.00
IsDB	7141.15	7559.65	9144.34	10,339.76	11,672.66	12,857.87	14,727.02	15,632.66	16,490.19	17,641.64
EBRD	22,819.02	28,927.88	32,357.32	27,568.48	30,655.08	33,719.91	35,052.58	29,888.71	28,490.19	28,651.49
NDB	–	–	–	–	–	–	–	–	–	–
AIIB	–	–	–	–	–	–	–	–	–	33.00
Regional	**575,031.00**	**608,285.30**	**669,183.77**	**706,851.32**	**776,233.78**	**848,258.10**	**886,220.63**	**841,428.72**	**785,237.08**	**784,200.92**
CABEI	3822.00	4166.00	4181.00	4664.00	5027.00	5358.00	5267.00	5575.00	5935.00	6310.00
EADB	187.00	140.00	105.00	99.00	67.00	81.00	101.00	108.00	162.90	185.00
CDB	750.00	769.00	818.00	993.00	1007.00	972.00	968.00	983.00	993.00	1017.00
CAF	9407.00	10,065.00	11,572.00	13,667.00	14,885.00	16,299.00	18,113.00	19,291.00	20,700.00	20,695.00
IIB	–	137.78	109.49	73.49	56.93	64.65	133.77	291.38	332.05	382.64
BADEA	845.00	948.80	1026.30	1088.40	1170.50	1237.80	1315.30	1377.00	1464.50	1559.20
NIB	19,124.05	18,179.22	19,826.98	18,400.81	18,312.57	19,963.84	20,227.26	18,400.90	17,013.11	17,540.22
PTA	276.70	542.80	611.90	821.40	1058.20	1278.20	1952.20	2443.10	2807.40	3136.70
BSTDB	706.84	901.98	865.05	832.85	870.79	972.66	1008.67	1100.22	1174.27	1216.01
ETDB	–	4.80	215.39	183.88	265.45	243.60	286.90	258.90	325.64	359.88
EDB	326.30	764.50	890.70	1104.70	1773.90	2267.10	2805.00	2392.50	1581.30	1580.20
Sub-regional	**35,444.89**	**36,619.88**	**40,221.80**	**41,928.53**	**44,494.35**	**48,737.85**	**52,178.11**	**52,221.00**	**52,489.18**	**53,981.85**
Total	**815,387.90**	**869,563.18**	**941,512.57**	**1,001,535.86**	**1,103,956.12**	**1,184,304.95**	**1,240,977.74**	**1,220,860.72**	**1,162,245.26**	**1,181,307.77**

Annex 7: Guarantees (Million USD)

	2007	2008	2009	2010	2011	2012	2013	2014	2015	2016
IBRD	938.00	788.00	1713.00	1726.00	1969.00	1753.00	1881.00	1804.00	1432.00	1506.00
IDA	189.00	209.00	292.00	279.00	258.00	299.00	359.00	424.00	411.00	1059.00
IFC	1414.00	1924.00	2055.00	2721.00	4081.00	4507.00	4933.00	4661.00	4091.00	4250.00
IFAD	–	–	–	–	–	–	–	–	–	–
Global	**2541.00**	**2921.00**	**4060.00**	**4726.00**	**6308.00**	**6559.00**	**7173.00**	**6889.00**	**5934.00**	**6815.00**
CEDB	–	–	–	–	–	–	–	–	–	–
EIB	5554.23	5682.31	4578.23	4110.15	4844.36	4847.48	6974.11	6635.06	10,031.28	10,695.95
IDB	659.00	870.00	834.00	814.00	847.00	641.00	546.00	191.00	817.00	658.00
AfDB	2.05	1.85	1.57	3.08	15.35	26.13	113.96	239.05	616.65	545.80
AsDB	1397.00	1616.00	1599.00	1969.00	1995.00	1905.00	1780.00	1740.00	1407.00	2105.00
IsDB	–	–	–	–	–	–	–	–	–	–
EBRD	521.12	364.63	468.20	621.33	715.53	827.26	864.70	762.45	627.09	595.57
NDB	–	–	–	–	–	–	–	–	–	–
AIIB	–	–	–	–	–	–	–	–	–	–
Regional	**8133.41**	**8534.78**	**7480.99**	**7517.56**	**8417.24**	**8246.87**	**10,278.76**	**9567.56**	**13,499.02**	**14,600.32**
CABEI	10.50	72.00	16.00	12.00	67.00	47.00	80.00	107.00	73.00	305.00
EADB	7.00	3.00	3.00	1.00	0.20	2.00	1.00	–	0.30	–
CDB	–	–	–	–	–	–	–	12.00	12.00	12.00
CAF	268.00	159.00	185.00	421.00	407.00	360.00	434.00	329.00	267.00	197.00
IIB	–	–	–	–	–	–	–	–	11.98	15.81
BADEA	–	–	–	–	–	–	–	–	–	–
NIB	25.00	17.00	–	–	–	–	–	–	–	–
PTA	156.80	118.60	217.00	166.30	240.30	503.00	597.40	490.00	351.00	348.40
BSTDB	–	–	–	–	–	–	–	–	–	–
ETDB	–	–	–	–	–	–	–	–	–	–
EDB	–	–	–	0.20	–	25.20	24.40	48.40	5.30	160.60
Sub-regional	**467.30**	**369.60**	**421.00**	**600.50**	**714.50**	**937.20**	**1136.80**	**986.40**	**720.58**	**1038.81**
Total	**11,141.71**	**11,825.38**	**11,961.99**	**12,844.06**	**15,439.74**	**15,743.07**	**18,588.56**	**17,442.96**	**20,153.60**	**22,454.13**

Annex 8: Undisbursed Commitments for Loan, Debt Security and Equity Investment (Million USD)

	2007	2008	2009	2010	2011	2012	2013	2014	2015	2016
IBRD	35,440.00	38,176.00	51,125.00	63,574.00	64,435.00	62,916.00	61,306.00	58,449.00	60,211.00	65,909.00
IDA	24,517.00	27,539.00	29,903.00	30,696.00	38,059.00	37,144.00	39,765.00	46,844.00	47,288.00	49,476.00
IFC	8723.00	11,399.00	10,547.00	11,250.00	12,158.00	11,521.00	12,319.00	12,206.00	11,591.00	11,874.00
IFAD	2287.00	2266.00	2405.00	2388.00	2442.00	2613.00	3143.00	3325.00	3558.00	3494.00
Global	**70,967.00**	**79,380.00**	**93,980.00**	**107,908.00**	**117,094.00**	**114,194.00**	**116,533.00**	**120,824.00**	**122,648.00**	**130,753.00**
CEDB	4762.24	4734.56	5122.77	5348.81	4984.10	3959.52	4250.39	3482.04	3395.66	4397.71
EIB	81,351.19	84,101.82	120,647.37	123,888.46	114,264.31	111,546.03	132,942.48	125,365.54	120,808.68	126,675.41
IDB	16,428.00	19,820.00	21,555.00	22,357.00	23,994.00	26,987.00	29,207.00	31,611.00	30,711.00	30,007.00
AfDB	2561.59	3932.31	7841.59	7476.85	8138.47	6859.27	6914.60	5434.49	6431.17	9146.82
AsDB	12,972.00	13,818.00	16,656.00	15,828.00	18,476.00	21,792.00	21,907.00	26,140.00	25,911.00	26,898.00
IsDB	8696.27	–	–	–	9339.05	10,472.57	–	11,424.30	13,363.70	12,228.03
EBRD	9955.81	8638.28	10,558.16	11,930.93	12,267.47	13,679.54	14,903.93	13,237.33	13,481.37	12,132.69
NDB	–	–	–	–	–	–	–	–	–	–
AIIB	–	–	–	–	–	–	–	–	–	334.00
Regional	**136,727.11**	**135,044.98**	**182,380.89**	**186,830.04**	**191,463.39**	**195,295.94**	**210,125.40**	**216,694.70**	**214,102.59**	**221,819.66**
CABEI	2548.00	1385.00	1230.00	1599.00	1516.00	1908.00	1780.00	2232.00	2682.00	2719.00
EADB	18.00	11.00	13.00	8.00	6.00	13.00	4.00	6.00	6.00	5.00
CDB	278.00	253.00	297.00	263.00	230.00	285.00	290.00	307.00	337.00	373.00
CAF	3917.00	5366.00	5592.00	9106.00	8376.00	7471.00	9620.00	10,287.00	9607.00	9950.00
IIB	–	29.23	11.52	14.70	28.47	26.39	73.09	83.77	56.61	34.79
BADEA	752.00	763.00	857.00	885.00	943.50	917.50	978.30	1047.00	1129.00	1114.00
NIB	1766.52	1974.82	1102.06	1575.38	2234.57	2128.19	1894.88	1597.76	1298.82	2101.88
PTA	63.30	245.10	136.20	158.20	160.80	522.60	915.60	649.00	740.20	901.60
BSTDB	120.28	188.53	138.74	109.97	222.55	141.04	204.24	110.36	223.73	168.87
ETDB	–	40.09	35.61	22.48	102.40	48.72	45.28	67.51	48.92	68.43
EDB	52.00	616.00	569.70	1144.90	1128.10	1348.00	1124.10	708.10	508.30	623.00
Sub-regional	**9515.10**	**10,871.77**	**9982.84**	**14,886.63**	**14,948.39**	**14,809.44**	**16,929.50**	**17,095.50**	**16,637.57**	**18,059.55**
Total	**217,209.21**	**225,296.74**	**286,343.72**	**309,624.67**	**323,505.78**	**324,299.38**	**343,587.90**	**354,614.20**	**353,388.16**	**370,632.21**

Annex 9: Total Assets (Million USD)

	2007	2008	2009	2010	2011	2012	2013	2014	2015	2016
IBRD	208,030.00	233,599.00	275,420.00	283,010.00	312,848.00	338,178.00	325,601.00	358,883.00	343,225.00	371,260.00
IDA	131,839.00	149,849.00	146,010.00	145,272.00	162,201.00	160,028.00	165,806.00	183,445.00	178,685.00	180,475.00
IFC	40,550.00	49,471.00	51,483.00	61,075.00	68,490.00	75,761.00	77,525.00	84,130.00	87,548.00	90,434.00
IFAD	7015.00	7474.00	7801.00	8232.00	8267.00	8956.00	9008.00	8228.00	8424.00	8206.00
Global	**389,441.00**	**440,393.00**	**480,714.00**	**497,589.00**	**551,806.00**	**582,923.00**	**577,940.00**	**634,686.00**	**617,882.00**	**650,375.00**
CEDB	27,247.10	29,786.56	32,744.84	33,032.20	33,748.79	35,435.13	33,767.26	31,014.18	27,343.79	26,988.12
EIB	457,540.46	489,824.12	556,513.86	596,641.36	662,018.76	749,173.79	754,231.17	739,142.87	686,483.05	669,267.06
IDB	69,907.00	72,510.00	84,006.00	87,217.00	89,432.00	92,209.00	96,987.00	106,277.00	111,116.00	113,325.00
AfDB	19,092.58	19,362.73	26,940.75	29,482.33	31,106.11	32,604.22	32,335.38	33,251.64	35,124.10	39,962.90
AsDB	69,549.00	78,722.00	85,667.00	100,170.00	113,310.00	119,864.00	115,868.00	115,660.00	117,697.00	125,854.00
IsDB	10,616.75	11,229.18	13,678.72	13,964.38	15,891.89	17,593.12	20,680.66	21,840.81	22,306.10	24,395.56
EBRD	48,836.92	45,991.51	46,875.68	52,548.74	60,859.88	67,476.75	67,517.98	63,724.47	59,906.81	59,187.72
NDB	–	–	–	–	–	–	–	–	–	10,054.00
AIIB	–	–	–	–	–	–	–	–	–	17,795.00
Regional	**702,789.81**	**747,426.11**	**846,426.86**	**913,056.01**	**1,006,367.43**	**1,114,356.02**	**1,121,387.45**	**1,110,910.97**	**1,059,976.84**	**1,086,829.36**
CABEI	4991.00	5451.00	5777.00	6468.00	6953.00	7506.00	7537.00	8044.00	8431.00	9194.00
EADB	276.00	244.00	224.00	237.00	206.00	219.00	254.00	294.00	381.00	394.10
CDB	1016.00	1177.00	1288.00	1269.00	1543.00	1641.00	1452.00	1378.00	1407.00	1599.20
CAF	12,590.00	14,272.00	15,887.00	18,547.00	21,535.00	24,818.00	27,418.00	30,458.00	32,470.00	35,669.00
IIB	–	428.64	433.62	469.01	459.33	484.22	566.81	741.82	880.76	928.66
BADEA	3412.40	3284.00	3386.00	3499.00	3519.00	3699.00	3902.00	4154.00	4269.00	4491.00
NIB	19,973.20	22,620.40	22,423.50	24,898.00	23,801.50	25,983.00	23,490.00	24,870.00	27,311.00	30,178.00
PTA	353.00	637.00	826.20	1056.00	1370.40	1843.70	2536.30	3544.00	4094.60	4261.30
BSTDB	891.68	1255.32	1148.49	1079.78	1082.74	1297.76	1285.60	1283.43	1403.66	1756.03
ETDB	176.48	252.29	477.63	554.55	681.06	689.15	700.24	665.58	646.47	637.72
EDB	1312.90	2007.60	2495.50	2552.60	2837.70	3884.00	4953.70	3915.50	2880.60	3255.10
Sub-regional	**44,992.66**	**51,629.26**	**54,366.94**	**60,629.94**	**63,988.73**	**72,064.83**	**74,095.65**	**79,348.32**	**84,175.09**	**92,364.11**
Total	**1,137,223.46**	**1,239,448.36**	**1,381,507.80**	**1,471,274.95**	**1,622,162.15**	**1,769,343.84**	**1,773,423.10**	**1,824,945.29**	**1,762,033.93**	**1,829,568.47**

Annex 10: Cash and Due from Banks (Million USD)

	2007	2008	2009	2010	2011	2012	2013	2014	2015	2016
IBRD	41.00	66.00	2380.00	1581.00	2312.00	5682.00	208.00	3606.00	311.00	1222.00
IDA	48.00	90.00	127.00	15.00	20.00	78.00	565.00	120.00	328.00	645.00
IFC	382.00	344.00	380.00	528.00	642.00	1328.00	616.00	819.00	1509.00	1391.00
IFAD	438.00	491.00	421.00	716.00	390.00	404.00	347.00	202.00	326.00	260.00
Global	**909.00**	**991.00**	**3308.00**	**2840.00**	**3364.00**	**7492.00**	**1736.00**	**4747.00**	**2474.00**	**3518.00**
CEDB	273.81	269.99	557.51	307.33	314.42	432.76	395.80	247.68	518.22	684.11
EIB	460.77	384.11	857.16	995.47	1799.81	1633.42	1741.80	1322.15	1322.77	1245.95
IDB	200.00	301.00	242.00	242.00	1189.00	1021.00	421.00	535.00	641.00	599.00
AfDB	150.12	913.38	500.09	609.85	528.13	1354.03	1469.16	589.67	1683.66	1757.04
AsDB	109.00	142.00	130.00	115.00	188.00	263.00	316.00	417.00	753.00	661.00
IsDB	158.03	113.98	100.33	749.99	1464.65	722.35	323.40	1512.56	327.03	1341.64
EBRD	6645.06	4653.84	4677.63	3973.86	6692.05	9915.29	10,020.54	12,884.03	12,763.92	14,873.35
NDB	–	–	–	–	–	–	–	–	–	2633.00
AIIB	–	–	–	–	–	–	–	–	–	3574.00
Regional	**7996.79**	**6778.30**	**7064.72**	**6993.50**	**12,176.06**	**15,341.85**	**14,687.71**	**17,508.08**	**18,009.60**	**27,369.09**
CABEI	495.00	595.00	697.00	829.00	662.00	748.00	719.00	958.00	1201.00	1506.00
EADB	70.00	83.00	102.00	119.00	132.00	117.00	129.00	152.00	182.00	174.70
CDB	8.00	16.00	98.00	9.00	79.00	96.00	68.00	34.00	65.00	94.00
CAF	329.00	1487.00	1268.00	1523.00	1801.00	1632.00	1692.00	1420.00	2806.00	1725.00
IIB	–	157.26	200.24	160.34	161.74	131.94	84.13	121.41	173.10	145.47
BADEA	515.70	435.30	372.00	262.40	188.00	170.00	147.00	200.40	140.00	157.00
NIB	6614.59	6648.15	1403.14	3641.95	3124.77	3717.01	2424.46	1989.91	2902.47	4697.07
PTA	33.00	60.00	171.30	156.60	214.70	462.60	404.00	439.00	643.50	595.00
BSTDB	8.37	8.78	17.56	113.71	15.40	24.01	20.55	77.70	54.11	73.79
ETDB	175.21	246.56	261.31	369.60	413.00	441.55	359.44	352.78	266.05	241.98
EDB	439.20	400.10	438.20	495.30	361.70	435.00	275.00	346.40	288.30	529.00
Sub-regional	**8688.07**	**10,137.16**	**5028.75**	**7679.90**	**7153.30**	**7975.12**	**6322.57**	**6091.61**	**8721.54**	**9939.00**
Total	**17,593.85**	**17,906.46**	**15,401.47**	**17,513.40**	**22,693.36**	**30,808.97**	**22,746.27**	**28,346.69**	**29,205.15**	**40,826.09**

Annex 11: Treasury Assets (Million USD)

	2007	2008	2009	2010	2011	2012	2013	2014	2015	2016
IBRD	23,336.00	26,598.00	41,045.00	36,301.00	32,645.00	33,675.00	36,874.00	45,482.00	49,951.00	53,522.00
IDA	17,432.00	29,161.00	26,488.00	26,343.00	29,818.00	30,865.00	30,741.00	34,162.00	33,173.00	31,493.00
IFC	14,527.00	12,381.00	20,787.00	23,967.00	26,310.00	29,832.00	30,686.00	33,287.00	34,731.00	31,212.00
IFAD	2504.00	2428.00	2488.00	2508.00	2766.00	2575.00	2359.00	2106.00	1734.00	1548.00
Global	**57,799.00**	**70,568.00**	**90,808.00**	**89,119.00**	**91,539.00**	**96,947.00**	**100,660.00**	**115,037.00**	**119,589.00**	**117,775.00**
CEDB	3597.81	4060.98	7606.37	10,085.64	6868.02	8089.24	8387.69	–	5786.44	5306.34
EIB	3346.08	3213.44	5994.34	16,546.16	19,285.58	24,299.39	36,714.40	37,932.13	54,423.02	54,560.22
IDB	16,165.00	16,234.00	20,114.00	16,356.00	13,703.00	14,399.00	21,015.00	27,395.00	27,901.00	27,292.00
AfDB	8419.57	7048.28	11,619.72	11,447.04	11,652.70	9970.00	9370.90	10,637.16	11,629.05	14,236.45
AsDB	13,297.00	15,412.00	14,124.00	18,253.00	21,508.00	23,886.00	24,545.00	23,088.00	23,309.00	26,025.00
IsDB	2996.15	3196.06	3870.63	2655.01	2461.04	3751.62	5078.92	4394.24	5177.09	5014.35
EBRD	15,003.64	6674.59	5249.55	14,525.83	16,030.13	17,165.39	17,630.41	14,319.10	25,925.21	25,316.32
NDB	–	–	–	–	–	–	–	–	–	–
AIIB	–	–	–	–	–	–	–	–	–	3180.00
Regional	**62,825.26**	**55,839.34**	**68,578.60**	**89,868.69**	**91,508.46**	**101,560.65**	**122,742.32**	**117,765.63**	**154,150.81**	**160,930.68**
CABEI	499.00	469.00	681.00	657.00	908.00	1025.00	1277.00	1148.00	1170.00	1223.00
EADB	–	1.00	1.00	1.00	1.00	1.00	–	–	0.40	0.20
CDB	171.00	259.00	241.00	103.00	244.00	400.00	289.00	233.00	214.00	340.00
CAF	2019.00	1734.00	2418.00	2604.00	3855.00	5554.00	6612.00	8728.00	7974.00	10,264.00
IIB	–	76.54	64.83	104.22	91.87	131.94	187.56	197.90	180.72	283.55
BADEA	2014.00	1870.70	1927.50	2121.60	2115.20	2252.00	2404.10	2512.00	2626.00	2705.40
NIB	2477.84	3616.33	8303.91	6990.06	5658.22	6959.84	7410.46	6699.40	6651.96	6957.06
PTA	3.60	–	4.40	2.60	3.00	–	–	216.00	241.80	214.70
BSTDB	158.64	309.13	248.95	234.90	182.18	264.54	217.62	91.06	151.66	436.92
ETDB	–	–	–	–	–	2.61	33.57	38.68	39.35	21.78
EDB	530.90	816.90	1137.90	878.50	626.60	1106.80	1462.50	1112.00	992.10	1124.50
Sub-regional	**7873.98**	**9152.61**	**15,028.48**	**13,696.89**	**13,685.07**	**17,697.73**	**19,893.81**	**20,976.04**	**20,241.99**	**23,571.12**
Total	**128,498.24**	**135,559.95**	**174,415.08**	**192,684.58**	**196,732.54**	**216,205.37**	**243,296.13**	**253,778.67**	**293,981.80**	**302,276.80**

Annex 12: Total Allowances (Impairment and Specific Provisions, Million USD)

	2007	2008	2009	2010	2011	2012	2013	2014	2015	2016
IBRD	1932.00	1370.00	1632.00	1553.00	1549.00	1690.00	1659.00	1626.00	1554.00	1571.00
IDA	12,216.00	13,096.00	10,577.00	8948.00	6947.00	6723.00	4005.00	4027.00	4144.00	3932.00
IFC	832.00	848.00	1238.00	1349.00	1307.00	1381.00	1628.00	1686.00	1743.00	1775.00
IFAD	155.00	177.00	117.00	105.00	77.00	78.00	54.00	30.00	24.00	17.00
Global	**15,135.00**	**15,491.00**	**13,564.00**	**11,955.00**	**9880.00**	**9872.00**	**7346.00**	**7369.00**	**7465.00**	**7295.00**
CEDB	–	1.39	1.44	2.67	2.59	2.64	2.76	2.43	2.18	2.11
EIB	54.47	23.66	152.70	122.93	249.72	403.74	448.21	506.28	532.37	502.81
IDB	51.00	136.00	116.00	145.00	150.00	180.00	244.00	370.00	444.00	532.00
AfDB	311.31	158.65	159.90	175.56	181.16	196.73	223.30	218.77	279.92	337.43
AsDB	15.00	9.00	103.00	42.00	35.00	43.00	36.00	35.00	34.00	45.00
IsDB	264.53	278.48	313.07	333.11	337.91	394.07	353.74	373.79	337.29	406.12
EBRD	182.54	502.40	1270.61	841.81	869.50	971.08	1126.72	1467.85	1179.06	1100.48
NDB	–	–	–	–	–	–	–	–	–	–
AIIB	–	–	–	–	–	–	–	–	–	–
Regional	**878.85**	**1109.58**	**2116.73**	**1663.08**	**1825.89**	**2191.25**	**2434.73**	**2974.12**	**2808.82**	**2925.94**
CABEI	140.00	162.00	203.00	200.00	178.00	168.00	159.00	168.00	177.00	194.00
EADB	53.00	31.00	32.00	33.00	12.00	8.00	6.00	6.00	3.10	5.00
CDB	–	1.00	2.00	2.00	5.00	8.00	5.00	6.00	6.00	6.00
CAF	168.00	143.00	144.00	141.00	131.00	126.00	38.00	56.00	59.00	64.00
IIB	–	84.89	149.82	163.02	152.68	160.97	–	4.86	10.89	17.92
BADEA	120.20	85.00	49.00	48.70	13.60	13.60	13.00	7.00	–	2.00
NIB	0.30	79.40	101.30	152.00	127.00	158.30	156.60	181.70	192.30	139.40
PTA	32.50	44.00	43.60	39.20	36.10	48.20	61.00	67.90	95.00	97.60
BSTDB	40.72	47.59	47.19	57.86	51.50	55.41	56.82	57.91	28.96	31.73
ETDB	–	0.15	0.31	0.46	0.46	0.46	0.46	0.29	–	–
EDB	0.60	1.40	6.60	19.20	–	31.00	142.30	42.60	132.80	83.40
Sub-regional	**555.32**	**679.44**	**778.82**	**856.44**	**707.34**	**777.94**	**638.18**	**598.26**	**705.05**	**641.05**
Total	**16,569.18**	**17,280.03**	**16,459.55**	**14,474.52**	**12,413.22**	**12,841.19**	**10,418.91**	**10,941.38**	**10,978.86**	**10,861.99**

Annex 13: Gross Income from the Loans, Debt Securities and Equities (Million USD)

	2007	2008	2009	2010	2011	2012	2013	2014	2015	2016
IBRD	5467.00	5497.00	3835.00	2493.00	3609.00	3680.00	3491.00	3271.00	1476.00	2277.00
IDA	744.00	921.00	801.00	837.00	897.00	914.00	1021.00	1015.00	1068.00	1154.00
IFC	3424.00	2878.00	462.00	2392.00	2427.00	2359.00	1573.00	2355.00	1511.00	1414.00
IFAD	53.00	54.00	57.00	51.00	55.00	49.00	49.00	52.00	58.00	53.00
Global	**9688.00**	**9350.00**	**5155.00**	**5773.00**	**6988.00**	**7002.00**	**6134.00**	**6693.00**	**4113.00**	**4898.00**
CEDB	980.42	1066.04	499.89	304.65	429.57	345.68	264.79	246.46	178.55	133.87
EIB	19,508.27	19,492.15	12,880.40	10,749.73	13,055.45	13,009.28	12,105.74	10,647.66	9042.74	8193.52
IDB	2436.00	2355.00	2002.00	1830.00	1742.00	1668.00	1858.00	1741.00	1946.00	2365.00
AfDB	548.35	514.45	464.04	462.01	491.29	547.14	535.92	509.98	462.83	512.19
AsDB	1506.00	1369.00	993.00	750.00	710.00	827.00	674.00	684.00	722.00	1133.00
IsDB	286.03	291.11	330.63	381.00	327.01	387.30	480.48	466.52	515.49	768.96
EBRD	2997.20	(573.38)	(123.89)	2101.84	746.58	1906.53	2079.68	519.63	1516.56	1563.23
NDB	–	–	–	–	–	–	–	–	–	–
AIIB	–	–	–	–	–	–	–	–	–	–
Regional	**28,262.26**	**24,514.37**	**17,046.06**	**16,579.24**	**17,501.91**	**18,690.95**	**17,998.61**	**14,815.25**	**14,384.17**	**14,669.77**
CABEI	274.00	278.00	266.00	273.00	268.00	297.00	298.00	286.00	309.00	331.00
EADB	22.00	21.00	16.00	11.00	8.00	7.00	7.00	10.00	11.80	17.50
CDB	46.00	47.00	46.00	43.00	40.00	40.00	39.00	40.00	38.00	32.00
CAF	734.00	584.00	417.00	351.00	402.00	468.00	486.00	525.00	568.00	706.00
IIB	–	9.74	15.85	8.02	3.88	5.28	8.27	10.93	16.33	21.08
BADEA	19.20	17.40	19.50	16.90	18.80	17.00	16.00	15.30	16.00	18.40
NIB	876.05	956.10	607.93	394.85	462.83	494.25	432.21	358.52	292.32	269.43
PTA	35.00	50.50	56.00	67.70	104.90	141.55	168.00	209.10	239.40	264.00
BSTDB	47.99	59.30	49.70	45.43	45.16	57.13	55.16	51.84	60.86	67.78
ETDB	–	–	1.87	4.00	5.07	8.76	6.93	8.98	8.59	10.08
EDB	42.00	68.20	67.40	83.20	118.70	156.10	222.10	240.30	201.80	161.20
Sub-regional	**2096.23**	**2091.24**	**1563.25**	**1298.10**	**1477.33**	**1692.07**	**1738.68**	**1755.98**	**1762.10**	**1898.47**
Total	**40,046.49**	**35,955.61**	**23,764.31**	**23,650.34**	**25,967.24**	**27,385.01**	**25,871.29**	**23,264.23**	**20,259.27**	**21,466.24**

Annex 14: Net Profit (Loss) (Million USD)

	2007	2008	2009	2010	2011	2012	2013	2014	2015	2016
IBRD	(140.00)	1491.00	3114.00	(1077.00)	930.00	(676.00)	218.00	(978.00)	(786.00)	495.00
IDA	(1081.00)	(283.00)	1850.00	(1077.00)	(2332.00)	(210.00)	(1752.00)	(1612.00)	(731.00)	371.00
IFC	2490.00	1547.00	(151.00)	1746.00	1579.00	1328.00	1010.00	1488.00	409.00	(34.00)
IFAD	322.00	(224.00)	119.00	(113.00)	(157.00)	(224.00)	(312.00)	(716.00)	(545.00)	(439.00)
Global	**1591.00**	**2531.00**	**4932.00**	**(521.00)**	**20.00**	**218.00**	**(836.00)**	**(1818.00)**	**(1653.00)**	**393.00**
CEDB	136.91	133.60	154.14	155.00	137.15	158.33	154.46	162.69	138.26	110.68
EIB	1,240.98	8845.65	(3286.01)	3534.25	4843.07	381.31	4024.21	819.52	4657.46	(294.09)
IDB	134.00	(22.00)	794.00	330.00	(283.00)	904.00	1307.00	548.00	960.00	848.00
AfDB	322.37	72.39	106.60	103.18	78.30	132.18	112.42	46.36	(42.96)	33.61
AsDB	765.00	1127.00	(28.00)	626.00	609.00	142.00	566.00	387.00	556.00	7.00
IsDB	258.37	299.12	195.65	261.19	167.34	199.80	261.80	239.05	216.17	412.71
EBRD	2773.44	(997.85)	(1312.39)	1639.52	223.84	1096.42	1271.53	(877.79)	481.21	847.50
NDB	–	–	–	–	–	–	–	–	–	228.00
AIIB	–	–	–	–	–	–	–	–	–	167.00
Regional	**5631.06**	**9457.91**	**(3376.00)**	**6649.14**	**5775.71**	**3014.03**	**7697.42**	**1324.83**	**6966.15**	**2360.40**
CABEI	81.00	84.00	71.00	114.00	103.00	103.00	118.00	103.00	159.00	115.00
EADB	(9.00)	(9.00)	2.00	2.00	7.00	7.00	8.00	10.00	7.00	7.60
CDB	35.00	43.00	22.00	41.00	41.00	15.00	3.00	49.00	10.00	(13.00)
CAF	401.00	311.00	235.00	166.00	153.00	160.00	207.00	138.00	78.00	123.00
IIB	–	(154.48)	86.87	31.00	3.11	3.03	4.14	4.86	2.18	1.05
BADEA	164.20	(91.00)	158.20	136.40	75.00	178.00	211.00	189.20	15.30	124.00
NIB	101.57	(391.49)	466.75	281.94	251.02	276.02	299.54	255.20	234.51	223.47
PTA	6.60	12.50	18.00	20.30	34.20	51.20	66.60	77.00	95.00	101.50
BSTDB	14.36	20.02	15.21	13.76	13.07	19.79	18.34	17.00	16.55	1.90
ETDB	4.26	4.49	6.09	(2.46)	8.14	10.45	6.78	7.39	8.87	10.08
EDB	39.30	40.50	39.80	15.80	24.50	12.00	(72.50)	17.80	(143.60)	163.50
Sub-regional	**838.30**	**(130.45)**	**1120.92**	**819.74**	**713.03**	**835.50**	**869.90**	**868.45**	**482.80**	**858.10**
Total	**8060.36**	**11,858.46**	**2676.92**	**6947.87**	**6508.74**	**4067.53**	**7731.32**	**375.27**	**5795.95**	**3611.50**

Annex 15: Total Operational Gross Income (Million USD)

	2007	2008	2009	2010	2011	2012	2013	2014	2015	2016
IBRD	6908.00	6863.00	5037.00	4108.00	4270.00	4389.00	2766.00	2951.00	2455.00	3507.00
IDA	1292.00	3421.00	3475.00	3183.00	2690.00	3303.00	2656.00	3165.00	3157.00	3606.00
IFC	4141.00	3464.00	1063.00	3383.00	3178.00	3120.00	2514.00	3415.00	2483.00	2419.00
IFAD	336.00	242.00	409.00	289.00	313.00	222.00	147.00	333.00	253.00	297.00
Global	**12,677.00**	**13,990.00**	**9984.00**	**10,963.00**	**10,451.00**	**11,034.00**	**8083.00**	**9864.00**	**8348.00**	**9829.00**
CEDB	1123.21	1260.88	583.44	356.77	514.97	400.44	281.34	272.69	200.32	129.65
EIB	20,685.95	20,850.45	24,677.48	25,862.15	32,278.92	33,419.08	31,937.20	27,575.85	24,374.90	23,383.10
IDB	2942.00	1393.00	2848.00	2482.00	1980.00	2189.00	2284.00	1943.00	2062.00	2733.00
AfDB	924.45	868.71	813.63	799.28	750.75	852.99	739.20	702.67	631.89	720.56
AsDB	2208.00	2065.00	1471.00	1142.00	1095.00	1238.00	1035.00	973.00	1029.00	1532.00
IsDB	437.73	392.77	398.04	424.12	376.14	462.92	526.68	572.28	620.81	918.18
EBRD	4008.53	201.80	347.18	2343.69	1023.47	2240.34	2347.23	665.33	1733.21	1790.92
NDB	–	–	–	–	–	–	–	–	–	28.00
AIIB	–	–	–	–	–	–	–	–	–	23.00
Regional	**32,329.87**	**27,032.61**	**31,138.77**	**33,410.01**	**38,019.26**	**40,802.77**	**39,150.64**	**32,704.82**	**30,652.14**	**31,258.41**
CABEI	322.00	309.00	286.00	295.00	282.00	319.00	314.00	298.00	323.00	360.00
EADB	25.00	24.00	17.00	12.00	12.00	14.00	11.00	15.00	18.00	25.20
CDB	56.00	54.00	52.00	46.00	43.00	43.00	43.00	43.00	40.00	36.00
CAF	824.00	653.00	484.00	386.00	429.00	520.00	508.00	570.00	621.00	813.00
IIB	–	22.27	21.61	10.69	10.35	11.87	17.93	20.64	29.39	33.73
BADEA	172.00	(108.70)	137.90	152.20	58.00	196.60	230.30	204.00	30.00	151.00
NIB	1269.54	1376.11	881.65	590.60	660.28	665.77	571.50	476.29	382.35	342.69
PTA	36.20	51.60	56.70	68.50	105.90	143.55	169.40	212.00	257.00	280.20
BSTDB	53.67	70.08	54.56	51.31	51.89	61.62	57.92	54.03	61.84	74.31
ETDB	5.68	9.60	12.18	12.32	19.81	20.29	14.94	16.66	15.80	15.73
EDB	59.30	113.50	111.50	109.80	149.70	186.30	248.10	264.90	226.00	193.50
Sub-regional	**2823.39**	**2574.46**	**2115.09**	**1734.42**	**1821.92**	**2182.00**	**2186.09**	**2174.52**	**2004.38**	**2325.36**
Total	**47,830.26**	**43,597.07**	**43,237.87**	**46,107.43**	**50,292.18**	**54,018.77**	**49,419.73**	**44,743.34**	**41,004.52**	**43,412.77**

Annex 16: Total Administrative Expenses (Million USD)

	2007	2008	2009	2010	2011	2012	2013	2014	2015	2016
IBRD	1065.00	1082.00	1244.00	1421.00	1457.00	1631.00	1761.00	1821.00	1949.00	2053.00
IDA	976.00	888.00	975.00	1585.00	1716.00	1674.00	1936.00	2004.00	1868.00	1765.00
IFC	500.00	552.00	616.00	733.00	809.00	894.00	1018.00	1061.00	1098.00	1118.00
IFAD	152.00	162.00	157.00	162.00	180.00	176.00	180.00	181.00	167.00	165.00
Global	**2693.00**	**2684.00**	**2992.00**	**3901.00**	**4162.00**	**4375.00**	**4895.00**	**5067.00**	**5082.00**	**5101.00**
CEDB	41.22	38.97	41.78	42.76	45.29	44.86	57.23	37.64	48.99	48.49
EIB	538.79	552.50	642.51	590.07	690.94	721.71	841.25	785.52	882.94	957.12
IDB	500.00	439.00	530.00	573.00	600.00	663.00	813.00	668.00	768.00	676.00
AfDB	66.37	72.39	98.76	115.50	121.29	164.45	170.94	178.20	169.06	174.76
AsDB	127.00	141.00	194.00	294.00	316.00	351.00	411.00	352.00	383.00	390.00
IsDB	98.45	97.04	104.25	111.34	129.27	139.55	154.00	159.37	151.04	201.65
EBRD	353.30	315.92	316.93	304.65	322.18	356.24	439.93	399.44	436.57	469.07
NDB	–	–	–	–	–	–	–	–	–	11.00
AIIB	–	–	–	–	–	–	–	–	–	31.00
Regional	**1725.13**	**1656.82**	**1928.23**	**2031.32**	**2224.97**	**2440.81**	**2887.36**	**2580.17**	**2839.60**	**2959.10**
CABEI	34.00	35.00	35.00	35.00	36.00	41.00	42.00	44.00	46.00	46.00
EADB	7.00	8.00	8.00	7.00	7.00	8.00	7.00	7.00	7.00	8.20
CDB	8.00	9.00	9.00	10.00	10.00	11.00	11.00	11.00	14.00	13.00
CAF	51.00	56.00	63.00	70.00	81.00	91.00	104.00	117.00	125.00	141.00
IIB	–	16.70	15.85	16.03	16.82	17.15	23.44	20.64	18.51	20.03
BADEA	10.00	11.20	12.00	12.20	12.50	13.40	14.00	14.30	15.00	18.00
NIB	40.48	42.17	44.08	41.96	42.70	45.26	48.54	45.41	45.73	44.48
PTA	7.40	8.50	8.20	10.60	12.10	12.30	15.80	19.30	21.00	31.50
BSTDB	17.36	17.25	17.71	18.84	19.80	20.32	22.48	20.03	19.38	19.40
ETDB	2.37	4.18	5.15	5.39	5.53	5.84	6.16	6.08	5.68	5.51
EDB	15.70	25.90	29.60	34.60	48.10	49.20	44.70	47.00	34.20	30.00
Sub-regional	**193.31**	**233.90**	**247.60**	**261.62**	**291.54**	**314.47**	**339.13**	**351.76**	**351.49**	**377.12**
Total	**4611.45**	**4574.72**	**5167.83**	**6193.95**	**6678.51**	**7130.28**	**8121.48**	**7998.94**	**8273.09**	**8437.22**

Annex 17: Gross Income from Treasury Operations (Million USD)

	2007	2008	2009	2010	2011	2012	2013	2014	2015	2016
IBRD	1281.00	1066.00	603.00	376.00	367.00	219.00	241.00	254.00	233.00	329.00
IDA	548.00	1396.00	1623.00	921.00	320.00	1013.00	105.00	634.00	522.00	881.00
IFC	618.00	473.00	474.00	815.00	529.00	313.00	500.00	599.00	467.00	504.00
IFAD	155.00	136.00	116.00	85.00	111.00	82.00	(17.00)	57.00	3.00	49.00
Global	**2602.00**	**3071.00**	**2816.00**	**2197.00**	**1327.00**	**1627.00**	**829.00**	**1544.00**	**1225.00**	**1763.00**
CEDB	287.06	324.27	82.11	52.11	85.40	55.41	15.17	26.10	21.77	(4.22)
EIB	1045.19	1283.15	11,735.13	15,050.96	19,222.18	20,378.13	19,799.74	16,895.42	15,393.13	15,122.12
IDB	487.00	(973.00)	831.00	631.00	220.00	495.00	402.00	158.00	95.00	344.00
AfDB	376.10	312.67	349.59	337.27	259.46	305.85	201.74	191.24	169.06	209.72
AsDB	683.00	677.00	459.00	368.00	365.00	390.00	339.00	305.00	322.00	399.00
IsDB	151.70	100.12	67.41	55.44	49.13	75.31	46.20	105.76	105.32	149.22
EBRD	1011.33	775.18	471.08	241.85	276.89	333.81	267.55	145.69	216.65	227.69
NDB	–	–	–	–	–	–	–	–	–	24.00
AIIB	–	–	–	–	–	–	–	–	–	23.00
Regional	**4041.39**	**2499.38**	**13,995.32**	**16,736.63**	**20,478.06**	**22,033.51**	**21,071.39**	**17,827.22**	**16,322.93**	**16,494.52**
CABEI	48.00	31.00	20.00	22.00	14.00	22.00	16.00	13.00	15.00	29.00
EADB	3.00	3.00	1.00	1.00	4.00	7.00	4.00	5.00	6.50	7.50
CDB	10.00	6.00	6.00	4.00	3.00	3.00	4.00	3.00	2.00	4.00
CAF	90.00	68.00	67.00	34.00	27.00	52.00	22.00	44.00	54.00	108.00
IIB	–	11.13	5.76	3.34	6.47	6.60	9.65	9.71	13.06	12.65
BADEA	153.10	(128.40)	118.30	133.40	40.00	178.00	213.30	188.30	13.00	132.60
NIB	393.35	420.29	273.71	195.09	196.03	170.99	138.60	115.83	88.40	71.68
PTA	1.30	1.10	0.60	0.70	1.00	2.00	1.40	3.00	17.30	16.50
BSTDB	5.68	10.78	4.86	5.88	6.86	4.49	2.62	2.19	0.98	6.54
ETDB	5.68	9.60	10.46	8.32	14.74	11.37	7.70	7.68	6.37	5.11
EDB	17.10	54.00	44.00	39.90	31.00	30.20	25.90	24.70	24.20	32.40
Sub-regional	**727.21**	**486.51**	**551.70**	**447.62**	**344.09**	**487.65**	**445.17**	**416.40**	**240.82**	**425.97**
Total	**7370.60**	**6056.89**	**17,363.02**	**19,381.25**	**22,149.15**	**24,148.16**	**22,345.57**	**19,787.62**	**17,788.75**	**18,683.50**

Notes

1. Since the financial year for IBRD (International Bank for Reconstruction and Development), IDA (International Development Association), and IFC (International Financial Corporation) ends every year on June 30, their numbers have been taken from their financial reports prepared as of June 30 of the relevant year and considered as the year-end figures; since it could not be taken either from their websites or published annual reports, IIB (International Investment Bank) data for 2007 and the data related with the undisbursed commitments of IsDB (Islamic Development Bank) for 2008, 2009, 2010, and 2013 have not been available. Since most of the reporting currencies are USD, the figures reported in a different currency were converted to USD using the relevant year-end exchange rate.
2. IBRD and IDB enjoy special legislation that permits the US Secretary of the Treasury to pay up to 25% of the country's callable-capital commitment to IBRD and over 10% of its commitment to IDB without congressional action. However, whether the secretary would do so, and under what conditions, is ambiguous.
3. Rating agencies also deduct demand notes and receivables on the assets side of the balance sheet. Such assets arise when members' currencies held by an MDB depreciate relative to the US dollar or other unit of account. Another adjustment is the deduction from equity of capital subscriptions paid in member countries' local currencies and restricted as to use, as it is uncertain whether these currencies could be used to meet debt-service payments.
4. "Mobilize domestic and foreign capital"; "co-financing together with multilateral institutions, commercial banks or other interested sources ... to facilitate ... the participation of private and/or foreign capital", as stipulated at EBRD's official documents: see http://www.ebrd.com/who-we-are/history-of-the-ebrd.html and the Agreement Establishing the European Bank for Reconstruction and Development, at http://www.ebrd.com/news/publications/institutional-documents/basic-documents-of-the-ebrd.html.
5. The related public disclosure requirements have been in effect since January 1, 2015.
6. In April 2016, the BCBS issued for consultation a proposed set of changes to the exposure measure, including an additional leverage requirement for global systemically important banks (BSBC 2016).
7. The Basel II accord (standard) applies a three pillar concept: (1) minimum capital requirements (addressing risk), (2) supervisory review, and (3) market discipline. The Basel I accord addressed only parts of these pillars.
8. BCBS defines Tier 1 capital as shareholders' equity and retained earnings. It measures a bank's financial strength and is used to absorb losses without ceasing bank's operations. Under the Basel III accord, the minimum Tier 1 capital ratio is 10.5%. It is calculated by dividing the bank's Tier 1 capital by its total risk-based assets.

Tier 2 capital includes revaluation reserves, hybrid capital instruments and subordinated term debt, general loan-loss reserves, and undisclosed reserves. Tier 2 capital is supplementary as it is less reliable than Tier 1 capital. In 2017 the Basel III accord set the minimum total capital ratio at 12.5%, which implies that the minimum Tier 2 capital ratio is 2%, as the Tier 1 minimum is 10.5%.

9. On-balance sheet exposures are generally included at their accounting value. However, exposures associated with derivatives and securities are covered by a separate treatment (amounts owed to a bank are excluded while any on-balance sheet collateral related to such transactions are included). Except in the cases of different treatment, no offset is permitted for physical or financial collateral held, guarantees in favor of the bank or similar credit risk mitigation instruments. Balance sheet assets that are deducted from Tier 1 capital may also be deducted from the exposure measure (BCBS 2011, 2014, 2017).
10. Off-balance sheet (OBS) items represent implicit obligations such as credit and liquidity commitments, guarantees, and standby letters of credit. The amount that belongs to the exposure measure is determined by multiplying the notional amount of an OBS item by the relevant credit conversion factor from the Basel II standardized approach for credit risk, subject to a floor of 10% (BCBS 2004).
11. A credit rating quantifies a borrower's overall creditworthiness to pay its obligations.
12. The Basel Committee applies a 0% risk weight to banks' exposures to MDBs that fulfill the following criteria: (1) very high-quality long-term issuer ratings, that is, a majority of an MDB's external ratings must be Aaa at the time of application and no lower than Aa3 afterwards; (2) either the shareholder structure comprises a significant proportion of sovereigns with long-term issuer external ratings of Aa3 or better, or the majority of the MDB's fund-raising is in the form of paid-in equity/capital and there is little or no leverage; (3) strong shareholder support demonstrated by the amount of paid-in capital contributed by the shareholders—regarding the amount of further capital, the MDBs have the right to call, if required, to repay their liabilities—and continued capital contributions and new pledges from sovereign shareholders; (4) adequate level of capital and liquidity (a case-by-case approach is necessary in order to assess whether each MDB's capital and liquidity are adequate); and (5) strict statutory lending requirements and conservative financial policies, which would include among other conditions a structured approval process, internal creditworthiness and risk concentration limits (per country, sector, and individual exposure and credit category), large exposures approval by the Board or a committee of the Board, fixed repayment schedules, effective monitoring of use of proceeds, status review process, and rigorous assessment of risk and provisioning to loan-loss reserve (BCBS 2017).
13. Typically, rating agencies use the following financial information to assess the capital quality of MDBs: (1) *Paid-in capital as a percentage of total subscribed*

capital: indicates the portion of subscribed capital that has been actually paid by members. (2) *AAA-rated callable capital as a percent of total callable capital:* indicates the quality of capital that has been subscribed but not paid-in by members. It shows the ability of members to meet a capital call in the unlikely event that an MDB cannot service its debt. (3) *Gearing ratios:* loans outstanding compared to the different types of capital available to the MDB (limited by MDBs' policies). These ratios include (a) *net disbursed loans as a percentage of paid-in capital plus reserves* (indicates the ability to absorb borrower defaults without resorting to capital calls, as paid-in capital plus reserves is a measure of funds actually available to the MDB); (b) *net disbursed loans as a percent of AAA callable capital plus paid-in capital and reserves.* (4) *Leverage:* the MDB's outstanding debt compared to the different types of its capital. Leverage limitations are established by most MDBs. Typically, the following ratios are used: (a) *outstanding debt as a percentage of paid-in capital plus reserves*; (b) *outstanding debt as a percentage of AAA callable plus paid-in capital and reserves.* (5) *Liquidity*: measures MDBs' ability to pay its current debt service and fund its lending. As MDBs' assets from lending are relatively illiquid, they rely on sufficient liquid assets, such as marketable securities. Typically, the liquidity is measured in *liquid assets as a percentage of undisbursed loans plus one year of debt service.* (6) *Administrative expenses ratio*: administrative expenses compared to total expenses. (7) *Profitability ratio:* although MDBs' primary objective is to promote economic and social development and not maximize profits, they do seek adequate income to cover operational costs and build reserves. *Net operating income as a percent of average assets* is the rate of return on MDBs' assets and is a key measure of MDBs' profitability.

14. Another form of commitment is the provision of funding to soft-loan and technical assistance (grant) windows, as these represent a key element in the franchise value of some institutions (mostly AfDB, 38 of the 53 regional members are eligible to borrow only from the soft-loan window, and IBRD, 66 of whose 145 eligible-to-borrow members could do so only from the soft-loan window).
15. To harmonize measuring of crowding-in of private investment, in 2016 the MDBs established the MDB Task Force on Measuring Private Investment Catalyzation.

References

BCBS, Basel Committee on Banking Supervision. 2004, June. *Basel II: International Convergence of Capital Measurement and Capital Standards: A Revised Framework.* https://www.bis.org/publ/bcbs107.pdf.

———. 2011, June. *Basel III: A Global Regulatory Framework for More Resilient Banks and Banking Systems.* www.bis.org/publ/bcbs189.pdf.

———. 2014. *Basel III Leverage Ratio Framework and Disclosure Requirements*. Basel (Updated 2017).

———. 2016, April. *Consultative Document Revisions to the Basel III Leverage Ratio Framework*. https://www.bis.org/bcbs/publ/d365.pdf.

———. 2017, December. *Basel III Finalising Post-Crisis Reforms*.

Buiter, Willem, and Steven Fries. 2002. *What Should the Multilateral Development Banks Do*. London: EBRD. http://www.ebrd.com/downloads/research/economics/workingpapers/wp0074.pdf.

Development Committee (World Bank and IMF). 2015. *From Billions to Trillions: Transforming Development Finance Post-2015/Financing for Development: Multilateral Development Finance*. Washington, DC: The World Bank. http://siteresources.worldbank.org/DEVCOMMINT/Documentation/23659446/DC2015-0002(E)FinancingforDevelopment.pdf.

Moody's. 2018. *Supranationals – Global, Basel III Risk-Weight Changes Benefit Single A-Rated Multilateral Development Banks*.

S&P Global Ratings. 2017. *Supranationals, Special Edition*. https://www.spratings.com/documents/20184/908545/US_SR_Event_Webcast_MultilateralNov17_Article2.pdf/fc892865-5302-4dd6-93ca-8469c8752818.

The World Bank. 2015. *Development Banks Working Together to Optimize Balance Sheets*. Washington, DC: Press Release. http://www.worldbank.org/en/news/press-release/2015/12/22/development-banks-optimize-balance-sheets.

4

Current Governance

Introduction

This chapter reviews the typical organizational structure of Multilateral Development Banks (MDBs). The conclusion presents recent challenges and developments, calling for better governance.

Sound governance is at the heart of MDBs' success. However, its importance and complexity are poorly understood and addressed. As all MDBs will strongly benefit from a better understanding and enhancement of their governance, the issue is of strategic importance and therefore reviewed thoroughly.

Corporate Governance (CG) emerged as a term in the 1970-es in the United States, in the context of efforts to impose responsible and transparent governance of corporations, to prevent abuse of the interests of shareholders and investors. The term was further conceptualized by Adrian Cadbury, President of the Committee on the Financial Aspects of Corporate Governance in Great Britain, who published the *Report of the Committee…*, known as the Cadbury Code (The Committee…, 1992). The Code is a key reference on the financial aspects of governance, defining CG as the system by which companies are managed and controlled.

Soon after, it was widely recognized that effective CG is critical to the proper functioning of the economy. As financial stability depends on the soundness of banks, their governance is very critical. Failures of systemic banks can transmit severe problems across international financial sectors and economies. This is why CG is of paramount importance to MDBs, given their role-model nature (OECD 2011, 2015).

I. U. Delikanli et al., *Multilateral Development Banks*,
https://doi.org/10.1007/978-3-319-91524-1_4

The Three-Tier Governance

The basic governance structure of all MDBs is virtually the same, with minor variations. Based on the design of the Bretton Woods institutions—the World Bank and the IMF—it has three tiers: (1) Board of Governors (BoG),[1] (2) Board of Directors (BoD),[2] and (3) senior management. Formally, all powers are allocated to the BoG as shareholder representatives. However, the BoG has a rather ceremonial role as it delegates most of these powers to the BoD. Thus, either the BoG or BoD elects the president/CEO, vice president(s), and other senior management positions.

While compositions of senior management vary from institution to institution, MDBs are typically headed by president/CEO, who chairs the BoD and the management/executive committee. As a rule, the formal (establishing) multilateral agreements specify only that BoG or BoD elects the senior management, without reference to nationality or quotas, as the latter are typically addressed, in many MDBs, by less formal "gentlemen's" agreements.

MDBs are overseen by the BoG, with a governor from each or a group of shareholder countries. In general, BoG (upon BoD's recommendation) is responsible for admitting or suspending member countries, increasing or decreasing capital, agreements for cooperation with other international organizations, supervising the BoD, approving strategies, financial statements, reserves, distribution of profits, and so on.

The BoD, to whom the BoG delegates oversight of day-to-day operations, supervises and guides the management. BoDs ensure the implementation of the decisions/strategies of BoGs by approving loans, guarantees, investments, technical cooperation, borrowing of funds, and so on. Daily operations are carried out by the management and staff of international civil servants (Fig. 4.1).

Both BoG and BoD members represent the respective shareholders/countries. They are typically accountable to cabinet ministers. In most MDBs (specifically the global and regional ones) only the largest shareholders are represented by a single director on the Board. The other countries often jointly appoint a director and an alternate director. Consequently, complex arrangements between these countries' ministers and respective director rotations are involved, to ensure adequate representation in the BoD as split voting is generally not allowed (e.g. a director, representing several countries should always vote with all votes of his/her constituency).

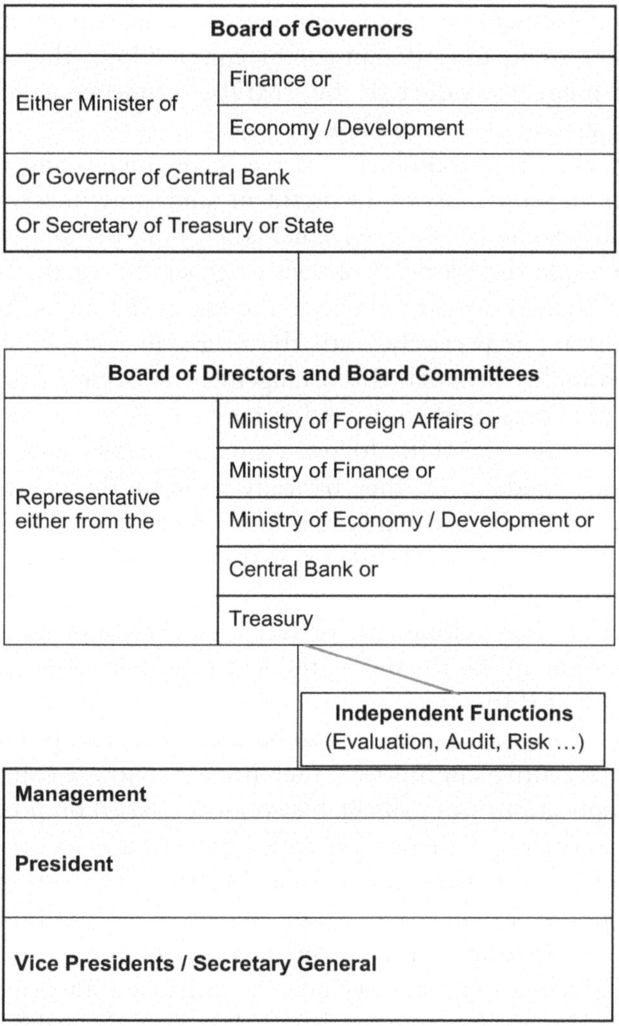

Fig. 4.1 Governance structure

Inherent Complexities

To comprehend MDBs' governance, one should bear in mind that historically these institutions evolved as international bureaucracies in the UN-style, rather than as corporate entities or banks. Therefore, the MDB-specific decision-making procedures are very complex and quite ambiguous to outsiders (often to insiders too), as many of them are part of informal agreements, rather than the respective establishing agreements and related by-laws, which are quite similar across MDBs.

Political appointment of senior managers is common in most MDBs, despite a recent trend toward transparent competition. This trend reflects critical assessments conducted by MDBs' Independent Evaluation Departments, shareholders, and NGOs.

In most MDBs the shareholders observe "gentlemen's" and other similar agreements on the nationality of the president (and sometimes other management positions). Some of these agreements are as old as the MDBs themselves—for example the World Bank, which generally sets the tone at other MDBs, agreed that its own and the IMF Presidents should be American and Western European, respectively, with the origin of Vice Presidents (VPs) reversed accordingly. Although this arrangement is being increasingly criticized, it has been consistently respected so far.

Most of the regional MDBs follow a similar model (agreed nationality options for the president), as they basically replicate the governance structures/processes of the World Bank. A minor exception is that some MDBs have broader boundaries on presidents' nationality; for example a president from non-borrowing shareholder countries at the EBRD (European Bank for Reconstruction and Development) or just member countries at the AfDB (African Development Bank), and a president from borrowing countries and an American VP at IDB.

Even when MDBs seek a geographical balance in the composition of senior management (executive committee), they usually follow a competitive process, taking applications from all eligible countries, based on professional criteria. However, there are a few exceptions of reserved seats for uncontested individuals from a particular country. Some MDBs, mostly sub-regional, have nationality/rotation schemes for senior management positions, implying direct non competitive appointments by member countries.

Most MDBs include in the management/executive committee merit-recruited (often promoted internally) senior professionals such as General Counsel, Chief Economist, and so on, but there are exceptions, usually in the group of smaller MDBs. The tenure of senior management positions is often five years, usually extendable or unlimited. Smaller MDBs indicate a similar pattern, albeit with some diversity, as illustrated by the following three "border" cases:

- CABEI, the Central American Bank for Economic Integration, with ten members: The election of Executive President follows a contest/competition that proposes the three best candidates from all founding member countries, from which the BoG elects one for a period of five years, eligible for another term. The choice of Executive VP (typically one) follows the same competitive procedure where any nationality from member countries, different from the one of the president, is eligible. Senior management includes a president, one VP, and nine other members (Chief Economist, General Counsel, Institutional Relations Officer, etc.).

- NIB, the Nordic Investment Bank, with eight members: no national quotas, either for the eight management positions or for any other staff position—recruitment is solely based on merit and is made through international competitions. There is no limitation on tenure—management members serve about eight years on average.
- CEDB, the Council of Europe Development Bank, with 37 members: The Governor (equivalent of President, heading the Governing Board) reports to the Executive Committee. The Governor and the three Vice Governors are elected by the Administrative Council (BoD equivalent) for a renewable term of five years. The Executive Committee comprises 13 members of the Administrative Council, elected by that Council reflecting the right of all member countries of sitting on the Executive Committee, with consideration of shares held and aiming at a balanced geographical representation. The senior management, reporting to the Governor, consists of six Director Generals and two heads of independent offices.

Board of Governors and Voting Powers

The highest level, where all powers are allocated and where all shareholders (member states) are represented, is the BoG. It acts as non-resident *external* multilateral supervision authority given the *self-regulation* of MDBs. All strategic issues such as the admission or suspension of shareholders, increase or decrease of capital, and so on, are approved by the BoG. It holds an annual meeting every year, with possible additional meetings, upon own decision, or request of BoD or a certain number or voting power of member states.

Every shareholder country assigns two official representatives at the BoG, one full member (Governor) and an alternate (Alternate Governor). Generally, MDBs do not have professional qualification requirements regarding those representatives. There are minor exceptions; for example NIB, EIB (European Investment Bank), and AsDB (Asian Development Bank) specify certain requirements regarding the Governors[3] but those are not *specific professional* qualification criteria. Likewise, the BoG of the CEDB is formed by the ambassadors at the Council of Europe—again, not a genuine qualification requirement.

The position of an MDB Governor is usually held by the country's minister of finance, governor of central bank, or an official of similar rank. Only a few

MDBs have term limitations for Governors, namely five years at the IBRD (International Bank for Reconstruction and Development) and AfDB. Governors and alternates serve without remuneration, there is only a reimbursement of certain expenses regarding their attendance of meetings.

The BoG agenda is usually prepared by the BoD. BoG meetings are typically presided by a Chair and two Vice Chairs, elected by the Governors for one year (except at IFAD—International Fund for Agriculture Development—and CEDB where this term is two and three years, respectively).

At the meetings, each Governor is entitled to cast the votes of the shareholder member state(s) he or she represents. The voting power of each member state corresponds to the number of shares held. As illustrated by Table 4.1, a quorum for a BoG meeting requires a qualified majority of the Governors, exercising not less than two-thirds of the total voting power in the global and regional MDBs, except IDB (Inter-American Development Bank; three-fourths of voting power) and AfDB (70% of voting power).

Sub-regional MDBs, with relatively fewer shareholder countries, have higher quorum requirements (100% at NIB; 80% of "A" shares and 50% of the other shares at CAF—Corporación Andina de Fomento; and 3/4 of the voting power at IIB—International Investment Bank—and EDB—Eurasian Development Bank). Hence, smaller MDBs typically seek consensus on key decisions. While in some cases this may be driven by a lower degree of trust, it also reflects the fact that for a smaller group of members it is easier and meaningful to aim at higher levels of presence and consent.

Decisions on regular issues require a simple majority, except at AfDB, CAF, IIB, NIB, and ETDB (over 51% majority). NIB is the only MDB which takes all decisions unanimously. As with the quorum thresholds, the respective BoG decision-making requirements are generally higher at the smaller MDBs, reflecting their inclination toward consensus and fewer disagreements among member countries. This is in line with certain regional cultural aspects; for example at NIB the members have equal votes regardless of actual shares and take decisions unanimously.

Actual voting powers reveal certain polarity and concentrations that have recently fuelled strong discontent among many (borrowing) member countries of larger MDBs. As shown in Table 4.2, all G7 countries have critically high (*veto*) voting power in all global and most regional MDBs, but very rarely in the sub-regional MDBs, as many of the latter were established in order to achieve a locally centered ownership and decision-making.

While the data in Table 4.2 is self-explanatory, it could be summarized as follows:

Table 4.1 Quorum and decision-making, Board of Governors

	Global				Regional								
	IBRD	IFC	IDA	IFAD	CEDB	EIB	IDB	AfDB	AsDB	IsDB	EBRD	NDB	AIIB
Quorum	2/3 of voting power	2/3 of voting power	2/3 of voting power	2/3 of voting power	2/3 of gov.		Gov. of regional states having 3/4 of total voting power	70% of total voting power	2/3 of total voting power	2/3 of the total voting power	2/3 of the total voting power	2/3 of the total voting power	2/3 of the total voting power
Decision	**Regular** Majority of votes cast **Special** 3/5 of gov. having 85% of voting power		**Regular** Majority of the votes cast **Special** 3/5 of gov. having 4/5 of voting power	Majority of the votes cast	Majority of 3/4 of the gov. having 3/4 of the votes cast	**Regular** 50% of subs. capital **Special** 18 gov. and 68% of subs. capital	**Regular** Majority of total voting power of member states **Special** 2/3 of gov. from regional states having 3/4 of voting power	**Regular** Majority of 66% and 2/3 of voting power of the gov. present or majority of 70% of voting power **Special** 2/3 of gov. having 3/4 of voting power incl. 2/3 of reg. gov. having 3/4 of voting power of reg. states	**Regular** Majority of the votes cast **Special** 2/3 of gov. having 3/4 of voting power	**Regular** Majority of the votes cast **Special** 2/3 of gov. having 3/4 of voting power	**Regular** Majority of the votes cast **Special** 3/4 of gov. (at least two from Central and Eastern Europe) having 4/5 of voting power	**Regular** Majority of the votes cast or 2/3 of total voting power **Special** Four of founder states	**Regular** Majority of the votes cast **Special** 2/3 of gov. having 3/4 of voting power

(*continued*)

Table 4.1 (continued)

	Sub-regional									
	CABEI	CDB	CAF	IIB	BADEA	NIB	PTA	BSTDB	ETDB	EDB
Quorum	One half plus one gov. incl. at least three gov. from founding members having 2/3 of voting power	2/3 of voting power	Gov. repress. 80% of Series "A" shares and 50% of the other shares	3/4 of voting power	2/3 of total voting power	All gov.	2/3 of total voting power	2/3 of the gov. having 2/3 of total voting power	Majority of gov. with all three gov. from found. Memb.	3/4 of voting power
Decision	**Regular** Majority of the votes cast **Special** Majority of gov. 3/4 of voting power including four gov. from founding states	**Regular** Majority of the votes cast **Special** 2/3 of gov. having 3/4 of voting power	**Regular** 60% of Series "A" shares + half plus one of the other shares **Special** 80% of Series "A" shares + half plus one of the other shares **To Amend** All Series "A" shares + half plus one of the other shares	**Regular** Majority of 3/4 of the votes **Special** Unani-mously	**Regular** Majority of the votes cast **Special** Majority of gov. having 3/4 of voting power	Unani-mously	**Regular** Majority of the votes cast **Special** 2/3 of gov. having 2/3 of voting power	**Regular** Majority of the votes cast **Special** Unanimously	Majority having 85% of the voting power	**Regular** Majority of the votes cast **Special** Majority of 3/4 of the votes

Table 4.2 Voting power of G7 and G20 countries at MDBs

	Voting power (%)												
	Global				Regional								
Country	IBRD	IFC	IDA	IFAD	CEDB	EIB	IDB	AfDB	AsDB	IsDB	EBRD	NDB	AIIB
Canada	2.5	3.02	2.67	3.42			4	3.89	4.48		3.44		
France	3.86	4.48	3.81	2.99	16.73	16.11	1.9	3.77	2.16		8.62		3.36
Germany	4.12	4.77	5.46	4.07	16.73	16.11	1.9	4.18	3.76		8.62		4.37
Italy	2.71	3.02	2.32	4.19	16.73	16.11	1.9	2.44	1.74		8.62		2.62
Japan	7.04	6.01	8.45	4.07			5	5.52	12.78		8.62		
United Kingdom	3.86	4.48	6.23	3.28		16.11	0.96	1.76	1.93		8.62		3.06
United States	16.32	20.99	10.21	6.96			30	6.61	12.78		10.12		
G7	**40.41**	**46.77**	**39.15**	**28.98**	**50.19**	**64.44**	**45.66**	**28.17**	**39.63**		**56.66**		**13.41**
Argentina	0.91	1.59	1.29	0.39			10.75	0.1					
Australia	1.37	1.77	1.25						4.93		1.01		3.65
Brazil	1.83	2.08	1.77	0.82			10.75	0.34				20	
China	4.55	2.3	2.2	1.44			0.004	1.19	5.45		0.001	20	27.52
India	2.99	3.82	2.86	1.43				0.27	5.36			20	7.92
Indonesia	1.01	1.19	0.88	0.73					4.65	2.25			3.34
Rep. of Korea	1.62	1.07	0.9	0.49			0.004		4.33		1.01		3.69
Mexico	1.65	1.15	0.53	0.55			6.91				0.01		
Russian Federation	2.85	3.82	0.34	0.33							4.05	20	6.25
Saudi Arabia	2.85	1.91	3.29	3.51				0.2		23.5	1.16		2.6
South Africa	0.78	0.67	0.26	0.26				5.08				20	
Turkey	1.12	0.61	0.6	0.39	7.09			0.34	0.57	6.45			2.66
Other G20	**23.53**	**21.98**	**16.17**	**10.34**	**7.09**		**28.42**	**7.52**	**25.29**	**32.2**	**7.241**	**100**	**57.63**
G20	**63.94**	**68.75**	**55.32**	**39.32**	**57.28**	**64.44**	**74.08**	**35.69**	**64.92**	**32.2**	**63.90**	**100**	**71.04**

(continued)

Table 4.2 (continued)

Country	Voting power (%)										
	Sub-regional										
	CABEI	EADB	CDB	CAF	IIB	BADEA	NIB	PTA	BSTDB	ETDB	EDB
Canada			9.24								
France											
Germany			5.56								
Italy			5.56								
Japan											
United Kingdom			9.24								
United States											
G7			**29.6**								
Argentina	3.51			9.27							
Australia											
Brazil			1.15	8.91							
China			5.56					4.74			
India											
Indonesia											
Rep. of Korea											
Mexico	7.42		2.81	1.23							
Russian Federation					11.10				16.50		65.97
Saudi Arabia						23.54					
South Africa											
Turkey									16.50	31.73	
Other G20	**10.93**		**9.52**	**19.41**	**11.10**	**23.54**		**4.74**	**33.00**	**31.73**	**65.97**
G20	**10.93**		**39.12**	**19.41**	**11.10**	**23.54**		**4.74**	**33.00**	**31.73**	**65.97**

- G7 countries have a very strong voting power in all global, most regional, and just one sub-regional MDB.
- The voting power of G20 countries is strong across all MDBs, with a few notable exceptions in the sub-regional group.
- In the relatively smaller regional and sub-regional MDBs, G20 is represented by just a few countries, showing lower presence, but also higher power concentration/domination at the country level.

It should be noted that all G7 and most G20 countries are usually large "donor", non-borrowing shareholders at most MDBs. The conventional rationale is that the prevailing decision-making power should stay outside the borrowing countries, to ensure financial discipline and lending prudency—as borrowing countries have interest to support higher risk or more concessional lending decisions.

G7 countries clearly have strong voting power in the global and regional MDBs, with full decision-making power at EIB and EBRD. The G20 countries could form a simple majority (51%) to take a decision in the global MDBs (except IFAD), as well as in CEDB, IDB, AsDB, NDB (New Development Bank) and AIIB (Asian Infrastructure Investment Bank), among the regional MDBs. However, all MDBs require a qualified majority (typically around 2/3 of votes) for (BoG) decision-making on special/fundamental issues such as amending establishing agreements. This, in combination with the growing discontent of many borrowing countries regarding the concentration of power at the non-borrowing ("donors") group, challenges any attempts to amend the status quo. In turn, it fuelled the creation of many sub-regional, as well as some new regional, MDBs, for example the NDB and AIIB.

Within G7, the United States has a sufficient share for a veto on strategic decisions that require a qualified majority in IBRD, IFC (International Financial Corporation), and IDB. The relatively high threshold of a qualified majority in these three, and some other, MDBs also allows many other shareholders to have a veto, if they act as a group. Hence, these MDBs are bound to seek broad consensus and political horse-trading if they attempt to reshape respective establishing agreements and other fundamental paradigms, including their governance system. This is possible, but very challenging.

While regional and sub-regional MDBs have lower thresholds for qualified majority, Japan enjoys similar veto power along the United States at the AsDB. Likewise, two or three countries among France, Germany, Italy, Japan, United Kingdom, and the United States can veto decisions at EBRD. CDB (Caribbean Development Bank) is similar regarding Canada, Germany, Italy, and United Kingdom. China has a veto power at AIIB, Russia at EDB, and Saudi Arabia at IsDB (Islamic Development Bank), and BADEA (Arab Bank for Economic Development in Africa). These are examples of polar models where voting power stays centered around a single or group of countries. While the discontent regarding this polar situation gave an impulse for the creation of subregional and other new MDBs, in the majority of the cases the *alternative* MDBs also carried the birthmarks of (reversed, retaliating) polarity (e.g. AIIB, EDB).

Board of Directors

BoD represents the governance layer between BoG and management, combining some oversight and executive roles. While all powers are vested at the BoG, most of them are actually delegated to the BoD.

The main BoD role is to ensure that the MDB is properly governed along the BoG-approved multilateral provisions of the *establishing agreements*. BoD guides and oversees executive management and independent control functions. It approves key policies on operational matters such as lending, recruitment, and so on, as well as supports the role and meetings of the BoG. Virtually any BoG issue is first addressed at the BoD as all fundamental BoG decisions are preceded by a BoD elaboration.

The members of BoDs are usually appointed upon nomination or election by shareholder countries. BoD members in the global and regional MDBs (except CEDB and EIB) are nominated by a group of countries due to the high number of shareholders (and a limited number of Directors). While many Directors represent a group of shareholder countries in these MDBs, some countries are directly represented (by either appointed or elected members), reflecting their higher voting powers and status stipulated in the respective establishing agreements. Others are elected by a group of countries assembled according to either regional similarities or borrowing/non-borrowing status or voting power.

At IBRD, IFC, and IDA (International Development Association), there are individual country-appointed Executive Directors for each of the five largest shareholders (United States, Japan, Germany, France, and United Kingdom). The rest of countries are grouped into constituencies, each represented by an elected Director. The Executive Directors of IBRD serve ex-officio to the Boards at IDA and IFC.

BoDs usually take decisions by consensus, rarely involving actual voting. However, the relative voting power of individual directors is a key mind factor when they contemplate whether or not to support a project or policy. This makes them inherent opinion leaders and power brokers. Typically, if there is a lack of a sufficient support for a project, its discussion is postponed rather than involving a divisive vote, triggering behind-closed-doors negotiations.

In contrast to group representations in global and regional MDBs, sub-regional MDBs have direct Board representation of the member countries (every member country has a director and is able to express its own opinion/vote).

As illustrated by Table 4.3, one BoD member represents approximately ten countries in the global MDBs, four to seven countries in the regional ones, and one single country in sub-regional MDBs. In the relatively smaller sub-regional MDBs, Boards are clearly more operational and inclusive, as allowed by their moderate size.

All global, many regional (IDB, AfDB, AsDB, EBRD, and AIIB), and some sub-regional MDBs (CABEI, CDB, and BADEA) have borrowing and non-borrowing (the latter are also called *non-regional* or *donor*) shareholder countries. BoD seats assigned to these two types of shareholders are specifically determined in the respective founding treaties.

As illustrated by Table 4.3, BoD seats of borrowing members at IDB, AfDB, and AsDB correspond to their voting powers. For example, 9 seats representing 64.2% of all seats and 65% of total voting power belong to regional (borrowing) countries at IDB; 13 seats represent 65% of all seats and 59.9% of the voting power at AfDB; 8 seats represent 66.7% of the seats and 65.2% of voting power at AsDB. BADEA is the only MDB with all BoD seats belonging to non-borrowing members since it has been established by members of the League of Arab States to finance development of African countries.

MDBs generally do not have any specific qualification requirements for the positions of director and alternate director. The establishing agreements of AfDB and IDB only require citizenship of a member country; EBRD, IDB, and BSTDB (Black Sea Trade and Development Bank) require high competence in economic and financial matters. Directors serve two to five years and may be re-elected or appointed without limitation, except at AfDB where the limit is two terms.

Many MDBs have resident BoDs with a remuneration determined by the BoGs. Other MDBs have non-resident BoDs, respectively without remuneration to directors (only an accommodation/travel allowance for the meeting days).

In the global MDBs (except IFAD) and most of the regional MDBs (except EIB, IsDB, NDB, and AIIB), the BoDs are resident. This involves substantially higher costs but allows for frequent BoD meetings. The non-resident Boards have minimum requirements for meetings, for example at least four to six times per annum. Non-resident Boards can make certain decisions by voting without a meeting (IsDB, NDB, AIIB, and sub-regional MDBs).

Table 4.4 outlines BoD quorum requirements. IBRD, IFC, and IDA have lower BoD quorum requirements relative to their respective BoG requirements.

Table 4.3 Composition of Board of Directors

	Global				Regional								
	IBRD	IFC	IDA	IFAD	CEDB	EIB	IDB	AfDB	AsDB	IsDB	EBRD	NDB	AIIB
Number of states	**189**	**184**	**173**	**176**	**41**	**28**	**48**	**80**	**67**	**57**	**65**	**5**	**56**
Non-borrowing							***22***	***26***	***19***		***28***		
Regional non-borrowing							*2*						
Non-regional non-borrowing							*20*	*26*	*19*		*28*		
Institutions											**2**		
Directors	**25**	**25**	**25**	**18**	**41**	**29**	**14**	**20**	**12**	**18**	**23**	**5**	**12**
Appointed by one member state (1)	*6*	*6*	*6*		*41*		*1*			*9*		*5*	
Elected by one member in BoG or appointed by BoG (2)	*2*	*2*	*2*			*28*	*4*	*1*	*3*		*8*		*2*
Representing non-borrowing shareholders (3)							*5*	*7*	*4*		*4*		*3*
Average number of countries represented by a member	*10.6*	*10.4*	*9.7*	*9.8*			*4.8*	*4.2*	*7.1*	*5.3*	*3.5*		*5.4*
Term (years)	2	2	2	3		5	3	3	2	3	3	2	2
Voting power of (%)													
Directors of (1) + (2)	45.6	48.8	40.0		100	100	34.0	6.6	31.0	83.9	53.2	100	35.4
Directors of (3)							49.9	41.1	34.8		18.8		22.7

	Sub-regional										
	CABEI	EADB	CDB	CAF	IIB	BADEA	NIB	PTA	BSTDB	ETDB	EDB
Number of states	**13**	**4**	**24**	**19**	**9**	**18**	**8**	**21**	**11**	**6**	**6**
Non-borrowing	***5***		***9***			***18***					
Regional non-borrowing			*4*								
Non-regional non-borrowing	*5*		*5*					*2*			
Institutions		**9**		**13**				**10**			
Directors	**12**	**9**	**19**	**19**		**11**	**8**	**10**	**11**	**6**	
Appointed by one member state (1)	*5*	*8*		*16*		*9*	*8*		*11*		
Elected by one member in BoG or appointed by BoG (2)	*2*		*9*								
Representing non-borrowing shareholders (3)	*4*		*5*			*11*		*1*			
Average number of countries represented by a member	*1.2*	*0.5*	*1.3*	*1.0*			*1.0*	*1.1*	*1.0*	*1.0*	
Term (years)	3	3	2	3		4	4	3	3	3	
Voting power of (%)											
Directors of (1) + (2)	68.4	87.0	64.8	92.4		93.0	100		100	100	
Directors of (3)	31.6		35.2			100		7.1			

Source: Authors' compilation

Table 4.4 Requirements for quorum and decision-making at Board of Directors' meetings

	Global				Regional								
	IBRD	IFC	IDA	IFAD	CEDB	EIB	IDB	AfDB	AsDB	IsDB	EBRD	NDB	AIIB
Meeting period	As often as the business may require				At least four times p.a.	At least six times p.a.		As often as the business may require				Quart.	As often as the business may require
Quorum	Not less than one half of the total voting power			2/3 of the total voting power	2/3 of directors	18 directors	Majority of directors including an absolute majority of dir. of regional members and not less than 3/4 of total voting power	Not less than 70% of total voting power	Not less than 2/3 of the total voting power				
Decision	Majority of the votes cast			3/5 of votes cast if more than one half of the total number of votes	Majority of the votes cast	**Regular** 1/3 of directors repres. 50% of the subscr. capital **Special** 18 directors and 68% of the subscr. capital	Majority of the total voting power of the member states	**Regular** 66.66% of the voting power of the members attending **Special** 70% of total voting power	Majority of the voting power present at the meeting	**Regular** Majority of the voting power of members present **Policy issues** Not less than 3/4 of the voting power of the members present		Majority of the voting power present at the meeting	

	Sub-regional								
	CABEI	EADB	CDB	CAF	BADEA	NIB	PTA	BSTDB	ETDB
Meeting period		At least every three months	As often as the business may require		Every four months	Eight per year	Quart.	As often as the business may require	
Quorum	Three dir. from founding states and two directors from other states	Seven directors including at least five from member states and at least one from a member of group of members other than member states	Not less than 2/3 of total voting power	Not less than half plus one of the member states present	Majority	Seven directors	Not less than 2/3 of the total voting power		Not less than 85% of the total voting power
Decision	Majority of the voting power present at the meeting	Majority of total voting power	Majority of the voting power present at the meeting	**Regular** Not less than half plus one of the dir. present **Special** Positive vote of at least half plus one director	Over 50% of the votes of the members present	Five directors	Over 50% of total voting power	**Regular** Over 50% of voting power of members present **Policy Issues** Not less than 2/3 of voting power of members present	Not less than 85% of voting power

Source: Authors' compilation

Five of the G7 countries (France, Germany, Japan, United Kingdom, and the United States) and three of the G20 countries (China, Russia, and Saudi Arabia) are directly represented in the BoDs of the global MDBs and have a combined voting power very close to reach the quorum requirement at IFC.

All regional MDBs apply same quorum and decision-making requirements to their BoDs and BoGs, respectively. Among them, IsDB stands out, as nine directly represented countries with more than 80% of the total voting power may call a meeting and make a decision. Similar is the case of EBRD, where six countries are represented directly at the BoD with more than 50% of voting power. These are two examples where directly represented shareholder countries have a low number of BoD seats but very high shares and voting powers. This illustrates a highly concentrated distribution of shares and voting power (to non-borrowing shareholders). At EBRD, shares and voting power for each of the five largest shareholders after the United States (Germany, France, Italy, Japan, and the United Kingdom) is 8.64%.

While sub-regional MDBs generally have identical BoG and BoD quorum requirements, at some of them (CABEI, CAF, and NIB) the BoDs enjoy lower thresholds. BoD meeting agenda is typically prepared by the president, who chairs those meetings in most MDBs. CEDB is an exception, as it has a part-time working official who chairs the BoD.

Directors who represent just one country vote in a straightforward manner. However, when a director represents a country group, it is important to articulate possible difference of opinions within that group. In this regard, there are two types of Boards. A director representing a country group in BoDs of the global MDBs and some of regional MDBs (AfDB, IDB) is unable to split his/her votes. In contrast, at other regional MDBs (AsDB, EBRD, and IsDB), a director is able to split his/her votes. The latter practice allows a fairer shareholder representation, particularly in respect to more controversial issues. Therefore the lack of a group vote splitting opportunity at the global and some regional MDBs represents a shortcoming, especially when country groups tend to be less homogeneous in terms of what they expect from an MDB.

Management

Typically, the management of MDBs consists of president, VPs, and secretary general. It is often referred to as executive or management committee (MC), in charge of conducting all MDB activities according to the directives and oversight of the BoD and BoG.

The management prepares the agenda for the BoD meetings in most MDBs, observing respective BoG/BoD directions. The agenda includes management-led initiatives such as recruitment, proposing policies and strategies, as well as loans/investments, for Board consideration and approval.

President

The president[4] reports to the BoD and is responsible for the day-to-day management. In most MDBs, except the global ones and CAF, the president is elected by the BoGs, usually following specific unwritten agreements, regarding nationality and nomination. IBRD and IDA share a president elected by the BoD of IBRD; in the case of IFC, he or she is elected by Executive Directors of IFC following a recommendation of IBRD's president.

As illustrated in Table 4.5, the formal qualification criteria for an MDB president are either absent or too general. At the global MDBs the requirement is simply not being a governor, an executive director, or an alternate to either.

The relatively few cases of professional requirements are very vague, such as a competence in matters related to the activities, management, and administration. Many MDBs have origin requirements including the nationality of either member country or regional member countries. As already noted, for several decades most MDBs observed unwritten (*gentlemen's*) agreements regarding the nationality of the president.

While IBRD and IFC do not require qualified majority voting (BoG) for the election of a president, the other MDBs apply certain levels of qualified majority. The prevailing term of service for a president is five years (with some cases in the range of three to six years) often allowing a re-election for a second term.

Vice Presidents

At most MDBs, the management team includes one or more VPs, typically appointed by the BoD or BoG on the formal recommendation of the president. The exceptions include IFAD, where the president appoints his/her VPs; and CEDB, where the Governing Board (equivalent of BoG) appoints Vice Governors (equivalent of VPs) on the recommendation of Administrative Council (equivalent of BoD).

IFC has the highest number of VPs. While there are 27 VPs at both IBRD and IDA, only 7 of them directly report to the president, 11 report to Chief

Executive Officer of IBRD/IDA, with the rest reporting to the Chief Financial Officer and Chief Administrative Officer of World Bank Group.

Like a president, a VP cannot simultaneously serve as a governor or director. Generally, each VP is responsible for certain division/field of activity such as finance or operations. In the absence or incapacity of the president, one of the VPs nominated by the president exercises his/her functions. VPs usually participate in the BoD/BoG meetings as part of the management, without voting power.

In several large MDBs (IBRD, IFC, EBRD, etc.), the VPs are generally selected/promoted from the professional staff, based on merit. In most regional and sub-regional MDBs, VPs are appointed either by each founding member state or a member state having high voting power—often implying a nationality rather than professional qualification criteria. Hence, VPs in those MDBs are often public officials nominated by the member countries, rarely having an MDB-relevant professional background. This also implies that they serve under pressure to observe national, rather than MDB, interests.

Committees and Independent Functions

Most MDBs delineate authority, by the use of various internal committees and independent functions, to ensure checks and balances of governance. The respective committees, such as executive/management, credit/investment, and assets/liabilities, typically include management/staff members that are not the same in each committee, although some of the members may take part in various committees. However, there are exceptions, at some of the largest and smallest MDBs. For example, the EIB has a more centralized approach where their MC deals with the issues that other MDBs allocated to distinct committees. Another example at smaller sub-regional MDBs is that while some of them have distinct committees, their members overlap substantially, thus compromising the "separation" principle.

In virtually all MDBs, the president chairs the MC.[5] However, at the larger MDBs, the other committees are usually not chaired by the president. EIB is an exception as there is only an MC, chaired by the president. The smaller MDBs have most of their committees chaired by the president.

While the MCs are typically composed mostly of senior management (VPs and secretary general), this is not always the case; for example, EBRD also includes the positions of Chief Economist and General Counsel, and NIB includes the General Counsel. The other committees normally include even a larger number of non-executive staff. For example, at EBRD the Credit

Table 4.5 Selection of president

	Global			Regional								
	IBRD IDA	IFC	IFAD	CEDB	EIB	IDB	AfDB	AsDB	IsDB	EBRD	NDB	AIIB
Authority	BoD of IBRD	BoD upon recom. of IBRD president	Governing Council	Governing Board	BoG upon proposal from BoD	BoG	BoG	BoG	BoG	BoG	BoG	BoG
Criteria	Not a governor or executive director or an alternate for either				High integrity and reputation; independence, competence and experience in financial, banking, and/or European Union matters, sufficient knowledge, skills and expertise to perform the duties		National of a regional member state. Highest competence in matters related with the activities	National of regional member	National of member country		National of the founder states; rotation; not a governor or director or alternate	National of regional member

(*continued*)

Table 4.5 (continued)

	Global		Regional								
	IBRD IDA IFC	IFAD	CEDB	EIB	IDB	AfDB	AsDB	IsDB	EBRD	NDB	AIIB
Decision	Majority of the votes cast	2/3 of total number of votes	3/4 of governors representing 3/4 of votes cast	Majority of governors having 50% of subscribed capital	Over 50% of total voting power having absolute majority of the gov. of regional members	Majority of the total voting power of the members incl. majority of the total voting power of the regional members	Over 50% of the governors having over 50% of the total voting power	Over 50% of the governors representing at least 2/3 of the total voting power	Majority of governors representing at least 50% of the total voting power	Over 50% of the votes cast	Vote of 2/3 of the governors representing at least 3/4 of total voting power
Term in years	Five (may be re-elected for same or shorter period)	Four (may be re-elected for only one further term)	Five (may be re-elected once)	Six (may be re-elected)	Five (may be re-elected for the following terms)	Five (may be re-elected but not more than two terms)	Five (may be re-elected)	Five (may be re-elected)	Four (may be re-elected)	Five	Five (may be re-elected once)

	Sub-regional										
	CABEI	EADB	CDB	CAF	IIB	BADEA	NIB	PTA	BSTDB	ETDB	EDB
Authority	BoG from a list of three nominees	Gov. Council	BoG	BoD	Council	BoG on the recom. of BoD	BoD	BoG on the recom. of BoD	BoG	BoG	Council
Criteria	National of one of the founder states, capacity and broad experience in economic, financial, or banking affairs		Experience in matters related to finance and dev. in the public or private sector			Non-member of BoD		National of member state; integrity and highest comp. in matters related with the activities, manag. and admin.	National of member country		
Decision	Majority of the votes of subscribed capital	At least 75% of the total voting power	At least 2/3 of governors having 3/4 of total voting power	At least half plus one of the directors	Unanimously	Over 50% of the votes present	Five directors	Majority of voting present	Over 50% of the total number of governors with over 50% of the total voting power	Majority of governors with 85% of the voting power	Majority of council members
Term in years	Five (may be re-elected once)	Five (may be re-elected)	Five (may be re-elected)	Five (may be re-elected)	Five	Three (may be re-elected for max. two terms)	Five	Five (may be re-elected for max two terms)	Four	Four	Four (may be re-elected)

Committee (named Operations Committee) includes Chief Economist, Director Risk Management, and Business Group Director Monitoring. The situation at IFC and NIB is similar. In contrast, some of the smaller MDBs compose all or most committees predominantly with senior management only (duplicating the MC). Examples of composition of different committees at several MDBs are illustrated by Table 4.6.

An important element of the checks and balances is delivered by an MDB-unique function of governance accountability and learning, known as Independent Evaluation (actual names vary, e.g. Office of Evaluation and Oversight at IDB, Independent Evaluation Group at IBRD and IFC, etc.). Unlike other independent control functions such as Internal Audit and Compliance, the Evaluation is very distinct for MDBs as it does not exist in any other bank. It was institutionalized a couple of decades ago in order to provide credible evaluations of the contribution of each MDB to their mandate (results on the ground) based on a comprehensive set of criteria and standards, common for the MDBs (MDB Evaluation Cooperation Group 2012; World bank 2003). This evaluation covers not only the project levels, but any other activity or system of the MDB, making a very important contribution to the institutional accountability and learning. To ensure independence and rigor, the Independent Evaluation Functions are reporting directly to BoD/BoG levels (most often to a dedicated BoD committee such as the Committee of Development Effectiveness), not to the management.

Self-Regulation and External Actors

Self-Regulation

MDBs, being international intergovernmental organizations (often referred to as supranational) are highly self-regulated complex institutions. Self-regulation is a process whereby MDBs create their own internal legislation and monitor their own adherence to legal, ethical, or safety standards, rather than have an outside, independent agency such as a central bank, to set, monitor, and enforce those standards. As most of the respective standards are actually set by the MDBs themselves, and are embedded in their various rules such as establishing agreements, policies, and procedures, the MDBs have specific independent control units and mechanisms to ensure compliance. While each MDB sets its rules of operation and governance, this is more a collective, rather than an individual process. MDBs usually operate in a similar manner, as a family of peer cross-referenced institutions adhering to common norms and standards, with large MDBs often acting as role models.

Table 4.6 Examples of MDB's committees

IMDB	Management Committee (MC)	Credit Committee (CC)	Asset/Liability Committee (ALCO)	Senior management	Note
EBRD	Most senior management, including Chief Economist, General Counsel. Chaired by President	Some VPs, General Counsel, Chief Economist, Director Risk, Business Group Director Monitoring and members of CC secretariat (observers)	Some VPs, Treasurer, Director Risk, Controller, Director Portfolio, Director Treasury Credit Risk, Deputy Treasurer and Head of Funding, and representatives of Banking, Chief Economist, General Counsel	President, 16 senior managers	Committees have different members. BoD gives final approval on operations above certain amounts
EIB	President and eight VPs	MC acts as CC	MC acts as ALCO	President and eight VPs	All powers in MC, some exceptions, delegated to BoD committees
IFC	Similar to EBRD, without Chief Economist and General Counsel, but including two CEOs (Executive VP/CEO and CEO IFC Asset Management Company)	Similar to EBRD	Similar to EBRD	President same with IBRD. Six VPs	BoD approves on operations above certain amounts
NIB	Senior management	Including technical staff	Including technical staff	Seven top management positions	President takes part in several committees. Committees include technical staff
CEDB	Senior management	Senior management	Senior management	Senior management of eight	As above, no technical staff in committees

As self-regulation may involve a conflict of interest, MDBs seek established best practice within the MDB family. Furthermore, MDBs apply self-regulation in view of their important public role to set highest standards as well as maintain a high credibility, as a system of interrelated institutions with common global goals.

Self-regulation extends well beyond setting up internal rules. MDBs impose various rules and requirements on corporate and sovereign borrowers, as part of the respective lending legal agreements. Thus, while not representing legislation per se, such standards and conditionality effectively become legally binding norms that are adopted, often beyond the expiry of respective lending agreements, by third parties such as partner organizations and borrowers (e.g. companies, banks, institutions) affecting wide segments of the institutional environment. For example, MDBs have a rather common set of requirements on good CG, as well as environmental and social norms, acting as a promoter (quasi-legislator) of such standards in many regions.

MDBs maintain control over the standards to which they adhere to by a complex process of cross-referencing. Self-regulation naturally requires expertise, as well as numerous independent functions within the governance structure, to ensure rigor and credibility. MDBs have very high visibility as standard-setters. Therefore, if they reveal any failure of the self-regulation/governance system, this usually triggers strong external pressures—for example by shareholder countries within and even outside their membership representation, relevant external authorities, as well as the wider public, academics, and NGOs.

While MDBs, as supranational institutions with privileges and immunities, are not overseen by banking and capital market authorities, except in the context of some specific treasury and other transactions, they observe best practice and relevant regulations on a voluntary basis. Furthermore, MDBs voluntarily comply with various norms and rules, such as the respective financial reporting and auditing standards, in the process of issuing audited financial statements.

One of the relevant international authorities that does not directly govern MDBs but is nevertheless referenced is the Basel Committee on Banking Supervision (BCBS).[6] While the Committee has no direct authority over MDBs, its role to enhance understanding of key supervisory issues and improve the quality of banking supervision and governance worldwide is reflected by the MDBs. MDBs voluntarily consult the Committee's guidelines and standards in many areas—for example capital adequacy and the Principles for Corporate Governance in Banking, addressed further (BCBS 2012, 2015). MDBs consistently self-regulate their own capital adequacy and risk appetite thresholds well above the levels set by the Committee.

BCBS aims to encourage convergence toward common approaches and standards. The Committee is not a classical multilateral organization, partly because it has no founding treaty. It does not issue binding regulation but acts as an informal forum where policy solutions and standards are developed. Hence, MDBs have often shared goals with some of those of the Committee.

The Peculiar Role of Credit Rating Agencies

Credit rating agencies have a high and often controversial impact on MDBs. While MDBs have no formal requirement to get ratings, they all do this in order to facilitate their borrowing from the international markets.

A credit rating quantifies a borrower's overall creditworthiness to pay its obligations. The borrower's capacity and willingness to pay its obligations are subject to a thorough assessment in establishing a rating. Credit ratings are vital to MDBs as they borrow in the market to finance their lending activities. The credit ratings of both non-borrowing (donor) and borrowing (regional) countries also influence MDBs' ratings. This reflects the assessment of shareholders as capital contributors to the MDBs, as well as borrowers affecting the respective loan portfolios. Therefore, the rating agencies assess not just the MDBs, but numerous relevant stakeholders, including the shareholder and borrower countries.

The credit rating of an MDB also depends on the robustness of its governance, as well as the evidence of shareholders' commitment. Key indicators of shareholder support to an MDB *by borrowing countries* include repaying the loans to the MDB, even in a time of financial distress (proof of respect of the MDB's *preferred creditor status*), as well as participation in the periodic capital increases. The latter reflects both the willingness and ability to pay (certain beneficiary countries in financial distress have either not subscribed to capital increases or are in arrears regarding payments for the capital increases of some MDBs—both situations signal compromised commitment, negatively affecting credit rating reviews).

A key indicator of shareholder support for non-borrowing (*donor*) shareholder countries is the willingness to increase contributions of *paid-in capital* and, secondarily, *callable capital*. The willingness to increase paid-in capital strengthens shareholders' equity and is a main criterion for commitment, for all types of shareholders. The willingness to contribute callable capital is an untested, less tangible, and harder to assess form of support, but also matters.

Another sign of commitment is the provision of funding to soft-loan and technical assistance (grant) windows, as these represent a key element in the franchise value of some institutions (mostly AfDB: 38 of the 53 regional members are eligible to borrow only from the soft-loan window; and IBRD, 66 of whose 145 borrowing members that could do so only from the soft-loan window).

While *rating agencies inherently play an invisible regulatory and oversight role over MDBs*, this process is controversial. The challenge stems from the very nature of MDBs as supranational institutions with *preferred creditor status*. This complexity is often poorly understood and reflected by the actual rating process that generally treats the MDBs as a simple mixture of banks (lenders) and sovereigns (shareholders)—and not as complex self-regulated public institutions with highly conservative approaches and systems regarding risk, leverage, prudence, and ownership support.

In the past, the rating was a rather simple process as most MDBs had a large number of AAA-rated shareholder countries and, with some exceptions, routinely got AAA or similar high credit rating. With the proliferation of MDBs, particularly sub-regional ones, as well as in light of the recent global crisis developments, rating agencies adopted a more stringent approach, severely shaking the easy access to AAA and similar ratings. Even large regional MDBs are currently likely to lose their AAA rating that was taken for granted for decades.

These rating challenges result in higher cost of funding that in turn puts a pressure on the MDBs' efficiency and competitiveness. This triggers an increasing attention on the importance and peculiarity of the rating process. It also affects the MDBs' governance and even their strategies. To issue high credit ratings, the agencies routinely put certain requirements on the banks, such as portfolio risk reduction, sector and country diversification, and so on. While this may be meaningful in the case of banks in general, it has a doubtful/controversial rationale and relevance vis-à-vis MDBs as they are special public mandate institutions, intrinsically different from banks and the associated risk mitigation needs. It is clear that rating agencies came short in understanding and reflecting adequately the very distinct public nature of MDBs, as highly capitalized conservative institutions with very committed sovereign shareholders, as well as preferred creditor status (implying that the debt to an MDB should remain due even if legislators impose restrictions such as foreign exchange or capital controls) and numerous other advantages relative to banks and even sovereigns.

While some rating agencies recently started to issue regular reviews on MDBs under a specific category of *supranationals*, the applied methodology is still short of reflecting the very distinct nature of MDBs and challenges the credibility of the ratings. On the positive side, these rating reviews just started to cover not only the financial features of MDBs, but also the *business profile*, reflecting some governance aspects. They also start to note the distinct nature of MDBs (rightly referred as Multilateral Lending Institutions—MLI, noting their institutional character; see *Supranationals, Special Edition* 2017).

The insufficient reflection by rating agencies of the very specific institutional nature of MDBs has already drawn the attention of MDBs and shareholders who are considering how to mitigate it. Some of the BRICS (Brazil, Russia, India, China, and South Africa) countries already announced the establishment of alternative rating agencies, calling for reconsideration of the rating system as such. Likewise, some MDBs took a course toward *sweating* their balance sheets, meaning a regrouping of their assets in order to boost the actual capital adequacy and thus make more resources available for lending.

Beyond the issue of how adequate the credit ratings are, there is a concern that the rating agencies are adversely impacting on the strategies and governance of MDBs, effectively undertaking the implicit role of regulators, although the latter have very little depth of knowledge on the MDBs' complexity.

Conclusions: Pressures to Improve Governance

While in principle only nation-states have the legitimacy to create international law, MDBs also assumed this role via their efforts to affect business practice, including CG. In turn, civil society and some governments called for more transparent and inclusive MDB governance. As a consequence, a number of UN and other intergovernmental organizations—including MDBs—have gradually improved their governance and disclosure.

During the last 20 years, various stakeholders have pressed the MDBs toward modernizing their governance (Buira 2000; Caliari 2002). These include both NGOs,[7] as well as MDB shareholders, increasingly criticizing various aspects of MDBs' governance. The most criticized elements include the outdated top-level hiring process, at (or based on) the IMF and the World Bank, mainly referring to President and VP positions (also where other management posts are based on national quotas rather than a merit-based competition), the concentration of voting power, mainly to G7/G20, the restrictions to information disclosure, and so on. The opponents to these management appointment practices have raised two main arguments:

- Any agreement stipulating a leadership position based on nationality must be abolished as outdated, counterproductive, and unfair, as the nationality principle limits the pool of potential talent, excluding those that may be better versed in the financial and development needs of the borrowing countries. Furthermore, the current system increases the political "horse-trading" among countries that divide up leadership positions.

- MDB Boards often chose candidates in secret closed-door sessions. This is non-transparent and undermines the legitimacy of the leadership. For any president and management to be successful, they must have the respect and confidence of both the MDB professionals and member countries. As about two-thirds of the World Bank members have expressed their view that the current process is controversial, any selection process that excludes the developing countries will be increasingly challenged in the MDBs that have not fully opened-up their leadership appointment practices.

The MDBs response to such criticism started in 2000 when an IMF Working Group reviewed the process for selection of the Managing Director. Their report was endorsed by the Board in 2001, as guidance for the future selection of Managing Directors, and focused on five recommendations:

- Executive Directors should establish clear criteria for identifying, nominating, and selecting qualified candidates for the post.
- Executive Directors should be informed in a timely manner regarding candidates, including their credentials and knowledge of the institution.
- There should be a channel for facilitating smooth communication.
- Transparency and accountability are critical.
- The selection at the IMF should take into account any impact on the selection process at MDBs.

The report recommendations represent a turning point for both the Bretton Woods institutions and the rest of MDBs, the effects of which are either taking place or yet to be seen. While the general consensus is that CEOs should be selected through a transparent merit-based process involving all member countries, the progress has been modest. However, the pressure is now escalating toward genuine geographical diversity in top positions and full abolishment of any national quotas,[8] culminating to the G20 initiative of 2017, calling for overarching governance reform of the MDBs, addressed below.

Many MDBs have recently moved toward a more transparent and competitive recruitment of senior management, slowly abolishing national quotas. There are however still many cases of preservation of quotas for the president/CEO, as well as other management positions, for example at CABEI, EIB, BSTDB, and so on, regardless of whether this is based on a written policy or otherwise.

The MDBs that continued to reserve senior management posts for certain (typically large) shareholders were subjected to pressure from shareholders and also have taken a course for reform. For example, the AsDB initiated a respective reform in response to a study of the Department for International Development (DFID, United Kingdom), representing a major shareholder. The study qualified the quota system for professional staff (reflecting country's shareholdings) and the reservation of certain posts for particular countries, as an anomaly (e.g. with presidency, treasury, and budget portfolios reserved for Japan, while the General Counsel's Office for the United States).

The latest bold call for governance reform was made by the G20 in April 2017, when the G20 Eminent Persons Group on Global Financial Governance was established. It includes eminent persons with deep knowledge and experience in global finance and MDBs, who would consult other external resources. *The group is expected to address the following key issues:*

- review the current and possible future challenges and opportunities facing the international financial systems, and the current state of the global financial architecture and governance
- outline the *optimal role of MDBs*, covering the interaction and coordination among them, as well as with the G20 and their memberships; their *capacity to catalyze private capital* flows and domestic resources; *their governance* and *accountability structures*, to ensure *efficiency, effectiveness, and transparency* in *addressing the pressing global challenges*
- recommend practical reforms of the global financial architecture and governance toward economic stability and sustainable growth, including an enhanced leadership and support by G20

The Group's findings and recommendations will be reported in late 2018 to G20 Finance Ministers and Central Bank Governors, while decisions on any MDB proposals should be made by their respective governing bodies.

As per their mandates, MDBs promote sound governance to their borrowing countries. Therefore, they need to lead by example by applying rigorous standards on themselves, to elevate their governance accordingly, demonstrating a visible commitment.

During last two decades, most MDBs made progress toward better governance. Yet, this fell short of matching the MDBs' governance requirements from their borrowers, outlined by the respective OECD (Organization for Economic Cooperation and Development) and Basel principles, implying a lot of work ahead.

Notes

1. Called differently in some MDBs: for example Governing Board in CEDB; Governing Council in IFAD; Council of the Bank in EDB and IIB; and Shareholders' Assembly in CAF.
2. Called differently in some MDBs, e.g. Administrative Council in CEDB; Executive Board in IFAD, no equivalent in IIB and EDB, where the "Board" is actually an executive (management) Board/committee.
3. The establishing agreement of EIB stipulates that the members of BoG must be ministers, at NIB that the members of BoG must be finance ministers, and at AsDB that BoG members should have a broad experience in economic and financial issues.
4. Called differently at some MDBs, for example as Director General at EADB (East African Development Bank) and BADEA; Chairman of Executive Board at IIB and EDB, Governor at CEDB, and so on.
5. As IFC and IBRD share the same president, it is the CEO/VP at the IFC who chairs their MC.
6. The Committee's Secretariat is located at the Bank for International Settlements (BIS) in Basel, Switzerland, but the BIS and the Basel Committee remain two distinct entities. BCBS was established by the central bank governors of the Group of Ten countries in 1974 to provide a forum for regular cooperation on banking supervisory matters.
7. On February 10, 2005, the International Financial Institutions (IFI) Democracy Coalition, a group of civil society organizations committed to improving governance at the IFIs, sent a signed statement to the Governors of the World Bank demanding transparency and accountability in selecting the organization's president. Over 60 civil society organizations and individuals from developing and developed countries have signed this statement which calls for a process based on "explicit [selection] criteria, including the commitment to a genuine democratization of the institution." The statement also insists that the process "be open to candidates from all countries", since the current tradition has it that the World Bank president is an appointee of the US government. The Coalition sees a transparent selection process as a step forward in minimizing the democratic deficit apparent in the Bretton Woods Institutions.
8. As initiated by the Reform Proposals for the Governance Structures of IFIs (Caliari and Schroeder 2002).

References

Arslan, Volkan. 2011. *The Analysis of the Representation and Governance Structures of the International Financial Institutions and Their Constituencies*. Treasury Expert Thesis, Undersecretariat of Treasury General Directorate of Foreign Economic Relations.

BCBS. 2013. *Principles for Effective Risk Data Aggregation and Risk Reporting*. Basel Committee on Banking Supervision, (Progress Report 2015).

———. 2015. *Guidelines: Corporate Governance Principles for Banks*. Basel: Basel Committee on Banking Supervision, Bank for International Settlements. https://www.bis.org/bcbs/publ/d328.pdf.

Bissell, Richard, and Suresh Nanwani. 2008. Multilateral Development Bank Accountability Mechanisms: Developments and Challenges. *Central European Journal of International and Security Studies (CEJISS)*. http://www.cejiss.org/static/data/uploaded/13835988693526/bissell-nanwani_multilateral_development_bank.pdf.

Buira, Ariel. 2000. *Reforming the Governance of the Bretton Woods Institutions in Financing for Development*. Proceedings of a Workshop of the G-24 (Published by the OPEC Fund for International Development).

Caliari, Aldo, and Frank Schroeder. 2002. *Reform Proposals for the Governance Structures of IFIs, A New Rules for Global Finance Briefing Paper*. New York: Friedrich Ebert Foundation. http://library.fes.de/pdf-files/iez/global/02057.pdf.

Carter, Colin, and William Lorsch. 2003. *Back to the Drawing Board: Designing Corporate Boards for a Complex World*. Cambridge, MA: Harvard Business School Press.

Higgs, Derek. 2003. *Higgs Report on Non-Executive Directors: Summary Recommendations*. http://www.berr.gov.uk/files/file 23012.pdf.

MDB Evaluation Cooperation Group (ECG). 2012. *Big Book on Evaluation Good Practice Standards*. https://www.ecgnet.org/document/ecg-big-book-good-practice-standards.

OECD. 2011. *OECD Guidelines for Multinational Enterprises*. Paris: OECD. http://mneguidelines.oecd.org/guidelines/.

———. 2015. *G20/OECD Principles of Corporate Governance*. Paris: OECD. https://doi.org/10.1787/9789264236882-en.

S&P Global Ratings. 2017. *Supranationals, Special Edition*, 2017. https://www.spratings.com/documents/20184/908545/US_SR_Event_Webcast_MultilateralNov17_Article2.pdf/fc892865-5302-4dd6-93ca-8469c8752818.

The Committee on the Financial Aspects of Financial Governance and Gee and Co. Ltd. 1992. *Report of the Committee on Financial Aspects of Corporate Governance*, London.

World Bank. 2003. World Bank Operations Evaluation Department: The First 30 Years. *The World Bank*. https://openknowledge.worldbank.org/handle/10986/15128.

5

Principles of Sound Governance

Introduction

This chapter elaborates a novel system of *Multilateral Development Bank (MDB)-specific governance principles*. The conclusion presents recent developments, an assessment of the adherence to the outlined governance principles, and areas for improvement.

A sound governance safeguards stakeholders' interest in conformity with public interest. For example, shareholders' interests at retail banks must be secondary to depositors' interest, and the latter's interest comes secondary to the overall public interest. In the financial sector, the governance determines the allocation and interaction of authority and responsibilities toward the activities of a financial institution conducted by its Board and senior management. This includes but is not limited to how Boards and management define strategy and objectives; select and supervise personnel; undertake decisions; meet shareholder obligations; align corporate culture, activities, and behavior with the required prudency; ensure compliance with laws and regulations; and nurture sound control functions.

In recent times, two major international organizations—the World Bank and the OECD,[1] followed by many MDBs—have proactively worked toward adoption of international Corporate Governance (CG) standards, to mitigate the risks of financial failures. Upon the World Bank's recommendation, in 1999 the OECD issued a milestone report of guiding CG principles, updated in 2004 and 2015 when the CG principles were formally adopted by OECD and G20 (G20/OECD, 2015). This is the sole internationally recognized reference on CG, aiming to establish a voluntary framework of standards

I. U. Delikanli et al., *Multilateral Development Banks*,
https://doi.org/10.1007/978-3-319-91524-1_5

applicable to various types of companies worldwide. While these standards are not directly aimed at public sector institutions and MDBs in particular, they serve as a guiding point. The OECD Guidelines and Standards on CG, such as those on Multinational Enterprises (OECD, 2011), were developed in cooperation with governments, international organizations, and the private sector. They refer to the six G20/OECD Principles of non-binding nature, outlined and promoted by the OECD to enhance regulatory frameworks in its member countries and beyond. The OECD cooperates with international organizations including MDBs, as well as with regional organizations and private sector, toward enhancing and disseminating the respective Principles, to protect shareholders' rights and values.

The six OECD/G20 Principles (OECD, 2015) were adapted by the Basel Committee on Banking Supervision (*Guidelines Corporate Governance Principles for Banks*, 2015). This resulted in 13 Basel Principles of CG, calling for better reliance on the bank's internal processes (*self-regulation*), rather than on *ex-post external supervision*. This is an unprecedented alteration of bank supervision toward better and timely *self-assessment*, supported by external authority guidance and validation—that is of particular relevance to MDBs as well. The Basel Principles underline the importance of having the appropriate levels, mixes, and interactions of authority, responsibility, accountability, and checks and balances, with a clear focus on the *soundness of Board of Directors (BoD) and senior management*, as well as key independent control functions (e.g. risk management, compliance, and internal audit).

The Basel Committee has noted that since the Principles were first stated in 2006, there is a strong evidence for banking sector strengthening, including a more robust oversight in many jurisdictions. As a result, "banks exhibit a better understanding of the important elements of corporate governance such as effective board oversight, rigorous risk management, strong internal controls, compliance and other related areas. In addition, many banks have made progress in assessing collective board skills and qualifications, instituting standalone board risk committees, establishing and elevating the role of chief risk officer (CRO), and integrating discussions between board audit and risk committees" (Guidelines Corporate Governance Principles for Banks, 2015).

This chapter reflects the need to critically revisit and substantially improve the MDBs' governance. It is based on a study of the relevance and implementation of the so far successful legacy of the 13 *Basel Committee Corporate Governance Principles*[2] (BCBS, 2015), to assess and enhance their substance and application, distilling new principles, matching the complexity of MDBs.

As neither the original OECD Principles, nor their Basel elaboration for the banking sector, made any reference to MDBs, the main contribution of this chapter is the elaboration of MDB-specific governance principles. The Basel Principles were used as a starting point. The elaborated new principles reflect the MDB nature of complex supranational self-regulated organizations, with distinctly different scope, scale, and governance. This effort resulted in the following seven MDB governance Principles:

Principle 1: Board's structure, qualifications, and role
Principle 2: Senior management
Principle 3: Risk management
Principle 4: Independent evaluation
Principle 5: Compliance and audit
Principle 6: Human capital
Principle 7: Governance accountability and disclosure

One of the primary objectives of the principles and their application in the MDB context is to explicitly reinforce the collective oversight and governance responsibilities of the Boards—Board of Governors (BoG) and Board of Directors (BoD). Another key objective is to address the components of strategy and institutional risk governance, with a focus on elevating institutional culture, in line with the very demanding global challenges faced by MDBs. The review of the principles should help to delineate the specific roles of the Boards, committees, senior management, and the control functions, in the very unique MDB context, with the ultimate goal of strengthening MDBs' relevance and efficiency.

The presentation of the seven MDB Principles is followed by a summary of stock-taking on the actual level of its implementation by MDBs, including relevant recommendations.

Principle 1: Board Structure, Qualifications, and Roles

The MDBs typical two-tier Board structure has all powers vested at the highest level—the BoG. However, most of those powers are delegated to the BoD, leaving the strategic matters and supervision, only formally at the BoG. Given this delegation of authority, this chapter uses the term Board as a reference to both BoD and BoG, with the understanding that most Board functions are de-facto conducted by the BoD, which often delegates some of its powers to the senior management.

Board Structure and Qualifications

Board members should be appropriately qualified, individually and collectively. They should understand their governance and oversight role and be able to conduct sound objective judgment about the operation of the MDB.

To ensure effective oversight, the Board should be composed of a sufficient number of independent (non-managing) directors. They should have a balance of skills, diversity, and expertise, collectively equipped with the necessary qualifications.

The following key requirements (BoD) should be taken into account:

1. Board members should have a range of knowledge and experience in relevant areas, as well as varied backgrounds to promote diversity of views. Areas of competence may include, but are not limited to, finance/reporting, development, multilateralism, information technology, strategic planning, risk management, compensation, regulation, CG, and management.
2. The Board collectively should have a reasonable understanding of regional and global economic and market forces and of the legal and regulatory environment, as well as sound international/development and governance experience, directly relevant to the complexity of MDBs as international self-regulated organizations.
3. Board members' attitude should facilitate communication, collaboration, and critical debate in the decision-making process.

The Board should have a comprehensive and rigorous process for identifying, appraising, and approving Board candidates. While Boards normally nominate/select candidates and ensure appropriate succession planning, in the MDB context this is done by the shareholders (formally represented by the BoG). In such cases, the BoD should still have a duty to ensure that members are qualified.

The selection process should review Board nominees on the following: (1) knowledge, skills, experience, and independence of mind (particularly for non-executive directors); (2) a record of integrity and good repute; (3) sufficient time to fully carry out their responsibilities; and (4) the ability to promote a smooth interaction with other Board members and management.

Board nominees should be free of any conflicts of interest that may impede their ability to perform their duties independently and objectively and subject them to undue influence from:

1. other persons (such as management or other shareholders)
2. past, present, or future positions held/aspired for
3. personal, professional, or other economic relationships with other members of the Board or management, or with other entities that may be related to the MDB

There should be a nomination committee, composed of a sufficient number of independent Board members, with the task to identify and nominate candidates as per these criteria. Should a Board member become poorly qualified or unable to fulfill his or her responsibilities, the BoD should take appropriate actions, which may include notifying the BoG.

To help Board members meet their skill and duty requirements, they should take part in relevant induction programs and ongoing training on key issues. Sufficient time, budget, and other resources must be allocated for this purpose.

Whenever there are shareholders with power to appoint Board members, as is the case in most MDBs, the Board should ensure that such individuals are fit for their duties. Board members are responsible toward the MDB's interests, regardless of who appoints them.

The BoDs should create relevant internal structure regarding their leadership, size, and Board committees, to effectively perform oversight and other responsibilities. This should ensure that the Boards have the time and means to cover all necessary matters and discussions in depth. The Board's rules, bylaws, or other similar documents should be regularly reviewed and updated. The Boards should conduct periodic assessments (using external experts if needed) of their structure, functioning, committees, and individual members, focusing on:

1. structure, size, and composition, including committees
2. suitability and performance of each Board member (reviewed at least annually)
3. regular review of own governance practices and procedures (improvements and updates)
4. use of the assessment results to improve BoD's performance and inform the BoG

The Boards should keep appropriate records such as meeting minutes, recommendations, decisions, differing opinions, and so on. These should be accessible by the BoG and relevant independent functions such as compliance, independent evaluation, and internal audit.

The chair of the Board (BoD) provides leadership to the Board and ensures its effectiveness, including nurturing of trustful relationship with Board members. He/she should have relevant experience, competencies, and personal qualities. The chair should ensure that Board decisions are taken on a rigorous and well-informed basis, including critical discussion and free expression of dissenting views. Sufficient time, skills, and effort is required for the proper exercise of his or her duties.

The chair should be an independent or non-executive Board member. In the cases where the chair may hold executive duties, there should be relevant safeguards to mitigate any compromise on the checks and balances, for example by designating a lead Board member, a senior independent Board member, or a similar position, as well as ensuring a larger number of non-executives on the Board.

Board Committees

The Board may establish certain specialized Board committees, to ensure focus and efficiency. The number and type of committees depend on many factors, including Board/MDB size, the mandate, and so on. Typical MDB committees include Audit Committee (AC) and Development Effectiveness Committee (DEC).

Each Board committee should have a charter or other document to determine its mandate, scope, and procedures, including reporting to the Board, committee member requirements, tenure limits, rotation of chair, and so on, to prevent undue concentration of power and to promote fresh perspectives.

The Board should disclose its committees, and their mandates, rationale, and composition. Committees should maintain appropriate records/minutes of discussions and decisions. A committee chair should be an independent, non-executive Board member. The members of the committee should not include any executive position or staff of the MDB. The respective secretariat/support functions should report only to the committee and not to the management. The same applies to key control functions that are supervised by and work with a Board committee, for example internal audit and independent evaluation.

Audit Committee

The main features and duties of the AC could be summarized as follows:

1. A dedicated AC is composed of independent or non-executive Board members, chaired by an independent Board director who is not a chair of the Board or of any other committee.

2. The AC members should have experience in audit practices, institutional performance, financial reporting, evaluation, and accounting. The AC should possess a collective balance of skills and expert knowledge, commensurate with the MDB.
3. The AC shapes the policy on internal audit and financial reporting, oversees the financial reporting process and the internal and external auditors (as well as the independent evaluation function of MDBs in the absence of DEC).
4. The AC approves or recommends to the Board the appointment, remuneration, and dismissal of external auditors.
5. The AC receives key audit/evaluation reports and prompts senior management to take corrective actions in a timely manner.
6. The AC oversees the accounting policies and practices and reviews third-party opinions regarding the overall risk governance framework and internal control system.

Given the inherent BoD composition by country representatives, it is recommended to ensure an AC composed of fully independent members, based on merit and international selection.

Development Effectiveness Committee

DEC assists the Board in ensuring that MDB's programs and activities are achieving desired development objectives and making efficient use of the human and financial capital. It works closely with the independent evaluation function to ensure its timely and effective use at the highest level.

DEC carries out the following responsibilities on behalf of the Board:

1. reviews and approves the annual work program and budget of the Independent Evaluation Department (IED) , as well as selects and oversees the IED head according to a credible process and criteria, reflecting respective international standards
2. reviews selected IED evaluation reports and the related actions taken by the MDB
3. reports to the Board essential operations evaluation matters with a significant impact on the relevance, efficiency, and effectiveness of the MDB, and makes recommendations on such issues to the Board, based on IED reports and recommendations
4. monitors and reports to the Board on the implementation of its decisions

Given the inherent BoD composition by country representatives, it is recommended to ensure a DEC composed of fully independent members, based on merit and international selection.

Other relevant committees may include the following:

1. *Risk committee*: deals with risk strategies/policies, capital and liquidity management as well as all relevant risks, such as credit, market, operational, and reputational, in interaction with the Risk Management Department, and AC.
2. *Compensation committee*: supports the Board in ensuring that the remuneration system is consistent with the MDB role, culture, mandate, performance, and control environment.
3. *Nomination/human resources/governance committee*: recommends to the Board new Board nominees and members of senior management, and reviews the role and responsibilities of the Board/management member, as well as the required knowledge, experience, and competences, ensuring that the Board is not dominated by any one individual or small group of individuals as this could jeopardize institutional interests. It may also assess Board and senior management effectiveness, as well as human capital policies.
4. *Ethics and compliance committee*: ensures appropriate means for proper checks and balances in decision-making, considering reputational risks, and compliance with laws, regulations, and internal rules.

Strategy, Oversight, Country Relevance, and Fair Forum

Further to the complexity of supranational governance, MDB Boards have to balance four key roles, outlined below. The first two are rather conventional as they also apply to corporations: *strategy* and *oversight*. The other two roles are inherent to intergovernmental organizations and MDBs: *country relevance* and *fair forum*.[3]

Strategy Formulation and Steering

MDB Boards have a visionary role, beyond their fiduciary duty of oversight. This includes a regular revisiting of the meaning and interpretation of the institutional mandate in the globally changing context of new challenges that require a multilateral response. The Boards' strategic thinking should foster possible and desirable advancements of the role and impact of the MDB.

Formulation of strategies and policies is an important element of the self-regulatory governance of MDBs. The Board should assess how the MDBs' goals and operations will be affected by changes in the external environment, formulating strategies, adapting goals and instruments, based on lessons from institutional experience.

To nurture strategic thinking, the Board should maintain frank and constructive deliberation among directors, as well as within the MDB. While this implies various features, it also suggests relatively small Boards,[4] in the range of 10–12 members (Carter and Lorsch 2003: 89–91). The empirical evidence suggests compromised effectiveness of larger Boards due to lower participation quality, cumbersome decision-making, free-rider issues, and so on.

Effective strategic thinking requires a Board with a high-caliber expertise, institutional memory, and experience. This implies relatively long terms over three years (Higgs 2003: 5) and loyalty to the institution, as well as merit-based recruitment of directors with MDB-relevant experience.[5]

Strategic thinking also requires *arm's-length distance* from day-to-day management. If involved in micro-management and routine operation approvals, Boards lose perspective of strategy. Therefore, Boards need to meet only a few times per year, hence giving advantage to non-resident Boards in this regard (the typical Board of a major corporation meets six to eight times per year) (Spencer Stuart 2006a: 21).

Effective strategy formulation also requires a critical mass of *independent* directors (i.e. directors who are free from any business or relationship which could materially interfere with their judgment) (*Guidelines: Corporate governance principles for banks*, Basel Committee, 2015: 16).

Independent directors deliver external objective views, counteracting potential conflicts of interest. In the private sector, independent, "non-executive" directors have become a standard and are instrumental for the proper functioning of Board committees.

Oversight

The Boards have fiduciary responsibility for the oversight of strategy and institutional integrity, key decisions such as those on Human Capital (HC), internal organization, governance structure and processes, mandate definition and interpretation, risk management, compliance, audit, independent evaluation, and so on. A Board may delegate some of its functions, but not its responsibilities, to dedicated Board committees.

The oversight role determines whether and how management and staff are carrying out the MDBs' functions in accordance with certain pre-set indicators and standards. Judgments should be based on performance standards that are set out *ex ante* by the Board, from the perspective of the institution, not of any individual national interest. The Board is responsible for setting the standards for regularly measuring management's performance. If performance is sub-standard, the Board should promptly undertake corrective action.

The responsibilities and actions of the CEO/president must be distinguishable from those of the Board. Otherwise the accountability is compromised by a conflict of interest as the Board would be unable to assess the CEO's performance without implying a judgment on its own performance. It is also essential that performance standards and indicators are set by the Board itself or an external relevant authority. Effective oversight also requires that the Board has sufficient access to information and independent evaluations regarding the performance of the institution and its management and staff. This implies the need of comprehensive reporting requirements for the CEO. Ultimately, the Board should be able to reward or sanction management on the basis of performance evaluations, including dismissing CEO/management[6] in cases of serious underperformance or misconduct.

A key role of the Boards is to conduct oversight of senior management, making its members accountable. The Boards should outline the possible consequences (including dismissal) if those actions are not aligned with well-defined performance benchmarks, with a specific reference to adherence to the MDBs' values. The oversight of management should:

1. assess if senior management's actions are consistent with the strategy and policies approved by the Board, including regular meetings and discussions, and critically review and question explanations and information provided by management
2. set appropriate performance and remuneration standards for management consistent with the long-term strategic objectives of the MDB
3. assess senior management's collective knowledge and expertise vis-à-vis the mandate, values, and products of the MDB; and develop succession plans for the CEO and other key positions

The Boards should establish and maintain adequate organizational structure, enabling effective decision-making and governance. This implies a clear definition of delineated responsibilities and authorities of the Boards, the senior management, and of those responsible for checks and balances, institutional accountability, and learning—for example risk management, internal audit, independent evaluation, and compliance.

Fundamental oversight responsibilities of the Boards that should not be delegated at lower levels include the following:

1. oversee implementation of strategic objectives, as per institutional mandate, reflecting past results and insights, as reported by independent evaluation
2. shape up and maintain institutional culture and values, for example adherence to development mandate and stakeholder needs, with a particular reference to multilateralism, development, *additionality*, and so on
3. oversee adherence to governance framework and periodically ascertain its relevance in the light of material changes to the MDB's mandate, scope, complexity, region, strategy, and stakeholder requirements
4. oversee a robust accounting and financial reporting, including annual financial statements, and conduct a periodic independent review of critical areas
5. approve selection and oversee performance of senior management and heads of key control functions: for example risk management, internal audit, independent evaluation, and compliance
6. oversee the reward system, including monitoring and reviewing executive compensation and assessing whether it is aligned with the MDB profile
7. oversee the integrity, independence, and effectiveness of policies and systems for whistleblowing with a focus on mandate fulfillment and respective accountability based on best practice and standards in independent evaluation
8. oversee key transactions, based on the internal independent functions, to ensure that appropriate restrictions are enforced (e.g. negative lists, etc.) so that resources are not misappropriated, misapplied, or unaccounted for, and there are no undue reputation risks

Country Relevance

Given the specific multilateral nature of MDBs, it is acknowledged that their Boards (BoG in particular, but also BoD) have a strong *political element* regarding member country representation. Directors have to promote particular country interests, on top of the common institutional agenda. Therefore they act as a *political counterweight* to the otherwise technical decisions of management and staff, to ensure that MDB actions and policies are in line (*relevant*) to the country needs/situation. In other words, directors weight and reflect, respectively, important actions and decisions, assessing if they are consistent with the interest of the country (or group of countries) they represent. If relevance is compromised, the director needs to align country interests with the operation of the MDB.

Ensuring *country relevance* as a measure of political counterweight reflects that Board directors are *state officials* who act primarily with their national interests in mind, as required by the governments that appointed or elected them. To perform this role effectively, the following conditions should be met:

1. Board directors should be primarily associated with and accountable to their national authorities (limited ability to act independently from those authorities). The relatively short tenures of directors support their loyalty to respective countries, rather than becoming too close to the MDB.
2. Directors should have adequate information about the MDB activities. This requires appropriate Board bureaucracy, including secretariat and advisors who process information regularly, from respective independent and credible sources.
3. The Board should have a close interaction with the key structures of MDB operations, to intervene promptly if *country relevance* is challenged.

Fair Forum

Further to the MDB complexity with a Board of country representatives, as well as guardians of the institution, the Board has a distinct role of a *fair forum*, where directors can freely present their views. This requires a process of Board decisions to become legitimate if they are based on deliberation in which all voices are respected and considered. This does not necessarily imply that directors always have equal voting power, but that they all have an *equal right to expression, respect, and attention.*

As only a very inclusive Board can act as a *fair forum*, it should represent well, directly rather than indirectly, the entire membership. The Board's rules should ensure the right of all members to participate equally in all deliberations and should guarantee that dissenting views are expressed and noted. Board records should accurately reflect the levels of agreement on decisions. The Board rules should limit situations in which a minority of the membership can impose a controversial decision without inclusive deliberation.

These requirements clearly favor a *relatively small Board* of one vote per each country. While the aim is a *fair forum* even if there is a weighted voting, the latter is a compromised solution, particularly when there are voting power concentrations. An unacceptable compromise is when decisions can be imposed by a small fraction of the membership. In these cases the largest voteholders have few incentives to consider the views of the others, jeopardizing the role of a *fair forum*.

In addition to sound rules, the culture of the Board should encourage meaningful participation, debate, and the voicing of disagreements. The chair's mandate and incentives should explicitly stimulate and facilitate a healthy debate, safeguarding the rights of minorities and dissenting voices. It is essential that directors are able to dissent without fear of retribution. By all means, Boards should not tolerate any form of *chilling effect* or *peer pressure*, as those undermine any rules.

Balancing the Four Roles

As the four roles, and the respective Board requirements, involve certain trade-offs, it is important to ensure a good balance among them. For example, the *strategy role* (and to some extent the oversight as well) requires a lean merit-based Board with independence, expertise, innovation, debate, and a distance from management. In contrast, *country relevance* and *fair forum* imply that each shareholder country should be represented and voiced—that is, a rather large politically based Board. *Country relevance* requires close involvement in day-to-day management, as well as strong relationship between the Board and political authorities. This is a serious challenge to expertise and independence, as well as the *strategy formulation* at arm's length. Ensuring a *fair forum* involves open debate and representation, but challenges the efficiency of decision-making.

Likewise, an effective oversight and institutional accountability is in conflict with political considerations required to align the MDB's operations with country perspectives.

Further to those trade-offs, it is clear that no Board can fully satisfy the respective requirements. Hence, MDBs should make a serious effort to assess and balance effectiveness, efficiency, accountability, and representation, reflecting the inevitable trade-offs. This requires a strong determination as well as utilization of independent evaluation and further methodological expertise, including comprehensive indicators of balance.

Institutional Culture and Values

MDBs need a continuous nurturing of a mandate-aligned institutional culture of reinforcing relevant norms for responsible and ethical behavior. These norms are critical for the MDBs' awareness regarding the complexity of the concept of risk—ranging from the mere financial risks to the multiple aspects of institutional and reputational risks of a highly visible role-model public institution that needs to walk the talk of ever higher development agenda.

Boards should set and reinforce the *tone at the top* to ensure a robust institutional culture that embraces the complexity of the development agenda and values at all levels. More specifically, they have the following key responsibilities:

1. Setting, articulating, and adhering to core institutional values that create a clear understanding that all operations should be conducted genuinely in line with the mandate of the MDB, overseeing the fitness and adherence to such values by senior management and employees. This requires adequate selection, elevation, training, and motivation of both *high-caliber leadership and staff at every level*, demonstrating genuine understanding and commitment to the MDB's mandate, as well as the relevant stakeholders' needs, including a high degree of ethics and cultural sensitivity.
2. Setting-up the risk appetite and funding frameworks and keeping management and staff updated on those. In the MDB context, this goes in line with stressing on the relevant public mandate, financial and non-financial *additionality*, *catalytic role* and absence of profit-maximization and dividend distribution.
3. Effective articulation and outreach of the institutional values, professional standards, codes of conduct, along with supporting policies. A code of conduct/ethics, or comparable policy, should clearly define acceptable and unacceptable values and behaviors.
4. Raising effective awareness among employees and management regarding the disciplinary or other actions that apply to unacceptable behaviors and transgressions, eroding the institutional culture standards, for example zero tolerance to disrespect of core values such as cultural sensitivity and multilateral development agenda, among others.
5. Taking steps so that employees can raise, confidentially and without the risk of reprisal, legitimate concerns about illegal, unethical, or questionable practices, based on a well-communicated policy and procedures, allowing sharing of material and bona fide concerns and observations of any violations in a confidential manner (e.g. whistle-blower policy). This includes communicating material concerns to BoD and BoG.
6. Performing effective oversight of the whistleblowing policy mechanism, ensuring that management addresses all raised legitimate issues. The Boards should ensure that staff who raise concerns are protected from detrimental treatment or reprisals. It should have regular direct interaction with relevant control functions, to obtain independent evaluation on the adherence to key institutional values.

Interaction with Independent Functions

The Boards should ensure a well-articulated system of accountability and sound control functions. They should define what actions follow when mandate goals and various safeguards are neglected. The Boards should approve and communicate sound policies on those functions.

The Boards have to assure the unobstructed functioning of the independent control units, with a focus on their independence from management and other units. This involves frequent direct interaction with the Boards and relevant committees, as well as highest levels of credibility and professional rigor.

The BoD should ensure that the risk management, compliance, internal audit, and independent evaluation functions are properly positioned, staffed, and resourced, and conduct their responsibilities independently, objectively, and effectively. It should regularly review key policies and controls with the heads of those functions to identify and address risks and issues as well as determine areas for improvement, based on highest professional standards, e.g. on independent evaluation (Evaluation Cooperation Group, 2012).

Conflicts of Interest

The wide range of activities and roles may cause conflicts of interest (e.g. if an MDB department lends to a firm while another department trades in securities issued by that firm). Further conflicts of interest may arise among the MDB or its customers and members of the Board or senior managers (e.g. a business relationship of the MDB with an entity in which one of those members has a financial interest).

The Board should oversee the implementation of policies to reveal potential conflicts of interest. If these conflicts cannot be prevented, they should be properly managed, involving disclosure and approval of relationships or transactions as per elaborate policies and standards. This requires a written conflicts-of-interest policy and implementation, covering a number of key issues:

1. duty to avoid, to the extent possible, activities that could create conflicts of interest or the appearance of conflicts of interest
2. examples of where conflicts can arise when serving as a Board member
3. a sound review and approval process for members to follow before they engage in certain activities (such as serving on another Board), to prevent a conflict of interest

4. duty to promptly disclose any matter that may result, or has resulted, in a conflict of interest
5. responsibility to abstain from voting on any matter where the member may have a conflict of interest
6. actions to be taken by the Board regarding any non-compliance with the policy

A potential conflict of interest appears when a bank is both owned by the state and subject to banking supervision of the state. In this regard, MDBs are even more prone to conflict, because of their inherent self-regulatory role. This requires a dedicated administrative separation of the ownership, management, and supervision/control functions, to mitigate political interference in the oversight and management of the MDB.

Principle 2: Senior Management

Senior management should manage the MDB's activities in line with the respective mandate and strategy, as well as all Board-approved policies, under the directions and supervision of the Board.

The Board should maintain comprehensive and transparent structure, procedures, and decision-making of senior management. The role, authority, and responsibility of the various positions within senior management, including that of the CEO, should be clearly outlined and articulated by the Board.

All members of senior management should have the required experience, competencies, and integrity to manage the operations and people under their supervision, in line with the core values and mandate of the MDB. They should obtain regular training, relevant to the MDB and respective duties. Members of senior management should be based on a rigorous recruitment process, addressing thoroughly the qualifications required for each position, involving a transparent merit-based international competition. A sound preselection and interview process should provide sufficient information to the Board about each candidate.

All members of senior management play a key leadership role and have a major impact on the MDB's governance and culture through personal conduct, acting as role models. Both the Board and the senior managers set the *tone at the top* and thus have a key responsibility for the institutional culture and the quality governance that often result in a hard-to-change legacy. As members of senior management should provide adequate oversight and guidance of those they manage, it is of paramount importance that the former are regarded as leading credible professionals and personalities. Their sound business acumen should be blended with a genuine dedication to the values and mandate of the MDB.

Senior management members should establish transparent and efficient management system, under which they delegate a balanced mix of authority and duties to remaining layers of management and staff, promoting accountability, transparency, and core values.

Guided by the Board, senior management implements the strategies, development mandates, risk management systems, processes, and controls. Independent control functions should operate rigorously and independently. Senior management should respect the independent duties of such functions avoiding any actual or perceived pressure or interference.

Senior management should provide the Board with the information it needs to carry out its oversight, enabling the effective supervision and assessment of the quality of management's performance. It should regularly update the Board on key matters, such as changes in strategy, independently evaluated performance, financial condition, compliance with limits or other rules, internal control obstacles, legal or reputational concerns, and issues raised by the MDB's whistleblowing, audit, and evaluation functions.

Principle 3: Risk Management

This principle requires an effective independent risk management function, under the direction of a CRO, with sufficient stature, independence, resources, and access to the Board.

This function oversees risk-taking activities across the MDB, with a focus on the following:

1. identifying and assessing risks, in the MDB-specific context
2. developing and implementing the risk governance framework, for Board review and approval
3. establishing an early warning system for breaches of the set risk appetite limits
4. influencing and, when necessary, challenging decisions that give rise to material risk
5. reporting to senior management and the Board on these items, including recommendations

While working closely with front units, the risk management function should be sufficiently independent of them. It should have access to all units that have the potential to generate material risk and should be fluent in *MDB-specific finance*, for example *additionality*, preferred creditor status, catalyzing, mandate-driven strategies, and so on.

The risk management function should be adequately staffed, including relevant MDB experience, qualifications, and product knowledge, understanding the multiple reputational dimensions of institutional risk. Staff should have the ability and skills to effectively challenge all operations regarding any aspects of risk.

Staff should be encouraged to gain experience in both business line and risk management roles, on a rotational basis. This can produce several benefits, including stature equivalent with business lines and other functions, promoting institutional dialogue regarding risk, and so on. To avoid conflicts of interest, risk managers should not oversee activities they previously dealt with.

The main duty of the CRO or equivalent is to oversee the development and implementation of the risk management. This includes improvement of staff skills and risk management systems, policies, processes, models, and reports. The CRO is responsible for supporting the Board in its oversight of risk appetite. Together with management, he/she should proactively monitor risk-taking and adherence to established limits. The CRO should not have management or financial responsibility related to any operational lines or revenue-generating functions, and should not have dual coverage (e.g. the Chief Operating Officer, CFO, chief auditor, or other senior manager should not also serve as the CRO).

While reporting lines may vary, the CRO should report and have direct access to the Board or its risk committee. The CRO should be free to interpret and articulate risk in a clear manner to engage the Board and management in discussion. The CRO should have the ability to meet with the Board or risk committee regularly and without management being present.

If dual coverage is unavoidable (e.g. in smaller institutions with resource constraints), dual roles should be compatible—not weakening checks and balances. In some cases, the CRO sits on the credit committee, responsible for approving credit exposures. While this may assist decision-making and also inform the CRO on potential exposures, it can trigger a conflict when he or she should assess the exposure in the future. Therefore, the CRO may have just a veto authority (as opposed to approval authority).

Appointment, dismissal, and other changes to the CRO position should be approved by the Board or its risk committee. When the CRO is dismissed, this should be disclosed publicly. The reasons for removal should be substantiated to the shareholders. The CRO's performance, compensation, and budget should be approved and assessed by the risk (or equivalent) Board committee.

The risk governance policies and procedures should reflect the MDB profile regarding risk identification, aggregation, mitigation, and monitoring. The Board and senior management, including the CRO, should regularly evaluate the risks, looking at both current and emerging risks, detected by all organizational units. Risk identification and measurement should include both quantitative and qualitative elements, including harder-to-quantify risks, such as institutional reputation risk.

Internal controls should ensure that each key risk is covered by a policy or other measure. They should verify both the implementation and the financial and management information. Key management decisions should be taken by more than one person.

The Board and senior management should give attention to the quality, completeness, and accuracy of the data used to make risk decisions. Ultimate risk assessment responsibility stays with the MDB, despite the use of various tools/data, for example external credit ratings or risk models (*Principles for effective risk data aggregation and risk reporting*, BCBS 2013–2015).

Risk measurement and modeling techniques should be used in combination with, but not as substitute to, qualitative risk analysis and monitoring. The Board and senior management should be informed of the assumptions used in and potential shortcomings of the risk models and analyses. Regular stress tests on potential risk exposures under a variety of adverse circumstances should be conducted and discussed with the Board or its risk committee.

Risk awareness requires open communication about risk-taking across the organization, both horizontally (among departments) and vertically. Senior management should consult with the control functions on risk-related plans and activities.

MDBs should avoid organizational *silos* that can disrupt sharing of information, as this may result in partially informed decision taking. Organizational silos often emerge when business units operate in isolation from each other, with limited information sharing and even incentives to hide information due to internal competition/tensions. The Board, senior management, and control functions may need to re-evaluate established practices to encourage effective communication.

Principle 4: Independent Evaluation

This principle requires an effective Independent Evaluation Department (IED), under the direction of a head with highest stature, credibility, ethics and independence, and adequate resources and direct access to the Boards. It is based on the

Good Practice Standards for Independent Evaluation, maintained by the MDB's Evaluation Cooperation Group (Big Book on Evaluation Good Practice Standards, Evaluation Cooperation Group, 2012).

Role and Independence

The IED provides an independent rigorous evaluation of the projects, programs, policies, governance, and activities, as well as the overall performance of the MDB. It serves two main functions, essential for the sound governance: *accountability and learning*. The IED is an institution within the institution with the challenging task to interface policy and reality by speaking truth to power (World Bank, 2003).

Independence from operations and management is essential to provide impartial, credible evaluation to improve the performance of the institution. The rationale for independence could be summarized as follows:

1. Independence ensures and safeguards the impartiality and credibility of evaluations and evaluators.
2. It is different from isolation, as a sound evaluation requires cross-fertilization of knowledge and experience, based on continuous interaction with all units across the MDB, and even among MDBs, reflecting the complexity of the development agenda and result-based governance.
3. Independence ensures credible assessment, as well as undisturbed dissemination of results across the MDB, its Boards and beyond.

The independence of the evaluation function has four dimensions: *organizational, behavioral, avoidance of conflict of interest, and protection from outside interference*. While independence could be ensured by different models, reflecting the MDB's structure, respect of these dimensions is important.

IED operates according to a Board-approved policy, outlining the IED mandate, responsibilities, reporting structure, and key operating principles. These governance arrangements should ensure independence and uncensored delivery of accountability and learning across the MDB.

For organizational independence, the IED is located outside the line and staff management function. It does not report to the management, but to the Board or a dedicated committee of the Board. It works with full autonomy but in close consultation with the other departments to achieve coherence of institutional values.

The IED evaluates a broad range of activities and issues such as operations, programs, strategies, policies, and so on. The evaluation policy defines the independence and reporting lines to the Board or a Board committee. It also describes the accountability and learning aspects of the evaluation function, as well as the difference and interaction between self-evaluation and independent evaluation.

The IED is overseen by the Board or its committee and reports without clearances to the BoD and BoG. To avoid isolation, it interacts regularly with all departments, management, and Boards, to discuss its evaluation findings and recommendations. In the cases of differing opinions, IED openly states differing views in its final reports. It provides evidence-based recommendations that are practical, feasible, and followed up in their implementation. All evaluation outputs should result in timely written management response/action.

To ensure independence and reflect the non-resident BoD, a dual reporting line is possible: to the president in his/her capacity as the BoD chair, for day-to-day matters; as well as to the Board or a Board committee which has an oversight role over the IED and safeguards its independence from pressures and interference.

The evaluation process and methods are governed by international standards, embedded in the BoD-approved evaluation policy, with a particular reference to the *Big Book on Evaluation Good Practice Standards* (Evaluation Cooperation Group, 2012). IED has unrestricted access to staff and information, prepares independently its work plan and relevant budget (for BoD approval), has full authority over the depth and scope of its evaluations, including the highest corporate level, and reports directly all evaluation findings to both BoD and BoG without any clearances.

The IED should have the capacity and resources to undertake a wide range of evaluation studies and institutional evaluations. Thematic, sector, and country-level evaluations, as well as evaluations of policies, strategies, and governance, are generally more useful than evaluations of individual projects. They match the role of the independent evaluation to support the Board, management, and staff in maximizing the relevance and effectiveness of the MDB.

IED is expected to face resistance regarding institutional level evaluations. BoD and IED should address this challenge seriously, mitigating any attempt to limit the scope of evaluation. Limitations can give the impression that evaluation and feedback may be avoided, thus undermining the MDB's efforts to build a sustainable learning culture.

Head and Staff

The head of the IED is competitively recruited by the Board or the Board committee that oversees the evaluation function, through procedures approved by that body. The recruitment panel may have a management representative and may be supported by outside search firms or consultants, provided that the Board or its committee retains control and final decision-making authority. If there is no resident Board, at least one Board representative should participate in a leading role in the recruitment process. Only the Board may terminate the contract of the head, based on a dedicated policy and duly substantiated evidence of poor performance or conduct.

The contract terms of the head should be in line with the overall staff policy of the MDB. It may be open ended or fixed and may include an option for renewal, subject to BoD decision. Open-ended tenure protection is an important safeguard of independence as expectations for renewal may trigger self-censorship. Upon termination of service as IED head, the individual should not be eligible for staff or management positions at the MDB, to assure independence. The head holds a grade-rank equal to the level immediately below vice president or higher, with commensurate compensation—to ensure credible standing in facing the challenges of independence. The IED head's performance is assessed by the BoD or its committee (or body designated by it for this purpose). Management, including the president, may provide inputs into this process by way of feedback, but should not be the assessor.

The IED staff is recruited by the head or his/her designee, in line with overall HR policies of the MDB. Such staff should have specific evaluation and personality skills and competencies, reflecting highest professional standards. Unlike the head, staff may be permitted to rotate within the MDB, subject to certain conflict-of-interest limitations.

IED head and staff should be protected by the respective policy from pressures and repercussions. This may include policy provision for the use of separate processes for assessing IED staff for changes in compensation, promotions, and job tenure, as well as handling employment issues. Such processes may be parallel to those for other staff, but should protect IED staff from potential career limitations for findings and recommendations in their evaluations.

The IED should have comprehensive policies and procedures to mitigate potential conflicts of interest. These should not allow staff to evaluate any projects, programs, or other activities for which they were previously in charge. Movement of evaluation staff into other units should be permitted only exceptionally, upon sound evidence that this is not representing a conflict of interest such as seeking or being invited for such promotions.

Stakeholders, Program, Resources, and Disclosure

IED's principle stakeholders are BoD and BoG. It reports to them accordingly, to facilitate their task of efficiently achieving results on the ground (mandate fulfillment). The IED interacts with many internal and external stakeholders. Internal stakeholders may include, but are not limited to management (which is acting on and following up evaluations); operations staff (obtaining feedback of evaluation lessons and findings); and other staff concerned with knowledge management and dissemination of evaluation products. Key external stakeholders may include, but are not limited to partner governments and institutions, borrowers, beneficiaries and targeted populations, co-financiers, and evaluation networks.

IED develops its own work program, which may be endorsed by the Board/committee. It may consult with staff and management, as well as the Board and outside organizations, but management does not interfere with the work program and its implementation. IED is free to amend and adapt the work program reflecting new priorities and developments. It independently determines the scope, themes, sampling, and depth of each evaluation.

The IED's budget is approved by the Board/committee, commensurate with the work program. Management does not approve the IED's budget. However, the IED may follow the MDB's processes of general applicability in presenting its budget and in accounting for the use of resources. The IED is subject to the auditing requirements of the MDB, but audits may be conducted by an independent auditor rather than the internal audit unit.

The IED has unrestricted access to MDB's staff, records, stakeholders (borrowers, co-financiers, etc.), and project premises. It transmits evaluation products to the Boards, normally after review and comment by management, but without any management clearance or restrictions on scope, content, or dissemination. Management responds to and implements IED recommendations. IED follows up the implementation of recommendations and updates the Boards accordingly.

Disclosure of evaluation findings is instrumental for accountability to stakeholders. It is a key element of the behavioral independence of evaluation and is governed by the Board-approved evaluation policy, consistent with the MDB's general disclosure policy. The IED head determines the appropriate types and level of external dissemination activities, without management interference. There should be no *dual coverage* by the head of the evaluation function, to avoid conflict of interest.

Principle 5: Compliance and Audit

BoD oversees the management of the compliance risks and control systems by establishing independent internal audit and compliance functions and approving respective policies.

Compliance

MDBs should have independent (from management) compliance function, reporting to the Board, ensuring integrity and compliance with applicable regulations and internal policies. The management is responsible for establishing a compliance policy to be approved by the Board. It stipulates how compliance risks are identified and managed through all levels, reflecting the self-regulatory nature of MDBs. This implies, inter alia, that the internal regulations need to reflect best practice of the external regulatory frameworks on a voluntary basis, rather than directly seek compliance with external regulations. Hence, the respective staff should possess a sound understanding and experience of the MDB complexity and governance.

The compliance function is the guardian of institutional values, policies, and processes, ensuring fulfillment of obligations. It advises the Board and management on compliance with applicable laws, rules, and standards, referenced to the self-regulatory infrastructure of the MDB. The compliance function also provides relevant guidance to staff, for example on codes of conduct. It reports to the Board and has sufficient authority, independence, and resources. There should be no *dual coverage* by the head of the compliance function, to avoid conflict of interest.

Audit

The internal audit function supports Board and senior management in promoting an effective governance process and the long-term soundness of the institution and provides independent assurance to the Board.

The internal audit provides assurance to the Board and management on the quality and effectiveness of the MDB's internal controls, risk management, and governance systems and processes. It should have a clear mandate, be accountable to the Board, and be independent of the audited activities. This requires sufficient skills, resources, and authority, as well as avoidance of dual coverage. The following features are essential for the internal audit function:

1. full access to records, data, and physical properties of the MDB, including management information systems and minutes
2. conducting independent assessments of the effectiveness and efficiency of the internal control, risk management, and governance systems
3. adherence to international professional standards, such as those of the Institute of Internal Auditors

4. audit staff should collectively have knowledge, skills, and resources reflecting the activities and risks of the MDB
5. timely and effective correction of audit issues by senior management
6. periodic assessment of the risk governance framework, including risk management and compliance, the risk reporting to the Board and management, and the internal controls
7. internal audit reports should reach the Board or its AC without management filtering (internal auditors should have direct access to the Board or the Board's AC but should not take part in those structures)
8. the head of the internal audit should report primarily to the Board (or its AC), which is responsible for the recruitment and oversight of the performance of the head of this function
9. if the head of internal audit is removed, this should be disclosed publicly

Principle 6: Human Capital

The main asset of an MDB is its Human Capital (HC) as it shapes the institutional culture and overall performance with long-term consequences. The proper selection, training, motivation, retaining, advancement, and rewarding of MDB-specific HC is of paramount importance.

Human Capital Policy

An elaborate HC policy should aim at highest quality MDB-centered HC. Given the international organization profile of MDBs, their HC represents a specific type of tenure-protected international public servants, rather than employees of a multinational company. This implies certain MDB-specific rights and privileges, in the context of extraterritorial supranational self-regulated jurisdiction. It also involves implicit and explicit tenure protection, regardless of actual contract terms and duration. The continuous process of HC selection, nurturing, motivation, and rewarding has long-term consequences for the MDB and is very hard to reverse or mitigate in case of failure. MDBs should establish and follow a rigorous and transparent internationally competitive recruitment process, which reflects the core values of the MDB and:

1. Is based on a comprehensive definition of the requirements and challenges of the respective international environment, with particular reference to the specifics of locations, cultures, and all other elements of long-term expatriate context;
2. Is based on a clear definition and criteria for solid evidence of *MDB-relevant international experience*, *commitment*, understanding, knowledge, and cultural sensitivity;
3. Is based on a comprehensive analysis of the international market for the required technical and personal skills of a similar level of international public servants, including peer institution packages and terms (beyond the current state of affairs, to foresee further trends and developments);
4. Has a genuine geocentric HC approach[7] that ensures hiring, motivating, and retaining the best talent worldwide, fitting with both the job and institutional values, for example a sound track *record of commitment to a good mix of development, multilateralism, cultural diversity, integrity*, and so on, on top of technical skills. Should certain nationality exceed a relevant threshold (e.g. 5%), this would signal an erosion of the merit-based selection process and may be due to uncompetitive reward package, poor search outreach, location challenges, implicit quota application, regionally biased requirements, or other deficiencies;
5. Has an HC policy that includes a good balance of incentives and tenure,[8] in due recognition of MDBs as international organizations with justified jurisdictional immunities, privileges, and competitive expatriate compensation packages. While some elements of the HC may have a short-term nature, it is essential to ensure a solid core of dedicated development professionals who demonstrate a genuine commitment to think and live the MDB values, often implying bold family decisions and facing expatriate challenges in locations of varying attractiveness;
6. Has MDBs aligning their strategy for headquarters and regional office locations, on one hand, with the various HC implications and risks, on the other, reflecting a range of factors such as security, family employment, and physical and institutional infrastructure (e.g. schools, hospitals, transportation, culture, etc.);
7. In which, based on MDB's mandate and profile, a critical mass of internal HC should be nurtured and retained, constituting a core of dedicated professionals who lead by example, safeguard, advance, and promote the institutional values and memory, as a counterweight to management shifts and political pressures.

Talent Management

Talent management should be driven by strategic rather than ad hoc transactional objectives. While each MDB may have specific qualification requirements, the selection criteria should include a balance of the five core areas of *behavior*, *attitudes*, *skills*, *motivation*, and *personality*. The focus should be on commitment to the MDB values, cultural adaptability, strong intercultural motivation and communication skills, technical competence, professional expertise, genuine global development experience, region-specific experience, interpersonal skills, language skills, and family flexibility. Both the recruitment and in-house advancement processes should aim at a good combination of key features, including:

1. advanced technical skills in relevant development background and context
2. excellent language and communication skills and a high degree of demonstrated tolerance toward other culture, race, creed, color, habits, and values
3. evidence of high level of relevant self-motivation, such as development volunteering and fluent interaction with diverse social circles
4. goal-oriented behavior, commensurate with the core MDB values and mandate, with a reference to comprehensive understanding of and commitment to relevant global initiatives, for example the UN Sustainable Development Goals
5. previous overseas experience, family circumstances, and cultural-adaptability

HC motivation and engagement is crucial. A respective survey should be regularly implemented with established procedures for follow-up. It should measure key engagement indicators, for example value/culture match (including trust and integrity), work relevance, career development, relationship with management, turnover intention, and so on.

There should be a methodology and process to monitor drivers of staff engagement over time and compare the responses of staff to those of comparator organizations. Management follow-up to the staff survey should be prompt and consistent. Staff motivation and engagement data should be used systematically to inform the update of relevant HC processes.

Talent management processes should be supported by a comprehensive career development framework—to assist HC in managing their development and motivation. Standardized learning programs may provide internal means of developing and enhancing technical and value-based skills, competencies, and behaviors across job families. Succession management should be backed by ongoing development and support, to prepare high potential talent for leadership roles.

Rewarding

The compensation system should ensure strong long-term commitment to MDB values as well as sound governance, risk management, and public accountability.

Reward systems are part of institutional governance and incentive structures as they allow the Board and management to promote good performance and ensure adequate operating and risk culture. The Board oversees the management's implementation of the remuneration system by regular (annual) reviews of outcomes with a reference to desired incentives for steering mandate fulfillment, risk mitigation, capital, and innovation.

MDBs should consider having a Board compensation committee to oversee the compensation system's design and operation. The Board (and a possible compensation committee), should approve the compensation of senior executives and control functions, and should oversee compensation policies, systems, and related control processes. Employees in control functions (e.g. risk, independent evaluation, compliance and internal audit) should have their remuneration determined independently of any business line overseen, and performance measures should be based principally on achievement of their own objectives, to safeguard their independence and authority.

The reward system should be in line with the MDB mandate, development and risk strategy, objectives, values, and long-term interests of attracting, nurturing, and retaining the best-fitting talent worldwide. It should embed measures to prevent conflicts of interest and encourage a sound risk and institutional culture, putting ethics, goals, and values ahead of personal and business line interests.

Result-based components in remuneration should be considered carefully, in order to align performance indicators with the MDB's strategies and mandates, not with simplistic volume or return objectives. Rewards for potential future results with uncertain timing should be carefully evaluated and restrained. Variable remuneration should take into account the full range of risks, including breaches of risk appetite limits, reporting metrics, internal values, or norms.

HC development must be the primary rationale for any performance management system. Performance ratings should have moderate impact on bonuses and annual salary increases. It is instrumental to minimize the required time and resources devoted to ranking and categorizing of HC. Performance management and talent management processes should be well integrated to ensure that learning reflects strategic and operational needs, as well as leverage career development opportunities as the main reward for good performance.

Employees with a significant influence on the overall risk/reputation profile (material risk-takers) should be assessed on the basis of a multi-year result horizon, involving the use of credible independent units. This implies the need to defer a sufficiently large part of the compensation until risk outcomes and sustainability of results become evident. This allows compensation to be reduced or reversed based on realized risks or conduct events (*claw-back* provisions), if there is evidence that compensation paid was based on erroneous assumptions, such as misreporting or poor quality at entry. *Golden hellos* or *golden parachutes*, by which new or outgoing executives or employees obtain large payouts irrespective of performance, are not consistent with sound compensation practice.

Administrative Tribunal

MDBs are *supranational extraterritorial* organizations. This exposes them to various political and legal challenges, with strong implications on their potential and actual HC. To safeguard their *supranational* nature, MDBs enjoy a range of *privileges and immunities*.[9] This implies a substantial loss of sovereignty for the host countries in many fields (e.g. the extraterritoriality of the international premises, as well as the immunity from national courts on multiple matters, including employment issues). MDBs are also immune from legal suit (known as *jurisdictional immunity*, sometimes raising interpretations but otherwise typical). Therefore they should ensure adequate internal legislation regarding relationships and disputes with employees. To this end, this principle requires the following elements of important self-regulation by MDBs:

1. The BoD-approved HC or related policy should establish a best-practice-based internal independent system for timely and fair justice to all possible infringements of staff rights.
2. That system should include an *International Administrative Tribunal* headed by an independent reputable judge, functioning according to prevailing best practice.
3. BoD policy and procedures should ensure timely escalation of legitimate appeals to the Tribunal, giving equal access to fair trial and immediate implementation of respective rulings and recommendations, including improvements in the MDB's governance.
4. The MDB staff should be supported to establish their own staff council or association, to represent individual and collective interests vis-à-vis all MDB levels of power.

5. A standing Grievance Committee or an equivalent body should handle competently and timely all grievances and complaints, following a comprehensive escalation and arbitration process whereby the rulings of the Administrative Tribunal should be credible and final to all involved parties. The Grievance Committee should include reputable members of the MDB and act as the body of first instance in the internal justice system with authority to jurisdiction over all elements of any grievance appeal.
6. The appeal system should be reviewed and updated regularly, to reflect concerns, as well as best MDB practice.
7. The Administrative Tribunal should maintain highest standards of natural justice and fairness as key principles of international administrative law. Exceedingly pedantic, voluminous, and formalistic approaches should be avoided as they deprive appellants from defending their rights naturally, justly, and fairly.
8. User-friendly guidance to staff and Grievance Committees on how to interpret relevant internal laws is important. MDBs must apply in good faith the general principles of international administrative law to its self-regulation toward filling any lacunas.

Principle 7: Governance Accountability and Disclosure

MDB Boards, upon assessments and recommendations of independent control/evaluation functions, should guide and oversee governance, and require improvement and remedial action as necessary. MDBs should ensure highest possible levels of disclosure and transparency regarding their governance, operations, and results, for information of and interaction with shareholders, stakeholders, and the public.

Due to their supranational and developmental nature, MDBs are highly self-regulated institutions with jurisdictional immunity, not falling under external (central bank) supervision. While the ultimate supervising authority is formally the BoG, in essence the accountability and control role is assigned to dedicated independent functions, empowered by and working with the Boards to facilitate disclosure and supervision. While most of these functions exist in conventional banks, one of them is MDB-specific. This is the independent evaluation, with a central role in assessing, reporting, and disclosing the MDB's fulfillment of its *raison d'être*, the respective development mandate of the institution.

Guidance and Assessments

The BoG and BoD, based on regular inputs from independent evaluation and other control functions, provide guidance or rules, requiring robust governance policies and practices. This is essential in the absence of directly applicable national jurisdiction, over a supranational MDB. It should ensure checks and balances and a clear allocation of responsibilities, accountability, and transparency among the members of the Board, management, and further.

The Boards should set and enhance sound processes to evaluate MDB's governance. Such evaluations may be conducted through regular reviews of documents and reports, interviews with Board members and personnel, with a particular use of the independent evaluation function and its institutional evaluations. There should be regular governance assessments, with relevant discussions among the Board, management, compliance, internal audit, external auditors, and the independent evaluation function.

The Board should evaluate whether an MDB has effective oversight mechanisms regarding the strategic objectives, mandate compliance, risk appetite, performance, capital adequacy, liquidity, controls, compensation practices, and the selection and evaluation of management. It should periodically assure the independence of oversight of the evaluation, risk management, and compliance and internal audit functions. This should include assessing the extent to which the Board interacts with and utilizes these functions.

Boards should evaluate the processes and criteria for the selection of Board members and management, as well as verify the adequacy of the respective expertise and characters, as outlined under Principle 2. The individual and collective suitability of Board members and senior management is a main oversight issue of the Boards.

The governance effectiveness of the Board and senior management, with a focus on mandate compliance, should be assessed regularly to determine the extent to which the Board and management demonstrate effective behaviors toward sound governance. This includes various aspects of attitude, such as how the *tone at the top* and the mandate values are communicated and implemented, how information flows to and from the Board and management, and how potential serious problems are identified and addressed. The evaluation of governance effectiveness includes various Board and management assessments, surveys, and other information often used by institutions reviewing their culture, as well as supervisory interviews, observations, and qualitative judgments. The consistency of treatment and behavior across the MDB is very important.

The Board should utilize the independent evaluation function and should have the necessary skills and motivation to address these issues, to produce complex and candid judgments regarding governance effectiveness.

The Board should interact regularly with senior managers and the key control functions through meetings and other means such as in-person talks, e-mail, telephone, and so on. The goal is a timely and open dialogue between the MDB and the Board on a range of issues, including strategies and risks, governance, culture, management, compensation, and incentives. This dialogue should also include independent evaluations on performance, relative to MDB peers, market developments, and emerging challenges.

Board and independent functions should address promptly governance needs, by suggesting specific measures toward improvement, and demand accountability for the state of governance. These may include, inter alia, amendments of policies and practices, as well as the composition of BoD or management.

Interaction with External Actors

In the self-regulatory context of MDBs, cooperation and information-sharing among relevant MDB units and authorities is important. This should include reference to best practice originating from distinguished authorities, including the Basel Committee and other relevant international bodies, recognizing the specific supranational nature of MDBs.

The interaction of MDBs with other institutions that often act as supervision/regulation proxies is important in the context of governance accountability and disclosure. Institutions that deserve a particular attention, due to their impact on MDBs, are the credit rating agencies (already addressed in Section "Interaction with External Actors"). While MDBs are not obliged to obtain credit ratings, they do so in order to borrow from international markets, to mobilize resources toward development.

Further to financial metrics, the *credit rating* of an MDB depends on the robustness of its governance, as well as shareholders' commitment. This, in addition to the very specific nature of MDBs, requires a deeper interaction with credit rating agencies. MDBs should establish a higher level dialog with a focus on governance as the key factor of resilience and success, including sustained shareholder support. The *preferred creditor status* of MDBs as supranational institutions should be enhanced and clarified in the dialogue with credit rating agencies, as it is often poorly understood and reflected by the rating process that generally treats MDBs as a mixture of banks (lenders) and sovereigns (shareholders).

A similar dialogue should also take place within the MDB and its Boards, to raise the importance of demonstrating sound governance, as well as evidence of shareholder commitment.

Disclosure

Sound governance and role modeling of the MDBs as high-profile public institutions require substantial transparency, to enable accountability and interaction with stakeholders. While this concerns the entire institution, the IEDs have a central duty to provide accountability within and outside the MDB, as stipulated by Principle 4. This is particularly important in the absence of applicable permanent external supervision authority such as a central bank, given the self-regulatory supranational nature of MDBs.

The unrestricted access to information on MDB strategies, operations, and results is essential for holding the Board and management accountable. Transparent governance, together with genuinely independent evaluation function, provides stakeholders with the information and analysis on the effectiveness of the Board and management.

Timely and accurate disclosure should cover all material issues, including mandate fulfillment, operational and financial performance, ownership, and governance. Disclosure should be assumed applicable to any record or information, unless specifically restricted by duly substantiated exception, for example private/trade data protection. A particular attention to timely and accurate disclosure should apply to the following information:

1. The criteria and process for the selection of members of the Board and for ensuring an appropriate diversity of skills, backgrounds, and viewpoints, as well as the function of Board committees and the number of times they meet.
2. The MDB's main objectives, performance indicators, organizational and governance structures, and policies (including remuneration policy and process).
3. The assurance of credible accountability process such as the independent evaluation.
4. Overview of the MDB's Accountability Mechanism (Bissell and Suresh 2008) that provides a forum where people adversely affected by MDB-supported projects can complain to seek solutions to their problems and report alleged non-compliance with respective MDB's policies and procedures (including problem solving and compliance review function).

5. Shareholder countries and voting rights, as well as relevant applicable limitations and possibilities, for example on new membership, vetoes, and so on.
6. Incentive and compensation policy, including an annual report on compensation (covering the decision-making process used to determine the compensation policy and the criteria for performance measurement; and aggregate remuneration data).
7. Key information on risk exposures and mitigation.

Disclosure should be timely, accurate, and user-friendly—at the MDB's public website, annual and periodic reports, or by other appropriate means. It is good practice to have an annual governance-specific statement in a dedicated section of the annual report.

Conclusion: Adherence to the Principles

The governance of the reviewed MDBs was compared to the seven governance principles, developed by the authors, to reveal adherence and disconnects, and suggest recommendations. The comparative process involved a substantial desk review, covering a wealth of MDBs' policies and procedures, as well as relevant reports, mostly originating from the respective independent evaluation units. The review also includes interviews with 140 managers and employees from 16 MDBs. Interviews with 62 external stakeholders (borrowers, government officials, academics, consultants) were also conducted and reflected by the assessment.

The levels of adherence to the seven principles were assessed in percentage terms of 5% intervals, where 100% implies a full adherence. As the results vary substantially across MDBs, they are presented as a *median*—the percentage value that is positioned in the midpoint of a frequency distribution of observed values, such that there is an equal probability of falling above or below it. For example, if the sorted adherence percentage values of seven MDBs are 35%, 50%, 50%, 55%, 60%, 60%, and 85%, the median value is the middle one (or the average of the two values in the middle): 55%. The assessment also presents the observed variance across MDBs—the lowest and the highest percentage values—to illustrate the degree of variance. Given the goal to enrich the understanding of MDB's governance as a family, rather than pointing out issues in any particular institution, the data are presented only in aggregated form. The results are summarized in Table 5.1. The recommendations are further elaborated in Chap. 7 (The Future).

Table 5.1 MDBs' adherence to the seven governance principles

Principle	Adherence	Rationale on deficiencies	Notes	Recommendations
1. BoD structure, qualifications, and roles	Median (M): 55% Variance (V): 45–70%	Often unaware or short of the four roles, focus on oversight, and country relevance. Over-delegation of some oversight tasks that should stay at BoD, for example values and culture (tone at the top), CG, management performance, whistleblowing; insufficiently competitive/open and merit-based recruitment of management; limited engagement with and support to control functions and their independence; administrative selection/qualification process regarding Board members	While resident Boards are generally more engaged, the benefits do not always outweigh the cost, in view of four roles' balance. BoDs with DEC delegate less	Gradually limit delegation and enhance four-role assessment and balance. Regular comparisons with the Principle. Enhance interaction/support of control functions. Improve qualification by dedicated focus and training on MDB matters. Consider addition of country-independent merit-based directors/advisors with remuneration. Improve recruitment/assessment of management vis-à-vis mandate requirements/performance
2. Senior management	M: 50% V: 40–65%	Often appointed by national quotas, not open competition; too general qualification/performance criteria; often lack of sound tone at the top; frequent micro-management, blame culture, reform fatigue issues	Wide variations across MDBs (more challenges at sub-regional ones); frequent inconsistencies across time and MDB	Move toward genuinely open merit-based internal/external competitive selections with clearly defined MDB-centered qualification requirements; reduce chronic issues, for example micro-management, poor value/culture setting, and so on
3. Risk management	M: 70% V: 60–85%	Generally sufficient adherence. Often focus on credit/product risks alone, overlooking operational and reputational MDB mandate-specific (reputation) risks	A banking rather than development approach. Limited communication	Widen risk horizons and implications in the specific MDB context. Enhance communication and interaction

(*continued*)

Table 5.1 (continued)

Principle	Adherence	Rationale on deficiencies	Notes	Recommendations
4. Independent evaluation	M: 65% V: 50–95%	The Evaluation Cooperation Group of MDBs (ECG) maintains high professional standards, generally implemented by its members, but not all other MDBs. Inconsistency across MDBs. Hidden challenges, pressures on independence, based on deficiencies of Principles 1 and 2 above	There are wide variations across MDBs. ECG membership is an good proxy indicator of adherence to high standards	Elevate the standards and their implementation with a focus on non-members of ECG, reflecting the question why membership was not possible. Focus on behavioral independence and detection of external or internal (self-) censorship elements
5. Compliance and audit	M: 75% V: 65–85%	Generally in line. Often focus on conventional audit/compliance, overlooking MDB self-regulation and complexity. Too centered on legal compliance and performance audit, overshadowing institutional CG and unduly duplicating the MDB-distinct independent evaluation	Frequent overlaps with other control functions, sometimes engagement in operational matters	Stay fully at arm's length from any operational matter and work groups, as well as performance audit. Reflect the very particular self-regulatory nature of MDBs, as well as their development agenda

6. Human capital	M: 50% V: 40–70%	Often there are waves of selection/contract fashions and reforms ranging from over-focus on simplistic competency/experience criteria to undermining long-term mandate/culture goals. MDB-specific external selection and internal nurturing are often imbalanced/compromised. Lack of MDB-centered education and definitions, alarming reform fatigue and widespred disengagement.	An HC survey (140 staff, 16 MDBs) indicates wide variations of often poor (36–61%) comprehension on, "development", "SDG" (UN Sustainable Development Goals), and even "MDB"	Revisit HC policies and practices toward the principle. Focus on proper selection and nurturing of culture-forming long-term core of HC, balancing performance metrics with genuine devotion and tenure. Zero tolerance to value conflicts, culture misfits/erosion, cynical attitude to development, and quota employment
7. Governance accountability and disclosure	M: 55% V: 40–65%	Institutional/governance level independent evaluation (including values and "tone at the top") are rarely conducted/disclosed fully and regularly. Some MDBs await external "regulations". Independence is often formal	Insufficient utilization of institutional independent evaluations. Limited MDB cooperation	Adopt regular independent evaluations and Board action on governance. Establish sound MDB cooperation. Utilize the capacity and lessons learned from evaluation units. Consider and eventually apply these seven principles

MDBs should apply rigorously their own governance yardstick onto themselves, not just the clients they serve. Otherwise, the noted poor record of adherence will shake the foundations of MDBs, both individually and as an institutional system. When governance is compromised by considerations other than those openly stated by policies and mandates, this erodes both the credibility and the effectiveness of the institutions. It is of paramount importance to drive governance and decisions by long-term goals and the core values that the MDBs need to promote and protect. This includes operational and financial resilience, positive public projection, shareholders' interest, and ultimately mandate-dedicated HC.

MDBs should be measured against an expanded standard of governance and excellence given their importance of role-model supranational public institutions with outstanding influence not only over financed projects, but also regarding the promotion of best practice in governance, transparency, and accountability. They should promptly refrain from any form of self-promotion—the selective use and disclosure of information toward presenting a better MDB image.

MDB governance needs consistent improvements with a particular orientation toward the public. While there are good examples of progress toward participation and transparency, these are often ad hoc measures of reactions to outside pressure from civil society and member governments. What is needed is a *systematic consistent approach to the issues of transparency, participation, and fair arbitration.*

A good step forward would be to consider and apply the outlined governance principles, in the current or amended form, at each MDB. As institutional evolutions vary, there should be a phased approach in implementing the principles, depending on individual situations. This will require several rounds of honest stock-taking, followed by respective enhancements of governance, toward elevating institutional values and performance.

Notes

1. The Organization for Economic Cooperation and Development (OECD) is a forum of 33 high-income countries committed to democracy and the market economy, providing a platform to compare policy experiences, seek answers to common problems, identify good practices, and coordinate domestic and international policies of its members.
2. The original 13 Basel Principles on CG of banks are: *(1) Board's overall responsibilities; (2) Board qualifications and composition; (3) Board's own structure and practices; (4) Senior management; (5) Governance of group structures; (6) Risk*

management function; (7) Risk identification, monitoring, and controlling; (8) Risk communication; (9) Compliance; (10) Internal audit; (11) Compensation; (12) Disclosure and transparency; (13) The role of supervisors.

3. Also referred as Political Counterweight and Democratic Forum roles; see *Governance of the IMF*, Independent Evaluation Office of the IMF, Washington, DC (2008).
4. At S&P 500 companies, average Board size is 10.7; at the United Kingdom's top 150 companies, it is 10.8; and among Italian blue-chip companies, the average is 10.7 directors (Spencer Stuart 2006a: 10, 2006b, c). Among the top 50 Japanese companies, average Board size is 13. The median Board size among the nearly 400 US non-profits participating in a recent survey declined from 17 in 1994 to 15 in 2004 (BoardSource 2004).
5. In private sector Boards (S&P 500) the average age of Board member was 50–61 years (S&P 500; top UK firms), implying experience of 25–30 years. In top UK firms, the average term for non-executive directors as of 2006 was 3.8 years (Spencer Stuart 2006b: 6). Independent directors should not have been former employees of the company in the previous five years, should not have a material business relationship with the company, should not be or represent a significant shareholder, should not have close family ties with any of the company's directors or senior staff, and should not have significant links with other directors through involvement in other companies. In S&P 500 firms, independent Board directors increased from 27% in 2001 to 81% in 2006. In the United Kingdom, 62% of Boards are composed by non-executive directors, nearly all of whom are independent (Spencer Stuart 2006b: 5).
6. CEO evaluation by the Board is a key aspect of oversight in both private and non-profit sectors. Over 95% of S&P 500 firms (and 80% of the non-profit US organizations) have a formal process to annually assess the CEO's performance (Spencer Stuart 2006a, b, c: 7; BoardSource 2004: 9).
7. The Geocentric Approach is a method of international recruitment where the MDBs hire the most suitable person for the job irrespective of their nationality.
8. Tenure is the duration and circumstances of employment in civil, judicial, academic, and similar public sectors for international civil servants. After a probationary period, it offers job security to these professions as a means of protecting those services and institutions from political influence, as well as ensuring long-term loyalty to a specific public mandate. It typically implies restrictions to firing—for example requiring strong evidence of material misconduct—and/or substantial compensation for losing a job.
9. Privileges are exemptions from substantive law of a state, while immunities are mostly exemptions from the administrative, adjudicatory, or executive powers of a state. Typical MDB privileges are partial exemptions from some areas of domestic law (e.g. taxation, customs, foreign exchange controls, immigration). An example of a key MDB privilege is the exemption from any direct taxation for the MDB itself and its employees (indirect taxes are often subject to reimbursement).

References

BCBS. 2013. *Principles for Effective Risk Data Aggregation and Risk Reporting*. Basel Committee on Banking Supervision, 2013 (Progress Report 2015).

———. 2015. *Guidelines: Corporate Governance Principles for Banks*. Basel: Basel Committee on Banking Supervision, Bank for International Settlements. https://www.bis.org/bcbs/publ/d328.pdf.

Bissell, Richard, and Suresh Nanwani. 2008. Multilateral Development Bank Accountability Mechanisms: Developments and Challenges. *Central European Journal of International and Security Studies (CEJISS)*. http://www.cejiss.org/static/data/uploaded/13835988693526/bissell-nanwani_multilateral_development_bank.pdf.

BoardSource. 2004. *Non-Profit Governance Index 2004*. Washington, DC: BoardSource.

Carter, Colin, and William Lorsch. 2003. *Back to the Drawing Board: Designing Corporate Boards for a Complex World*. Cambridge, MA: Harvard Business School Press.

Evaluation Cooperation Group of MDBs (ECG). 2012. *Big Book on Evaluation Good Practice Standards*. https://www.ecgnet.org/document/ecg-big-book-good-practice-standards.

G20, OECD. 2015. *G20/OECD Principles of Corporate Governance*. Paris: OECD Publishing. https://doi.org/10.1787/9789264236882-en.

Higgs, Derek. 2003. *Higgs Report on Non-Executive Directors: Summary Recommendations*. http://www.berr.gov.uk/files/file 23012.pdf.

IMF. 2008. *Governance of the IMF, Independent Evaluation Office of the IMF*. Washington DC: IMF.

OECD. 2011. *OECD Guidelines for Multinational Enterprises*. Paris: OECD. http://mneguidelines.oecd.org/guidelines/.

Spencer Stuart. 2006a. *Board Index, 2006: The Changing Profile of Directors*.

———. 2006b. *UK Board Index, 2006*.

———. 2006c. *Board Index: Italia 2006*.

World Bank. 2003. World Bank Operations Evaluation Department: The First 30 Years. *The World Bank*. https://openknowledge.worldbank.org/handle/10986/15128.

6

Clients' Perspective

Introduction

This chapter provides an overview of the typical operations and financing cycle at Multilateral Development Banks (MDBs). The main goal is to highlight issues from the borrowers' perspective and offer guidance on the process of application and financing.

The chapter offers information about the variety of financing instruments, products, and terms, as well as related procedures and requirements, applicable to both state and private sector clients, with a focus on the latter. A step-by-step guide to the stages of the loan cycle and a brief overview of key documents and terms are also offered. Although most aspects of the lending cycle are comprehensively covered, the aim is to ensure a generic understanding applicable to most MDBs, rather than an exhaustive description of details. This is supplemented by suggestions to streamline and harmonize the application process across MDBs, as well as to broaden the range of offered financing products and services.

Application and Financing Cycle

MDBs have rather elaborate and complex financing cycle—the process that covers the financing of a project from its design and assessment to actual funding and full repayment. While the cycles vary by detail and terms used by MDBs, a generic one typically includes the components outlined in Table 6.1. The indicative duration of each phase varies substantially across MDBs,

I. U. Delikanli et al., *Multilateral Development Banks*,
https://doi.org/10.1007/978-3-319-91524-1_6

Table 6.1 Phases in the financing cycle

Phase: description and elements	Weeks	Key actors
1. Preparation (also identification, design, initiation, concept, etc.) Identification and early review of concept: • Define projects, sponsors, goals, beneficiaries, loan size, and so on • Preliminary feasibility assessment (concept note), briefly outlining mandate, economic, technical, social, environmental relevance, and risks	2–12	Applicant/sponsor, MDB, co-financiers
2. Appraisal (ex-ante evaluation, assessment, final review, etc.) Detailed assessment of the application/ proposal (business plan in case of private sector) that results in additional requirements, rejection, or interim approval by credit committee and/or management: • Rigorous assessment of all elements of phase 1 • Financial and legal analysis and due diligence • Assessment and articulation of expected outcomes (economic, technical, environmental, social, and fiduciary aspects) • Outlining relevant institutional and business arrangements, for example responsibility, contracting, reporting, time tables, and so on • Detailed program/project appraisal document (final review document, etc.) and draft financing legal agreements[a] (term sheet, mandate letter, loan agreement, co-financing agreement, etc.) • Compliance tests on credibility of involved companies/businesses	6–24	Applicant/sponsor, MDB, co-financiers, external consultant, lawyers, MDB independent departments, for example risk, evaluation, compliance
3. Negotiation Resolution of outstanding issues from the appraisal phase, for example environmental and other reporting, collateral and security, financing and disbursement arrangements, terms and conditions, timetable, and so on. This phase may overlap with phases 2 and 4	2–10	Applicant, co-financiers, lawyers, and so on

(*continued*)

Table 6.1 (continued)

Phase: description and elements	Weeks	Key actors
4. Approval(s) At least two reviews and approvals of project and financing documents: (1) internal—by credit/management committee or similar; (2) external—by MDB's Board of Directors (or by the management in certain cases such as smaller size projects)	3–12	MDB committees and Board of Directors
5. Signing Signing of legal/loan/guarantee agreements, discussed earlier	2–8	Applicant, MDB
6. Effectiveness Verification by the MDB that agreed (precedent) conditions have been met to begin disbursements, for example reports, securities, statements, and so on	2–12	As above
7. Disbursements, repayments, restructuring, cancellations • Disbursements as per agreed applications, reporting and covenants • Repayments as per agreed schedule and terms • Restructuring may be required if covenants/performance not met • Cancellations by MDB or borrower: pre-payment of outstanding loan	As per terms, for example 5–20 years	As above
8. Completion, ex-post evaluation, and final repayment • Completion is typically when financed project becomes operational • Ex-post evaluation by the Independent Evaluation Unit, reported to Board • Final repayment date—as specified in the financing agreement	As above	As above, Evaluation Unit, Board
Time range from start to first disbursement (weeks):	17–78	

Source: MDB policies and procedures, authors' assessment

[a]*Legal contract* setting out the terms and conditions of the loan or another financial product. It includes eligible activities to be funded; reporting, environmental, procurement and fiduciary requirements; disbursement conditions, timetable, financial terms, and so on

depending on size and complexity of the project. Typically large scale sovereign infrastructure projects such as roads, dams, and airports involve substantial preparation and many stakeholders, while smaller size private sector loans such as trade finance may be financed within a couple of months.

The preparation of sovereign projects is initiated by the respective country, often in cooperation with and guidance by the respective MDB. In contrast, private sector applications are developed by the prospective borrowers, in response to various marketing activities of the MDB or referrals of other relevant partners, sometimes a partnering MDB.

Applications by private companies are normally sent directly to the regional or central office of the MDB, following certain templates and guidelines. They should include a number of key documents such as a business plan, audited financial statements, and other relevant information regarding the project and sponsors. The initial information has to be sufficient to enable the MDB to determine whether the proposed operation fits its mandate, policies, and strategies, to proceed with further assessment. The applicant has to provide the name and address of a central contact point for the entire communication period. All correspondence and supporting documentation should be submitted in the operating language of MDB, typically in English.

The differentiation between the initial screening during phase 1, and the subsequent thorough appraisal ensures that the MDB's resources are not wasted on applications with negligible likelihood of approval, or are considered less attractive in comparison with other mandate-relevant opportunities. The reviews at the preparation phase focus on:

- Consistency with the MDB mandate, policies, or strategies
- Disqualifying legal or eligibility issues (e.g. negative list of activities that cannot be financed)
- Ensuring prompt feedback to applicants, to update the project if relevant

Eligibility and Concept Review

Each MDB has a set of eligibility criteria, to be met by applicants for borrowing or another form of financing. While those vary, the following overview provides an orientation regarding typical requirements. It should be noted that each institution has various programs and instruments that would have different eligibility criteria. As the criteria may change over time, it is useful to consult the respective websites, as well as the local representative offices, for details on the applicable requirements and opportunities. Nevertheless, it is a good strategy to be aware of the application and implementation process beforehand, as well as the usual pitfalls.

For each application, MDBs assign a team of specialists with specific technical and legal expertise, to conduct relevant assessments and interact with the applicant. While MDBs have many common requirements, each institution has a specific profile and orientation. In addition to the regional dimension, MDBs have priority sectors and strategies, for example in financing predominantly public or private sector operations, or both. MDBs also differ in their appetite for risk—those that are focusing on the private sector (e.g. International Financial Corporation—IFC; European Bank for Reconstruction and Development—EBRD; Black Sea Trade and Development Bank; Nordic Investment Bank; etc.) generally deal with higher risk levels, in contrast to sovereign lending operations. The unique combination of well-established relationship with governments and other MDBs, as well as the preferred creditor status and dedicated expertise, allow MDBs to address risks and situations that are often beyond the capability of other financiers. This is the essence of the MDB's *additionality*—to complement rather than displace other sources of finance. In other words, MDBs perform eligibility test to verify if they can provide added value, by supporting projects that could not otherwise obtain financing on similar terms.

The *Eligibility Review* is an important initial step of phase 1, ensuring consideration and feedback. To assess the eligibility of a project, MDBs typically require the following information:

- a brief description of the project, specifying the use of the loan
- information on the sponsor, including experience, financial status, and contribution to the project (equity, management, operations, production, etc.)
- details on product or service to be developed and produced
- market analysis: customers, competition, share, sales, pricing, distribution
- financial information: project costs, additional funding, use of funds, financial projections
- implementation overview: contractors, procurement, and so on
- environmental and regulatory issues: for example audits, impact assessments
- applicable licenses, subsidies, trading tariffs, and so on

While each MDB has its own eligibility criteria, they revolve around a core of principle requirements, for example:

- The proposed operation fits the MDB mandate and strategies
- Sound social and economic development potential
- Strong potential to facilitate mobilization of domestic and foreign capital
- Economically and operationally sustainable, meeting high environmental and social standards
- Does not finance goods or activities excluded by the MDB's *Environmental and Social Exclusion List*
- Within financial and maturity ranges of the MDB

Soon after the eligibility test, the applicant receives a negative or positive reply. In case of further processing, a confidentiality agreement between the (private sector) applicant and the MDB may be signed, if required by the prospective borrower. The *Concept Review* is another internal step that provides a brief outline of the key aspects of the application, after successful clearance on eligibility:

- Description of the operation, including objectives, MDB role, feasibility screening, identification of potential development goals and indicators, marketing, and so on
- Assessment of consistency with the institution's developmental strategies, with reference to the mandate, country and sector strategies
- Information on the borrower and all parties involved
- Key terms and conditions of the financing facility requested
- Preliminary assessment of financial performance and projections, as well as anticipated security arrangements
- Review of impact on the MDB's exposure limits (sector, country)
- Anticipated risk areas and respective mitigation options
- Social and environmental issues and safeguards, as per respective policies
- Timetable, budget, consultant needs, and so on

The preliminary financial assessment of private sector applicants normally requires financial reports prepared and audited as per the International Financial Reporting Standards. If the operation does not pass the Concept Review requirements, the applicant is informed accordingly. Otherwise, the process continues with a preliminary contract of engagement—typically referred to as a *Mandate Letter*, to be signed by the applicant as a commitment to bear certain obligations and cost related to the application. The pre-approvals achieved are valid for a certain period of time, generally 6 to 12 months (Fig. 6.1).

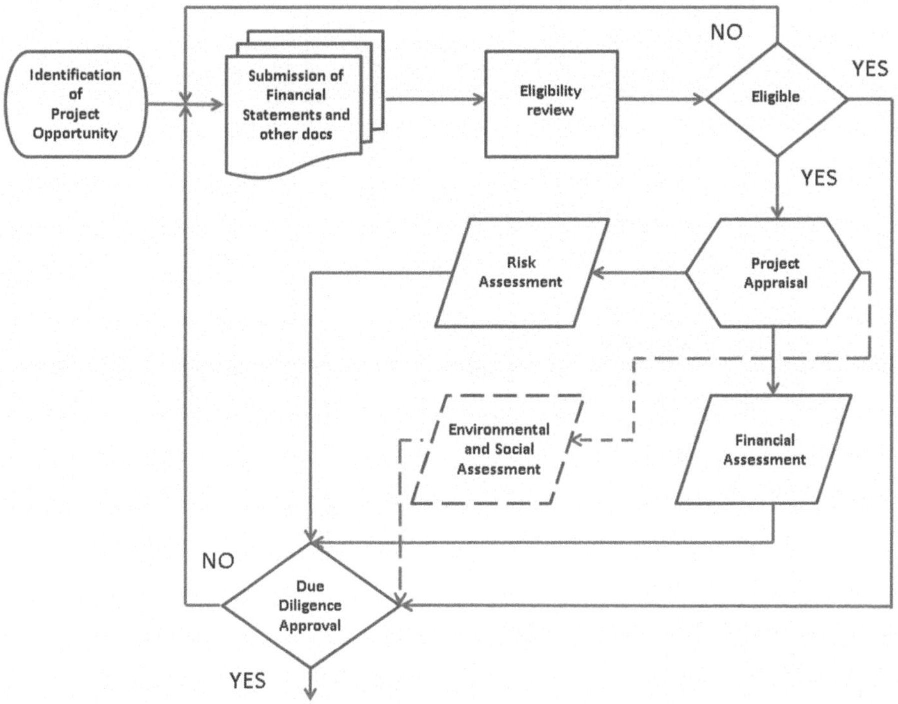

Fig. 6.1 Eligibility and concept review

Appraisal and Due Diligence

The Appraisal and Due Diligence phase determines the MDB's prospective commitment, elaborating upon key issues and details on the operation, the borrower, the financing plan, the market, the key risk areas and respective mitigation. The (private) borrower is expected to present a comprehensive proposal, including all necessary financial, technical, and other information. MDBs often require amendments and updates on the proposal. Technical assistance financing may be provided by some MDBs for specific elements of the process, such as feasibility studies, reporting, improvement of corporate governance, and so on (Fig. 6.2).

The appraisal normally involves a visit to the site of the operation by the designated team of the MDB. Depending on the size, type, and complexity of the operation, the availability of required information and the quality of the proposal, the time period for the appraisal would normally vary from one to six months. The Appraisal and Due Diligence stage results in an internal Final Review Document, presenting the operation to be financed in a standard template, providing details on a number of elements, as follows:

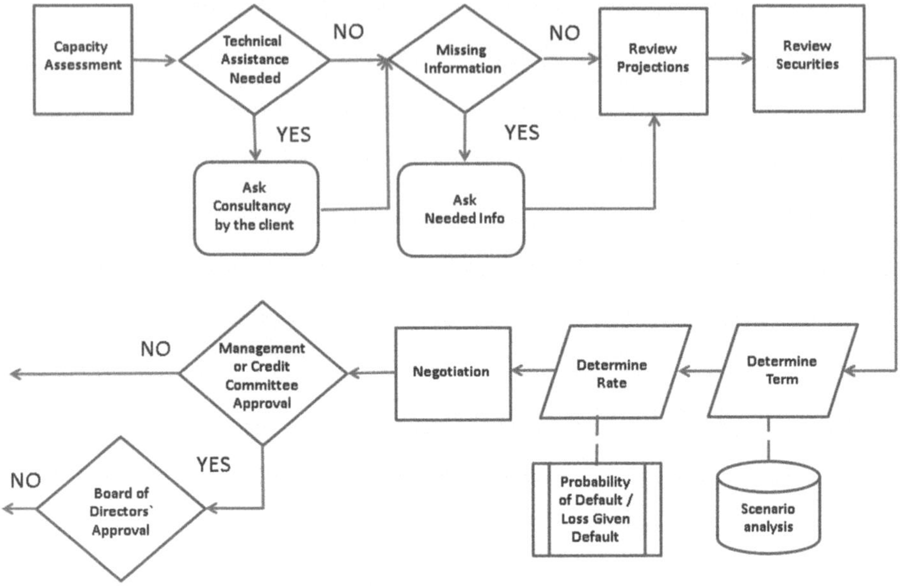

Fig. 6.2 Appraisal and due diligence

- Description of the operation
- Development goals and indicators
- Operational and financial goals and indicators
- Market analysis
- Creditworthiness assessment of key parties involved (including ultimate beneficiary)
- Terms, conditions, and covenants of the financing requested (or exit strategy in case of equity investment)
- Financial and risk analyses and specific mitigation elements, including security package and loan covenants
- An assessment of other relevant issues (e.g. legal, regulatory, technology, etc.)
- Disbursement plan
- Assessment of corporate governance, environmental and social aspects
- Implementation plan, including key monitoring indicators and timetable

This stage typically includes the preparation and signing of *Term Sheet* with private sector borrowers. This is a formal document describing concisely the terms and conditions under which the MDB intends to provide financial support to the operation. It includes amount of financing, interest rate, commissions, tenors, security, co-financing, securities, main requirements, and so on.

Approval, Signing, and Disbursements

Following the internal approval by credit or management committee, the Final Review Document is presented for Board approval. This is a rather formal process of endorsement as Board rejections are very rare. The Board approval is normally valid for a period of time typically ranging between 6 and 12 months. If the *Loan Agreement* (or similar legal agreement) is not signed within that period, MDBs normally update earlier reviews and approvals and decide whether to resubmit the operation for re-approval by the Board.

Signing of the legal agreement normally takes place soon after Board approval. The legal agreement(s) comprise various formal documents, including but not limited to the following:

- Operation Agreement (e.g. loan agreement, fund agreement, etc.)
- Security Agreements
- Co-financing Agreement
- Agency Agreement
- Other contractual arrangements

The disbursement of the funds, entirely or in agreed tranches, takes place upon verification by the MDB that all relevant pre-conditions set by the legal documentation are fulfilled.

Financing Products and Terms

This section covers a range of typical financial products offered by MDBs, without the intention to provide complete or very detailed description, as the product range includes many variations and updates. Larger MDBs with a focus on public sector operations, such as the IBRD (International Bank for Reconstruction and Development), offer eligible member countries a broad spectrum of flexible and low-cost loans, hedging, and guarantees. Concessional lending opportunities are offered by some members of the MDB family such as IDA (International Development Association), targeting the poorest developing countries with loans with negligible or no interest, as well as grants. Other products administered by many MDBs include guarantees and grants offered through *Trust Funds* or other special arrangements with donors.

Most MDBs offer on-line orientation and application support regarding the available financial products and services. Some (IBRD, IDA) even offer their own mobile applications that enable borrowers to instantly access information such as financial terms and rates and to prepare amortization schedules. Client forms and reference documents are broadly available but are not harmonized across MDBs and are often hard to comprehend by prospective applicants.

Loans

Virtually all MDBs offer a variety of loan products. Most *global and regional* MDBs provide loans for project, program, or policy purposes, as well as guarantees and hedging products to manage currency and interest rate risk exposures. By using their AAA credit rating, MDBs offer loans (mostly to the public sector) that are more competitive and flexible relative to lower rated financiers and sovereign borrowers. The specific loan terms, such as currency, maturity, interest rate, and so on, are determined at the time of loan negotiation.

MDB loans are generally structured with substantial flexibility to match project needs. Private sector loans reflect the conservatively estimated cash flow of the project and the repayment capacity of the borrower. The credit risk is typically covered entirely by the MDB but in some cases is partly syndicated to the market. Private sector loans are typically secured by a borrower's assets but may also be converted into equity shares under certain conditions (debt-equity conversion options).

Typical loan terms and requirements for private sector borrowers include the following:

- a minimum amount, for example USD 3–5 million, offered in major foreign and some local currencies
- a fixed or floating interest rate (market based, referenced to the London Interbank Offered rate, LIBOR, or the EURO Interbank Offered Rate, EURIBOR)[1]
- senior, subordinated, mezzanine, or convertible debt
- various maturities, for example from 1 to 20 years, with tailored *grace periods*
- various fees and charges including *risk margins* (reflecting country and project risks), appraisal fees, front-end fees, syndication fees, commitment fees (on committed but undisbursed amount), loan conversion fees (for interest rate or currency conversions), pre-payment and cancellation fees, late payment fees, as well as some preparation costs
- recourse to a sponsor (may or may not apply)

- specific performance and completion guarantees plus other forms of support (limited recourse finance)
- insurance against standard risks (fire, theft, construction), but not political or currency risks
- security mostly based on project assets, for example mortgage on fixed and movable assets, assignment of receivables, pledge of company shares, and assignment of contractual benefits such as insurance policy
- various project finance covenants, for example on debt limits, financial ratios, hedging, and so on
- repayment, which is normally in equal, semiannual installments, but some flexibility applies

Equity

Many MDBs (IFC and EBRD in particular) with private sector focus offer direct equity investments in the range of USD 1–100 million. These cover a variety of sectors such as industry, infrastructure, and financial institutions. Equity investments typically acquire minority shares with a clear exit strategy.[2] The equity and quasi-equity products may have different forms, including listed or unlisted ordinary shares, subordinated and convertible loans, income notes, redeemable preference shares, and underwriting of share issues by public or privately owned enterprises. Other forms of financing could be arranged on a case-by-case basis.

MDBs also participate in equity funds, which have regional or sector focus, with strong local presence. These funds are required to apply the MDBs' screening and investment criteria.

Guarantees

As noted in Chap. 3 (Financial Dynamics), virtually all MDBs offer unfunded participation products such as guarantees, although their share is rather small. The provision of guarantees ranges from all-risk guarantees, whereby the MDB covers lenders against default regardless of the cause, to partial risk-specific contingent guarantees covering default arising from pre-determined causes. The common denominator of all guarantees is that the maximum exposure is specified and the credit risk falls within (MDB) pre-set limitations.

Co-financing

As MDBs aim to mobilize and catalyze capital, as well as cooperate with peers and crowd-in the private sector, most of them focus explicitly or implicitly[3] on co-financing. This increases their resources available for other projects. It also helps to introduce borrowers to the international debt markets. Co-financing partners vary from other MDBs to commercial banks, governmental agencies, bilateral development financial institutions, export credit agencies, and so on. By the involvement of such co-financiers MDBs aim to broaden and deepen the provision of finance to mandate-relevant operations and regions, toward the intention to do more with less, by crowding in substantial private investment flows.

Co-financing arrangements may include numerous options such as A/B loans (where the MDB finances part of the loan and syndicates the rest to commercial lenders), parallel loans, export credit guarantees, political risk insurance, loans and equity from international financial institutions and grants. MDBs typically build long-term partnerships with other institutions to increase the availability and flexibility of financing and improve the investment climate in their regions.

Other Products

MDBs offer many other products and combinations. For example, recently they have begun to support initiatives such as the Climate Investment Funds[4] that includes the Clean Technology Fund (CTF), providing grants,[5] loans,[6] and guarantees. The CTF provides resources to scale up the demonstration, deployment, and transfer of low carbon technologies with a significant potential for long-term greenhouse gas emissions reductions.

Concluding Remarks

Approaching the MDB services from the client's perspective is often a challenging experience—particularly for private sector borrowers or other non-governmental applicants. This is largely due to the lack of harmonized templates and processes among MDBs, as well as due to the technical jargon used by those institutions, even in borrowers' handbooks that often contain 100 page texts full of MDB-specific terms.

In reference to Chap. 3 (Financial Dynamics), it is suggested that unfunded products such as guarantees, should increase their presence as they constitute a key avenue toward the intended larger scale crowding-in of the private investments toward developmental goals.

While this chapter is expected to represent a comprehensive generic summary of the application and financing labyrinths, it is also a call for certain harmonization among MDBs. Ultimately, there is a clear need and opportunity to broaden the demand for MDB services by becoming more accessible to potential and actual clients, with a focus on private sector borrowers. MDBs should cooperate to harmonize and modernize their interface procedures so that borrowers are able to promptly navigate their application and project cycles.

Notes

1. Variable rate includes a contractual Lending Margin + Maturity Premium + Actual Funding Margin (MDB's average borrowing margin relative to LIBOR for a preceding period). Fixed rate includes Contractual Lending Margin + Maturity Premium + Market Risk Premium + Projected MDB Funding Cost + Basis Swap Adjustment if any.
2. MDBs usually exit their equity investments within four to eight years, depending on the nature and scope of the project. Exit strategies typically involve selling the MDB participation to the project sponsors or via a public offer.
3. For example, some MDBs, such as EBRD, typically finance about 35% of the project costs. This implies that the sponsors should find own funds or other lenders for the remaining 65%.
4. The Climate Investment Funds, funded by the IBRD, African Development Bank, Asian Development Bank , European Investment Bank, and Inter-American Development Bank operates with USD 8.3 billion. It includes the CTF (5.8 billion, see http://www-cif.climateinvestmentfunds.org/fund/clean-technology-fund).
5. CTF project preparation grants are available for financing project feasibility studies and associated analysis, as well as investment plans and CTF co-financed projects.
6. There are two CTF loan programs, based on an analysis of the financial internal rate of return of each project without CTF co-financing: (1) harder concessional loans for projects with rates of return near or above normal market threshold, but below risk premium for project type, technology, country, or acceleration in deploying low carbon technology; (2) softer concessional loans for projects with negative rates of return or below normal market threshold.

7

The Future

Introduction: The Increasing Importance of MDBs

Multilateral Development Banks' (MDBs) unique role in inspiring and advancing sustainable economic development through knowledge and funding is gaining further importance at a time of unprecedented rise of global challenges. To illustrate the pressure on the world's development agenda, it is sufficient to look at the UN Sustainable Development Goals (SDGs), to be reached by 2030, as agreed worldwide.

The vast financing needs to achieve the SDGs in 15 years exceed by far the current level of development finance. The United Nations Conference on Trade and Development estimated that achieving the SDGs will require global investments in the range of US$5 to $7 trillion per year (UNCTAD 2015). The annual investment gap in developing countries is estimated at about $2.5 trillion, to cover mainly basic infrastructure (roads, rail, and ports; power stations; water and sanitation), food security (agriculture and rural development), climate change mitigation, and adaptation, health, and education.

In contrast, the official development assistance peaked to $142.6 billion in 2016 (OECD/DAC 2017). This implies that the development funding may not cover even 5% of the actual needs to achieve the SDGs. Even if the full average MDB lending of about $150 billion p.a. is added (although part of it is already counted as official development assistance), the total of development funding will reach about US$2 trillion by 2030, or under 2% of the required financing of the Millennium Development Goal (MDGs). As MDBs invest in non-SDG areas as well, the actual contribution to the SDGs will be even lower than those estimates. With regard to the new development agenda,

I. U. Delikanli et al., *Multilateral Development Banks*,
https://doi.org/10.1007/978-3-319-91524-1_7

this gap, to a great extent, will have to be covered by the respective countries, to achieve the SDGs. In most cases, national budgets will be burdened with large amounts, easily reaching over 5% of GDP or 20% of the entire state budget, for many years ahead (Gable et al. 2015).

MDBs should increase and refocus their potential by attracting more capital, enhancing financial leverage to mobilize substantial private resources. A recent study by the Business & Sustainable Development Commission estimates that implementing the SDGs could trigger up to $12 trillion of market opportunities in food and agriculture, cities, energy and materials, and health and well-being alone, as well as create 380 million new jobs by 2030 (BSDC 2017). To this end, MDBs should mobilize their wide range of partners and know how, as well as their credibility of honest brokers toward the massive financial challenge, focusing on some SDGs that resonate with respective institutional mandates. A forward-looking concept to be considered is *social impact investment*—presenting a social or economic problem as a matter of financial efficiency, whereby development challenges such as unemployment or public administration efficiency are represented as a cost. The financial gains that would be generated by resolving the problem represent an investment opportunity for the private sector, guaranteed and repaid with a premium by government with potential MDB involvement. Such approaches have been piloted in several high-income countries, and have a strong potential elsewhere. In other words, development finance should be articulated into investing in the future with sound financial and social returns.

While the SDGs represent a paramount funding challenge, some specific needs deserve a particular MDB attention, for example:

- The cost of providing adequate infrastructure across 50 countries by 2040 is estimated at US$94 trillion, according to forecasts of the G20's Global Infrastructure Hub (GI Hub 2017). If the SDGs on universal provision of clean water, sanitation, and electricity are added, the total cost rises to US$97 trillion. The GI Hub analysis reveals a shortfall in needed spending of $18 trillion—19% of the forecast need for infrastructure alone.
- Ensuring more peace and stability in today's world requires strong multilateral effort. MDBs represent a logical viable platform toward achieving a more peaceful world and endeavoring investors, to close the outlined financial gaps.
- The World Bank just released a report estimating that climate change will force 140 million people to migrate in the next 30 years (World Bank 2018).

Obviously it will be naïve to offer simplistic solutions to complex issues of immence financial magnitude as those outlined above. Therefore, the proposed approaches require further rounds of high-level discourse and consideration in multilateral settings. It is clear that MDBs have a key role to play, looking at novel avenues, products, and entire paradigm shifts—centered around new governance and human capital models, toward innovative ways of catalyzing private capital, as sketched further.

One possible approach is taking social impact investment into a new environment. It is already gaining popularity in OECD (Organization for Economic Cooperation and Development) countries; it may require substantial MDB involvement to crowd-in investors in riskier regions. MDBs can lead by example, as well as refocus their attention on guarantees and similar unfunded risk products, multiplying the current leverage levels, to protect, encourage, or *risk-share* viable investments.

While innovation involves certain risks, it is clear that some SDGs represent unprecedented opportunities to the MDBs to test and tune novel approaches and products, broadening their partnerships. Achieving the SDGs requires much more than finance. Without a global change of mindsets, approaches, and accountabilities, with strong MDB leadership and innovation, the prospects are grim. This is particularly relevant in the complex geopolitical context of *international development* and *multilateralism* as they have never been more important, yet very challenged. The rapid transformations toward political and social upheavals, driven by populism and nationalism, deserve unprecedented debate about poverty, inequality, peace, and sustainability. This makes MDBs particularly relevant and important, at a time when they are pressed to deliver faster, deeper, and wider, with even more limited resources.

From Learning Organizations to Agents of Change

The MDBs, individually, and even more so as a system, are important agents of regional and global change, with a particular reference to their influence on socioeconomic development. While a lot has been achieved in this domain, as noted by other chapters, it is essential to strengthen their institutional learning function by incremental application of the governance principles outlined in Chap. 5. It is important to enhance the role and use of the internal independent evaluation units across MDBs. Another important improvement is required toward attracting, nurturing, and retaining core human capital with MDB-relevant value systems.

MDBs have unique position to elevate international governance standards in the context of their efforts to affect business practice. However, to lead by example they have to reshape their own governance. While many MDBs moved toward a more transparent and competitive recruitment of senior management, slowly abolishing national quotas, the pace and depth of this process is insufficient. There are still many cases of preservation of quotas for the president/CEO, as well as other management positions, that contradict key governance principles.

The latest bold call for governance reform, made by the G20 in April 2017, is a good opportunity to address overdue constraints to *optimize MDBs. Clearly, a better and deeper* interaction and coordination among institutions is necessary, toward utilizing the system's collective *capacity to catalyze private capital* flows and domestic resources. Otherwise, MDBs will be unable to address *the pressing global challenges.*

Alignment of Governance and Finance

As per their mandates, MDBs promote sound governance to borrowing countries. To lead by example, they should apply rigorous standards on themselves, elevating their own governance accordingly. One specific recommendation is to undertake action toward implementation of the seven governance principles developed in Chap. 5, as follows:

- ***Board of Directors***: Gradually add more independent directors, a fully independent merit-based Audit Committee and/or Development Effectiveness Committee. Enhance and balance the four Board roles (strategy, oversight, country relevance, fair forum). Regular comparisons with the principle should provide stock-taking across MDBs. Enhance interaction with and use of control functions, with a focus on the learning aspects of independent evaluation. Improve qualification by dedicated focus and training on MDB matters. Improve recruitment/assessment of management vis-à-vis mandate requirements/performance.
- ***Management***: Conduct merit-based internal/external competitive selections with clearly defined MDB-centered qualification and performance requirements. Address openly and mitigate chronic issues, for example micro-management, poor value/culture alignment and setting, reform fatigue, and so on.
- ***Risk Management***: Widen risk horizons and implications in the specific MDB context. Enhance communication and interaction with a focus on external actors such as Basel Committee and rating agencies. Improve risk

mitigation by wider risk sharing and utilization of balance sheet, special credit status, and other means.

- ***Independent Evaluation***: Elevate the standards and their implementation with broader outreach, focusing on behavioral independence and detection of (self-) censorship elements, toward a stronger learning function at institutional and Board levels. Evaluation metrics can be broadened and further harmonized across MDBs, for example including *additionality*, investment mobilization and leverage, SDG relevance, impact of safeguards, institutional indicators, and so on. Efficiency and effectiveness can be enhanced by some degree of pooling—a shared evaluation pool that will conduct meta-evaluations on the MDB system, assessing gaps and overlaps, using the outputs of the MDBs' independent evaluation functions. For example, a small reduction/relocation of evaluation resources at each MDB can be used to support a shared umbrella team who would compare MDB results and guide eventual specialization based on comparative advantages of the institutions.
- ***Compliance and Audit***: Stay at arm's length from operational matters and work groups, as well as performance audit. Reflect the particular self-regulatory nature of MDBs, as well as their development agenda, broadening the aspects of compliance.
- ***Human Capital***: Revisit policies and practices toward the principle. Focus on proper selection and nurturing of culture-forming long-term core, balancing performance metrics with genuine mandate-devotion and tenure. Important capabilities such as sound international and development commitment and experience should be among leading criteria of both selection and tenure. This implies zero tolerance to value conflicts, culture misfits/erosion, and cynical attitude to development, national quotas, or concentrations.
- ***Accountability and Disclosure***: Adopt regular independent evaluations and Board action on governance. Utilize the capacity and lessons learned from evaluation units. Consider and review openly these seven principles.

MDBs should apply rigorously their own governance yardstick onto themselves, not just the clients they serve. A poor record of adherence will shake their foundations both individually and as an institutional system. When governance is compromised by considerations other than those openly stated by policies and mandates, this erodes both the credibility and the effectiveness of the institutions. It is of paramount importance to drive governance and decisions by long-term goals and the core values that the MDBs need to protect. This includes operational and financial resilience, positive public projection, shareholders interest, and ultimately mandate-dedicated human capital.

MDBs should be measured against an expanded standard of governance and excellence given their importance of role-model supranational public institutions with outstanding influence not only over financed projects, but also regarding the promotion of best practice in governance, transparency, and accountability. They should abolish any form of self-promotion—the selective use and disclosure of information toward presenting a better MDB image.

A good step forward would be to consider and apply the seven governance principles, in the current or amended form, at each MDB. As institutional evolutions vary, there could be a phased approach in implementing the principles, depending on individual situations. This will require several rounds of honest stock-taking, followed by respective enhancements of governance, toward elevating institutional values and performance.

Both the governance and the financial dynamics of MDBs are very distinct relative to other financial or public institutions. This calls for a dedicated mindset shifting, with particular reference to issuers of credit ratings and standards. While self-regulated, MDBs maintain high-profile mandates and observe prudent and conservative banking principles, require sound security and collateral in the assets of investment projects, and self-impose highest risk-mitigation and transparency requirements, well beyond the regulatory norms applicable elsewhere. As MDBs are intrinsically different from commercial banks, this should be demonstrated to and reflected by key market players, such as rating agencies and Basel guidelines. The key goal will be to enable borrowing from the international markets at better terms while maintaining highest credit rating. This requires a new dialogue with policy makers and involved actors, to develop and articulate the intrinsically strong risk resilience of MDBs. Beyond the issue of how adequate the credit ratings are, there is a concern that the rating agencies are impacting on the strategies and governance of MDBs, effectively undertaking the implicit role of regulators, who however have very little depth of knowledge on the MDBs' complexity and intrinsic risk mitigation.

Addressing the MDB group disparities and taking a course toward boosting overall complementarity and efficiency should become a priority. Looking at the examples of the *regional group*, as well as IBRD (International Bank for Reconstruction and Development), it is clear that MDBs could operate successfully with generally lower levels of *paid-in capital* (around 5%), while increasing the share of *callable capital*. The inherently high level of retained earnings is a key engine of capitalization of MDBs, consistently increasing their equity and resilience. As the equity/capital ratio of *sub-regional* MDBs is particularly high, this factor should be used, along with others, to close the many gaps between this group and the other two, with reference to ratings and Basel risk treatment in particular. As the sub-regional MDBs have more limited access to capital markets and consequently have to maintain higher liquidity levels, they should enhance and tailor the capacity of their treasury functions, to improve efficiency.

MDBs are very conservative in terms of leverage as even the lowest ratio figures are over five times above the Basel minimum requirement of 3%. As with many other aspects, MDB groups differ substantially in terms of leverage—with a threefold magnitude. While *regional* MDBs are highly leveraged (lending is over six times their equities), *global* and *sub-regional* MDBs are on the lower end. This puts the regional group in the lead in meeting the mandate goal of mobilizing external resources. Other MDBs should, respectively, try to utilize better their own equity toward doing more with less, noting that there is a large further potential to increase leverage ratios, relative to the Basel standards. The necessary increase in MDB's effectiveness and efficiency, including the use of higher leverage and balance-sheet optimization, requires revisiting of the legacy of institutional and regulatory deficiencies (namely Basel standards and credit rating process), as well as updating their treasury policies accordingly.

Through their *additionality*, MDBs mitigate both *market and institutional failures* and inefficiencies. This requires further balancing and articulating the two aspects of *additionality*—financial and non-financial, based on comparative advantages across MDBs. A review of the MDBs' returns reveals strong divergence, implying varying levels of subsidy and *additionality*. Another factor that deserves attention is the relatively high level of administrative expenses, particularly at global MDBs (over six times above the regional group). Given their relatively small size, the inefficiency of the sub-regional group is mostly attributed to lack of economy of scale and scope—implying a call for growth and intra-MDB cooperation.

To improve their impact and efficiency, MDBs should complement higher levels of borrowing (leverage) with more effective crowding-in of strategic private investments, with a focus on specific measures that enhance catalyzing. These may include closer cooperation with potential investors already in the early project phases, to outline and implement factors that are essential in delivering follow-up investments.

Overall, the *regional* MDBs demonstrate leadership in many domains, over the last decade. Their share in total assets, lending operations, and borrowings exceeds 60% of all MDBs, respectively. As they have been operating with relatively modest *paid-in* capital (as share of subscribed capital), those institutions achieved higher mobilization and efficiency, relative to other peers. While performance varies across MDBs, the regional group leads in many aspects because of their stronger local presence, their size (not too big or small), as well as sound track record.

Alignment with Relevant SDGs

MDBs are gradually engaging toward substantial contribution to the UN SDGs and related public discourse. Through their organizational learning and knowledge sharing, they play a key role in promoting essential multilateral values and achievements, across the world. Last but not least, the MDBs have an increasing role and impact on improving the corporate governance for companies as well as policy-making institutions, with a specific focus on a range of publicly important safeguards, outlined in the next section.

Through the rigor and independence of the embedded evaluation units, the MDBs utilize a sound assessment framework that provides critical insight on their outreach and impact. This constitutes an essential measure of their actual and possible role as *agents of change*. The ex-post evaluation of results, regularly reported and disclosed by MDBs, is vital to understand and enhance institutional impact. This ex-post evaluation is based on the OECD Development Assistance Committee criteria of Relevance, Effectiveness, Efficiency, Impact, and Sustainability[1] that need further elaboration in the MDB context as suggested by one of the governance principles already. The focus on MDBs as agents of change requires a specific attention to their impact, toward improving the global and regional systems that ensure sustainable delivery of the multiple aspects of the MDBs' safeguards and standards. Development impact is the measure associated with being an agent of change. It depends on the mandate of each institution but typically includes key elements such as contributing to employment, government/tax revenues, investment outcomes, environmental and social outcomes, business and social innovation, as well as catalyzing and mobilizing of financial resources. Evaluating development impact plays a vital role in generating learning information by assessing the implementation and results of a project, program, or policy. It also provides the basis for improved governance and decision-making through accountability and transparency to shareholders and stakeholders. As development impact is often elusive and therefore not easy to measure, MDBs have to confront the complexity of the measurement challenges, distinguishing private sector from public sector operations, with a focus on additionality and evidence.

The development outcomes are normally not reported in the context of global goals, such as SDGs. However, the SDGs and the post-2015 development agenda provide an ambitious framework and are more broadly relevant across the goals and mandates of the MDBs than were the earlier UN MDGs. Understanding how these institutions contribute to global development goals hinges to the relevance and future of MDBs.

In this context it is important to enhance MDBs as learning organizations, acting as genuine *knowledge banks*, with dedicated human capital, engaging in crowding-in novel activities, aiming at catalytic finance and innovation. This requires a tailored leveraging that brings different parties together for the same investment by sharing or co-development of products and services. It is important to reveal and articulate comparative advantages among MDBs, to understand who should provide leadership, and ultimately what are the best channels for a sound knowledge transfer. In other words, the issues of mandates, safeguards, and specialization intrinsically dive into the murky waters of *additionality*, attribution, and contribution.

From Safeguards to Change

The rather recent role of MDBs to improve corporate governance at country, sector, and company levels (Institutional development Impact) opens up a wider intervention avenue. As borrowers from public and private sectors have to comply with multiple MDB safeguards, the latter are reviewed in order to highlight their role toward institutional change, based on a wealth of evaluation studies, conducted by the MDBs. While those safeguards are not completely articulated or harmonized, the review addresses their general pattern, looking at the MDBs as a system, rather than individually.

The safeguards review was performed in the overall context of governance, looking at the broader relevant frameworks, including MDBs' respective environmental and social policies, as well as risk mitigation and the specific requirements to borrowers. Recently, most MDBs have been taking action to elaborate and enhance their environmental and social safeguard policies, with some of them making an effort to reflect relevant SDGs. While the IBRD is among the leaders in this field,[2] there are substantial differences among the institutions regarding the current state, as well as the plans to move forward. As safeguard policies have evolved with different focus and speeds, MDBs recognized the need to harmonize them within and vis-à-vis peers, reflecting regional and mandate differences.

MDBs' safeguard frameworks largely depend on the specific institutional governance and timing of adoption. While pioneering safeguard systems at IBRD are structured more horizontally as stand-alone policies, the regional and even more so the sub-regional MDBs adopted a more hierarchical approach, as they typically have an umbrella policy that consolidates environmental and social review procedures. Consequently, the IBRD framework consists of integrated requirements regarding both the lender and the borrowers, while most other MDBs have a more differentiated approach, better outlining the "change" factors (Table 7.1).

While safeguards are an important change driver, compliance costs may be reduced by harmonization among MDBs, for example a common minimum standards policy and templates. It is essential that harmonization does not turn into unification as project-specific needs require a tailored approach. Upon co-financing among MDBs, only one institution should address safeguards. The key is to articulate safeguards as investment assets, not just costs, particularly from the view-point of borrowers. This will require a concerted effort on the MDB side, as well as better use and coordination of relevant functions such as environmental/social, procurement, compliance, and evaluation. A further focus of independent evaluation functions on this matter—to reveal actual cost and benefits of compliance versus perceived, as well as offer more synergies—would be useful. Another possible measure of efficiency may include pooled institutional arrangements, regarding safeguards and related compliance. The use of common resources and getting uniform results may substantially reduce costs and risk of interpretation.

Technology and Development

The required paradigm shift involves novel socioeconomic concepts and approaches, going beyond the *Washington Consensus* and the complacency of success. New thinking is critical to restore the shaken fundamentals of *multilateralism* and *globalization*. This partly concerns the need to comprehend the impact of financial de-regulation that is associated with the latest financial turmoil, with a particular attention to the role of technological advancements. In this context, MDBs should regain the reputation of knowledge banks, demonstrating engagement with (financial) technologies and other advancements inspired by the private sector.

In the macroeconomic domain, it is important to refocus from growth to its more even and fair allocation, as growth alone, like investments alone, is no substitute of sustainable development. Widening disparities in otherwise

Table 7.1 MDBs' safeguards

Safeguard group	Potential	Recommendation
1. **Environmental and social**: MDBs differ substantially regarding the tailoring and applicability of Environmental and social (also referred as Environmental, Health and Safety), as well as other safeguards. Some MDBs have specific standards for private and public loans, others have generic frameworks. In some cases, MDBs allow application of national/borrower standards, mostly in public sector	Very high	Limit acceptance of borrowers' standards—allow only if MDBs do policy lending to improve those standards
2. ***Ecosystem services/natural habitats***: *Some MDBs* refer to ecosystem services in general, while others include those (e.g. "environmental flows") as critical indicator-based inputs regarding both environmental and social impacts	High	As above
3. **Climate change**: Often included in Environmental Assessments (e.g. greenhouse gas emissions and project footprint). A few MDBs use more specific and detailed requirements to both the institution and the borrower (assessing greenhouse gas emissions and the impacts of projects, as well as climate change on project viability)	Very high	Integration and explicit targeting. Focus on dedicated vehicles with mobilizing potential, for example Green Funds
4. ***Community health, safety and security***: *Large variations across MDBs. Some focus on specific issues such as* dam safety, but omit other key areas, for example infrastructure and equipment safety; hazardous materials management; emergency response; exposure to disease	Very high	Harmonize and broaden scope toward specific sectors and projects
5. **Corporate governance**: Most MDBs, particularly those dealing with the private sector. See Chaps. 4 and 5. Wide variations across MDBs. In many respects MDBs do not meet the standard they impose on borrowers and this is a serious credibility issue	Very high	Lead by example—enhance MDB governance and broaden outreach
6. ***Gender***: MDBs either have generic or project-focused gender policies. There are large variations, from elaborate policies to complete absence. Systematically integrated gender considerations (within overall safeguard requirements) are rare	Moderate	Integrate and provide guidance on applicability. Lead by example

(*continued*)

Table 7.1 (continued)

Safeguard group	Potential	Recommendation
7. ***Core labor rights***: *While MDBs focusing on public sector rarely have specific reference to* "core labor rights" or similar as defined by the International Labor Organization, those with private sector orientation often do so (International Financial Corporation, and European Bank for Reconstruction and Development). The covered issues include freedom of association; the right to organize and bargain collectively; discrimination in employment; wages and working conditions; retrenchment and contract, migrant and supply chain labor issues, and so on	Moderate	Elaborate further, particularly in context of corporate governance requirements to private sector
8. ***Human rights***: While many MDBs address this issue partially in the context of 5 (Corporate Governance) or 7 (Core labor rights), only one institution (European Investment Bank) has a cross-cutting policy requiring "human rights" compliance (as per the EU Charter of Fundamental Rights). Some MDBs refer to this issue between the lines by mentioning the responsibility of clients to respect human rights. The IBRD only refers to "human rights" in its Operational Policy OP 4.10, Indigenous Peoples. Nonetheless, it has recognized the relevance of human rights and is supportive of and encourages respect for them in its operations. MDBs seem constrained by the requirement to avoid political interference	Very high	Overcome controversy of addressing and articulating the issue
*9. **Exclusion lists**: These include activities and items that cannot be financed and often refer to* environmental and social safeguards. Not all MDBs have consolidated list with categorically excluded items, for example IBRD has a qualified prohibition on tobacco projects in a separate operational policy (OP 4.76. Tobacco) and excludes other items via its procurement policy. Most MDBs have formal Exclusion or Prohibition lists as part of their environmental and social safeguard policies that go well beyond the products and activities excluded by the IBRD's procurement policy	High	Harmonize and elaborate toward project levels, reflecting context

growing economies can and do cause turmoil and undermine social fabrics. The key issues are not just income and wealth inequalities, but mostly the inequality of opportunities and access to basic resources, including education, mobility, clean air, self-determination, and decent work—to mention a few. Such growing inequalities fuel rapidly the risks of populism (promising simplistic quick fixes to complex and often exaggerated problems) and in turn, conflict.

MDBs have to think big and long term, open to learn from the most curious and bold entrepreneurs and philanthropists—to reshape the environment they are created to improve upon. The suggested governance principles could be combined with a variety of innovation approaches, provided that the reforms are participatory and inspire engagement of human capital with highest relevant values, rather than trigger resistance as often happened so far.

MDBs should focus on the wide range of opportunities associated with the digital revolution. The new wave of automation, digital information, and the democratization of knowledge trigger unprecedented potential to affect many relevant sectors, including healthcare, communication, education, energy, and so on. A number of technological advancements, including genomics, energy storage, and automation are expected to drive major economic and social transformations in the future. The McKinsey Global Institute estimated a potential economic impact between $14 trillion and $33 trillion a year, reaching 1/3 of global GDP by 2025 (McKinsey 2013).

MDBs need to respond to the tech-driven society accordingly, both internally and externally (through their operations). This implies a refocusing to cultivate and use new forms of knowledge, toward promoting innovation and catalyzing economic development. Reflecting the challenges and opportunities of the digital revolution as agents of change within innovation ecosystems, MDBs should consider two main intervention avenues:

- ***Support entrepreneurship, partner with the private sector, fostering inclusion and diversity***: MDBs should seek new forms to foster entrepreneurship, inspiring and nurturing innovative thinking within and outside. Many startups already demonstrate an ample ability to trigger social change, involving social entrepreneurship and other novel ventures. The MDB mandates require an application of knowledge at the intersections of diverse disciplines, to deliver social and economic accelerators. MDBs should explore new partnerships with leading companies, foundations, and other institutions, relevant to the development agenda of the rapidly changing world. It is critical to broaden the diversity of resources and perspectives into the core MDB activities. Expanding the opportunity for diverse voices and ideas, from governance to technology, is necessary to keep the pace with the tech-driven society and economy. Expanding the pool of technologically diverse human capital is critical for the future of technological innovation.

- **Address the nexus of technology and development**: While technology does not automatically benefit society, MDBs have to reveal and explore possible applications toward development. This requires a broad interaction with thinkers, philosophers, policy experts, economists, and cognitive scientists and sociologists, to connect technology with development finance. A particular focus on the effects of technology on increase in inequality is inevitable, as the new landscape implies a growing gap in earnings between the best educated and the least educated. Labor economists predict that the rapid innovation will continue to exacerbate inequality and social tensions. The rapidly changing job market requires a prompt response in education and vocational training, as qualification requirements are changing faster than the models of education worldwide. Preparing for the unprecedented shifts in job profiles will be a critical investment to foster development in due time. Assessment and adoption of relevant (financial) technology, for example block-chain, smart contracts, distributed work spaces, machine learning, and so on, should be explored within MDBs as well as in their operations. Getting ready for the future will require immense intellectual resources and the capability to devote them to the MDBs' mandates—toward addressing the challenge of technologies, ensuring that the new economy leaves no one behind. While leaders in industry, government, and education engage on the future of work and other important topics at the latest World Economic Forum in Davos, MDBs should adequately address these challenges and the opportunities they present. To deliver their mandates, MDBs should nurture new talent in their sectors and regions to balance opportunities in the new economy.

The MDBs are unique institutions, but bear the legacy load of outdated governance. Their know-how in linking finance with reform of policies should evolve in line with needs—toward strengthening project design and evaluation (*additionality*), to improve specialization, focus, and effectiveness. MDBs should seek new institutional arrangements to provide international public goods and mitigate cross-border externalities.

A better division of labor among the MDBs will require coordination and open dialogue. In this regard, *sub-regional* institutions can naturally focus on what they already provide best—cover specific regional needs, themes, and the private sector, using limited capital and higher leverage. Likewise, regional MDBs should be differentiated from global ones, by looking to less policy and more cross-border issues, building upon their leadership in financial leverage.

A possible avenue for greater focus and effectiveness could be the shift from policy-based lending toward the promotion and demonstration of higher standards (based on the safeguards and governance principles addressed) and the provision of other relevant international public goods. While MDBs are generally not equipped to provide international public goods on their own, they could broaden their cooperation in strategic partnerships with other regional and international organizations, as they have done with the OECD on corporate governance. This should be addressed in the context of newly emerging needs and opportunities within the global development agenda, implying respective evolution of the roles and capabilities of the MDBs.

Notes

1. http://www.oecd.org/dac/evaluation/daccriteriaforevaluatingdevelopmentassistance.htm.
2. The IBRD issued its latest full Operational Policy related to safeguards (Physical Cultural Resources, http://web.worldbank.org/archive/website01541/WEB/0__-1123.HTM), in 2006. Most other MDBs have revised their safeguard policies accordingly, often introducing additional operational requirements regarding environmental and social impacts and risks arising with lending. Some of these additional requirements include material provisions beyond the IBRD's safeguard policies.

References

BSBC. 2017. *Better Business Better World, The Report of the Business and Sustainable Development Commission*, London. http://report.businesscommission.org/uploads/BetterBiz-BetterWorld_170215_012417.pdf.

Gable, Susanna, Hans Lofgren, and Israel Osorio Rodarte. 2015. *Trajectories for Sustainable Development Goals: Framework and Country Applications*. Washington, DC: World Bank. https://openknowledge.worldbank.org/handle/10986/23122.

GI Hub (G20). 2017. *Forecasting Infrastructure Investment Needs and Gaps*. https://outlook.gihub.org/.

McKinsey Global Institute. 2013. *Disruptive Technologies: Advances That Will Transform Life, Business, and the Global Economy*. https://www.mckinsey.com/~/media/McKinsey/Business%20Functions/McKinsey%20Digital/Our%20Insights/Disruptive%20technologies/MGI_Disruptive_technologies_Full_report_May2013.ashx.

OECD/DAC. 2017. *Development Aid Rises Again in 2016 But Flows to Poorest Countries Dip, Paris*. http://www.oecd.org/dac/development-aid-rises-again-in-2016-but-flows-to-poorest-countries-dip.htm.

UNCTAD. 2015. *World Investment Report 2014*, Geneva. http://unctad.org/en/PublicationsLibrary/wir2014_en.pdf.

World Bank. 2018. *Climate Change Could Force Over 140 Million to Migrate Within Countries by 2050: World Bank Report*. Washington, DC: World Bank. http://www.worldbank.org/en/news/press-release/2018/03/19/climate-change-could-force-over-140-million-to-migrate-within-countries-by-2050-world-bank-report.

Glossary

Additionality *A* core principle at virtually all MDBs, stipulating that their operations should be *additional* to what is already available in the market. It implies that MDBs should not compete with (or crowd out) market participants (banks) as their role is to offset market and institutional deficiencies by offering unavailable products and services. While *additionality* is a broad concept, it generally has two aspects: (1) financial, for example offering of products with certain financial terms that are not available (e.g. longer loan maturity, broader risk coverage, etc.); and (2) non-financial such as know-how, advise, honest brokerage, and enhanced social, environmental, and other development features of the financed operations.

AfDB The African Development Bank was established in 1964. Its membership includes 80 shareholders and its headquarters are in Abidjan, Côte d'Ivoire.

AIIB The Asian Infrastructure Investment Bank was established in 2015. Its membership includes 64 shareholders and its headquarters are in Beijing, China.

AsBD The Asian Development Bank was established in 1966. Its membership includes 67 shareholders and its headquarters are in Manila, Philippines.

Authorized Capital The total capital approved to be available to be ***subscribed***.

BADEA The Arab Bank for Economic Development in Africa was established in 1973. Its membership includes 18 shareholders and its headquarters are in Khartoum, Republic of the Sudan.

Basel Committee See BCBS.

Basel I, II, and III Standards The Basel II accord (standard), maintained by ***BCBS*** applies a three pillar concept: Pillar 1—minimum capital requirements (addressing risk); Pillar 2—supervisory review; and Pillar 3—market discipline. The Basel I accord addressed only parts of these pillars. The latest Basel III accord further specifies capital and risk requirements of banks—the minimum ***Tier 1 capital*** ratio is 10.5%. It is calculated by dividing the bank's ***Tier 1 capital*** by its total risk-based assets. ***Tier 2 capital*** is supplementary as it is less reliable than ***Tier 1***

I. U. Delikanli et al., *Multilateral Development Banks*,
https://doi.org/10.1007/978-3-319-91524-1

capital. In 2017 the Basel III accord set the minimum total capital ratio at 12.5%, which implies that the minimum ***Tier 2 capital*** ratio is 2%, as the ***Tier 1*** minimum is 10.5%. See: BCBS, Basel Committee on Banking Supervision, *Basel III Finalising post-crisis reforms*, December 2017; BCBS, Basel Committee on Banking Supervision, *Basel III leverage ratio framework and disclosure requirements*, Basel 2014 (updated 2017); BCBS, Basel Committee on Banking Supervision, *Basel III: A global regulatory framework for more resilient b anks and banking systems*, June 2011, www.bis.org/publ/bcbs189.pdf; BCBS, Basel Committee on Banking Supervision, *Consultative Document Revisions to the Basel III leverage ratio framework*, April 2016, https://www.bis.org/bcbs/publ/d365.pdf; BCBS, *Basel II: International Convergence of Capital Measurement and Capital Standards: a Revised Framework, June 2004*, https://www.bis.org/publ/bcbs107.pdf.

Basel Principles on Corporate Governance See ***OECD/G20 Principles on Corporate Governance***. The 13 Basel Principles on CG of banks address the following matters, in order to ensure quality of bank governance: *(1) Board's overall responsibilities; (2) Board qualifications and composition; (3) Board's own structure and practices; (4) Senior management; (5) Governance of group structures; (6) Risk management function; (7) Risk identification, monitoring, and controlling; (8) Risk communication; (9) Compliance; (10) Internal audit; (11) Compensation; (12) Disclosure and transparency; (13) The role of supervisors. Published by* ***BCBS****, (2015) as Guidelines: Corporate governance principles for banks, Basel Committee on Banking Supervision, Bank for International Settlements, Basel,* https://www.bis.org/bcbs/publ/d328.pdf.

BCBS Basel Committee for Banking Supervision.

Bilateral Having two sides, in the international context—involving two countries. In contrast to ***Multilateral***, where at least three parties/countries are involved.

BoD Board of Directors.

BoG Board of Governors (the highest governance authority at an ***MDB***).

BRICS A grouping acronym that refers to Brazil, Russia, India, China, and South Africa.

BSTDB The Black Sea Trade and Development Bank was established in 1997. Its membership includes 11 shareholders and its headquarters are in Thessaloniki, Greece.

CABEI The Central American Bank for Economic Integration was established in 1960. Its membership includes 13 shareholders, and it has currently two headquarters, one in Tegucigalpa, Honduras, and another one in San Salvador, El Salvador.

CAF The Development Bank of Latin America (formerly referred to as the Corporación Andina de Fomento) was established in 1970. Its membership includes 32 shareholders, and its headquarters are in Caracas, Venezuela.

Callable Capital To assure the MDBs more advantageous access to the international markets, their shareholder countries subscribe most of their contributions in the form of *callable capital*, a commitment by each shareholder to make additional capital available, only if and when it is required (*called*) to avoid default on the MDB's borrowing or guarantee. Its use is limited to pay off bondholders if the institution has no liquidity.

Capital Increase A new funding plan, to which member countries "subscribe" when they make their contributions (in some cases such as concessional MDB programs, the term is "replenishment"). This includes subscription to the *initial* capital, *voluntary capital increases, special capital increases (e.g. when adopting new members)* and *general capital increases.*

Catalyzing Private financing triggered by the development impact of an MDB operation or other activity (e.g. an improved investment climate, risk sharing, better infrastructure, new skills, etc.). It includes ***Co-financing and Mobilization.***

CDB The Caribbean Development Bank was established in 1969. Its membership includes 28 shareholders, and its headquarters are Wildey, St. Michael, Barbados.

CEDB The Council of Europe Development Bank was established in 1956. Its membership includes 41 shareholders and its headquarters are in Paris, France.

CG Corporate Governance.

Concessional Lending Provision of loans at soft terms, partly or fully subsidized, not charging the market interest rates and/or other fees. See Sound Banking Principles as they are opposite to Concessional financing.

Conditionality See ***Safeguards.***

Constitution See ***Establishing Agreement.***

Corporate Governance Corporate Governance (CG) emerged as a term in the 70s in USA, in the context of efforts to impose responsible and transparent governance of corporations, to prevent abuse of the interests of shareholders and investors. The term was further conceptualized by Adrian Cadbury, President of the Committee for Corporate Governance Financial Aspects in Great Britain, who published the Report of the Committee…, known as the Cadbury Code (1992). The Code is a key reference on the financial aspects of governance, defining CG as the system by which companies are managed and controlled.

Credit Rating A credit rating quantifies a borrower's overall creditworthiness to pay its obligations. It is assigned by ***Credit Rating Agencies.*** While MDBs are not obliged to seek credit ratings they do so in order to facilitate borrowing from international markets.

Credit Rating Agency A company that provides ***Credit Ratings.***

CRO Chief Risk Officer.

Development Denoting the concept of ***International Development***—also referred to as ***Global Development.*** A broad concept concerning level of socioeconomic development, categorizing countries as developed, developing, and least developed, based on many schools and respective criteria. It is often largely synonymous with economic development but recently broadened to a multi-disciplinary context of human development, competitiveness, quality of life, and so on. International development is typically associated with institutions and policies that arose after the Second World War, with a focus on alleviating poverty and improving living conditions in previously colonized countries. The concept is also covered by academic and other programs of research focusing on but not limited to global inequalities, ranging from their causes, characteristics, and possible solutions.

International Development Studies are very multidisciplinary as they examine a broad range of topics like poverty, conflict, security, social and gender inequality, sustainability, education, the environment, and the relationship between local, national, and global processes.

Donor Country Non-borrowing member shareholder of an ***MDB***. In a broader context, a country that offers funds/aid for development, bilaterally or via an MDB.

EADB The East African Development Bank was established in 1967. Its membership includes 13 shareholders, and its headquarters are in Kampala, Uganda.

EBRD The European Bank for Reconstruction and Development was established in 1991. Its membership includes 67 shareholders, and its headquarters are in London, United Kingdom.

EDB The Eurasian Development Bank was established in 2006. Its membership includes six shareholders, and its headquarters are in Moscow, Russia.

EIB The European Investment Bank was established in 1958. Its membership includes 28 shareholders and its headquarters are in Luxembourg.

Equity Equity (of MDB shareholders) is composed of capital, retained earnings, and fair value gains on available-for-sale equity investments.

Establishing Agreement The Agreement for Establishing an MDB, also referred to as the MDB ***Constitution***, is the highest level of self-regulation rules governing the functioning of the MDB and the role of its shareholders and governing bodies such as the ***BoG/BoD***, as well as all ***privileges and immunities*** of the institution and its staff. It is a multilateral agreement signed and ratified by the member countries of the MDB.

ETDB The ECO Trade and Development Bank was established in 2005 (ECO stands for Economic Cooperation Organization). Its membership includes ten shareholders and its headquarters are in Istanbul, Turkey.

Extraterritorial MDBs have extraterritoriality of the international premises, as well as immunity from national courts on multiple matters, including employment issues. MDBs are also immune from legal suit (known as "jurisdictional immunity", sometimes raising interpretations but otherwise typical). See Privileges and Immunities.

Financial Leverage See ***Leverage***.

G20 **G20** (or G-20 or Group of Twenty) is an international forum for the governments and central bank governors founded in 1999 and gaining increasing importance. The G20 discuss policy for the promotion of international financial stability, seeking to address issues that go beyond the responsibilities of any organization. Membership consists of 19 individual countries plus the European Union (EU, represented by the European Commission and by the European Central Bank). The G20 economies account for around 85% of the gross world product, 80% of world trade, two-thirds of the world population, and about half of the world land area.

Gearing (ratio) See ***Leverage***.

Global Development See ***Development***.

Global MDB MDB lending to several continents, covering them almost entirely (this categorization is relative, as there are overlapping and border cases, see Global and Regional).

Governance See ***Corporate Governance.***

Hard Loan A loan provided on the basis of ***Sound Banking Principles*** in line with market pricing and rates, as opposed to ***concessional*** or ***soft*** loan.

IDB The Inter-American Development Bank was established in 1959. Its membership includes 48 shareholders and its headquarters are in Washington, DC, United States.

IFAD The International Fund for Agricultural Development, established in 1977. Its membership includes 176 shareholders and its headquarters are in Rome, Italy.

IIB The International Investment Bank, established in 1970. Its membership includes nine shareholders, and its headquarters are in Moscow, Russia.

Immunity See Privileges and Immunities.

Independent Evaluation Function (Department) It is very specific for MDBs and provides independent rigorous ex-post evaluation of the projects, programs, policies, governance, and activities, as well as the overall performance of the MDB. It serves two main functions, essential for the sound governance: *accountability and learning*. It is an institution within the institution with the challenging task to interface policy and reality by speaking truth to power. Independence from operations and management is essential to provide impartial, credible evaluation to improve the performance of the institution.

International Development See ***Development.***

IsDB The Islamic Development Bank was established in 1975. Its membership includes 57 countries and its headquarters are in Jeddah, Saudi Arabia.

Leverage ***Financial leverage*** (known as *gearing* in the United Kingdom and Australia) represents use of borrowed funds to invest in assets, typical for banking and non-banking lending institutions. The rationale is that the after tax income from the asset (e.g. loans or equity) will exceed the cost of borrowing. Normally, the lending institution has its own limit, based on regulations and internal policy, regarding the level of risk it is prepared to take. The latter determines the limit on leverage, as well as other measures such as type and value of collateral (security) for the borrowing and lending. For MDBs, leverage relates to ***Mobilization*** and ***Additonality***. Banking institutions (but not MDBs) are subject to many regulatory requirements, including leverage limits, as set by the ***BCBS*** and respective national central banks. This is because leverage involves substantial individual and systemic risk as it enables both gains and losses to be multiplied. Leveraging may result in a loss in two ways: when borrowing costs exceed the income from lending, or when the lending becomes impaired and non-collectible.

Liquidity Liquidity describes the degree to which a financial asset can be quickly bought or sold in the market without affecting the asset's price. Cash is treated as the most liquid asset, while real estate, or fine art, is not considered liquid. Accounting liquidity measures the ease with which a company can meet their financial obligations with the liquid assets available to them. There are several ratios that express accounting liquidity.

MDB Multilateral Development Bank, a ***Development*** Institution with special ***extraterritorial*** status, established by three or more countries (multilateral), to finance and promote socioeconomic development in specific sectors and regions. While bearing the name of a Bank, these institutions are not meeting the definition of a bank and are not subject to any regulation and supervision, other than their own *self-regulation.*

Mobilization A private financing on commercial terms due to direct involvement of an MDB (involving a mandate letter or other evidence of direct involvement; it does not include sponsor financing but includes guarantees on the loan or equity). See ***Private Co-financing.***

Multilateral/Multilateralism In broad terms, multilateralism means international governance, or governance by many parties. It is considered more democratic, opposite to bilateral as the latter is assumed to enhance the leverage of the powerful over the weak, tending to increase international conflict. It implies coordinating national policies in groups of three or more states. Multilateralism as membership in international institutions binds powerful nations and discourages *unilateralism* by giving small countries a voice and influence that they could not otherwise exercise. Small countries group together to collectively bind a larger country. Likewise, multilateralism allows a great power to influence another great power, as seeking control through bilateral ties could be costly. International organizations, such as the United Nations (UN) and MDBs are multilateral in nature. The main advocates of multilateralism have traditionally been the middle powers, such as Canada, Australia, Switzerland, and the Nordic countries. Larger countries often act unilaterally, while smaller ones have little direct power in international affairs except their participation in the United Nations and to some extent in MDBs. Multilateral institutions are not imposed on countries, but are created and accepted by them to increase their ability to pursue their own interests through the coordination. They serve as frameworks that constrain opportunistic behavior and encourage coordination.

NDB The New Development Bank (formerly referred to as the BRICS Development Bank) was established in 2014. Its membership includes five shareholders, and its headquarters are in Shanghai, China.

Negative List A list of activities that are not eligible for financing by MDBs, typically including business dealing with alcohol, tobacco, armament, nuclear energy, and so on. This is related to the MDBs' ***Safeguards.***

NIB The Nordic Investment Bank was established in 1976. Its membership includes eight shareholders, and its headquarters are in Helsinki, Finland.

OBS Off-balance sheet (OBS) items represent implicit obligations such as credit and liquidity commitments, guarantees, and standby letters of credit.

OECD Organization for Economic Co-operation and Development has the mission to promote policies that will improve the economic and social well-being of people around the world. It provides a forum for governments to work together and share experiences and seek solutions to common problems. OECD sets international standards on a wide range of issues, from agriculture and tax to the safety of chemicals.

OECD/G20 Principles on Corporate Governance Upon the World Bank's recommendation, in 1999 the OECD issued a milestone report of guiding CG principles, updated in 2004 and 2015 when the CG principles were formally adopted by OECD and G20 (G20/OECD Principles of Corporate Governance, 2015). This is the sole internationally recognized reference on CG, aiming to establish a voluntary framework of standards applicable to various types of companies worldwide. While these standards are not directly aimed at public sector institutions and MDBs in particular, they serve as a guiding point. The OECD Guidelines and Standards on CG, such as those on Multinational Enterprises (2011), were developed in cooperation with governments, international organizations, and the private sector. They refer to the six G20/OECD Principles of non-binding nature, outlined and promoted by the OECD to enhance regulatory frameworks in its member countries and beyond. The OECD cooperates with international organizations including MDBs, as well as with regional organizations and private sector toward enhancing and disseminating the respective Principles, to protect shareholders' rights and values. The six OECD/G20 principles (2015) were adapted by the Basel Committee—see **Basel Principles on Corporate Governance**.

Paid-up and Paid-in Capital The MDBs' shareholders subscribe some of their capital contributions as *paid-in capital*, in a fixed ratio (often ranging from 5 to 50%) with the callable share. The difference between the *paid-up* and *paid-in* shares reflects the shares to be issued on payment of subsequent installments. Thus the paid-up include the commitment to pay-in, while the *paid-in is what is actually paid already*, according to the agreed payment schedule.

Preferred Creditor Status A special status of virtually all MDBs, implying that the debt to an MDB should remain due even if legislators impose restrictions such as foreign exchange or capital controls. Conventional financial institutions do not have such privilege and are exposed to risks of capital or foreign exchange controls and limitations.

Private Co-Financing Financing from private sources (including sponsor and third parties) committed along a specific MDB financing, including ***Mobilization***.

Privileges and Immunities (of MDB) Privileges are exemptions from substantive law of a state, while *immunities* are mostly exemptions from the administrative, adjudicatory, or executive powers of a state. Typical MDB privileges are partial exemptions from some areas of domestic law (e.g. taxation, customs, foreign exchange controls, immigration). An example of a key MDB privilege is the exemption from any direct taxation for the MDB itself and its employees (indirect taxes are often subject to reimbursement).

PTA The Eastern and Southern African Trade and Development Bank or the Preferential Trade Area Bank, established in 1985. Its membership includes 31 shareholders, and its headquarters are in Bujumbura, Burundi.

Regional MDB MDB lending to just one continent, covering it almost entirely (this categorization is relative, as there are overlapping and border cases, see Global and Regional).

Risk Weight (of assets) Risk-weight of assets is used to determine the minimum amount of capital that must be held by banks and other institutions to reduce the risk of insolvency. The capital requirement is based on a risk assessment for each type of bank asset. For example, a loan secured by a letter of credit or unsecured is considered riskier than a loan secured with liquid assets of high value, or a mortgage loan secured with collateral. The ***Basel Committee*** applies a 0% risk weight to banks' exposures to MDBs that fulfill certain criteria.

Safeguards Also known as ***Conditionality***. An MDB system of policies and requirements applicable to the MDBs and their borrowers, aiming to set and comply with high standards on various matters such as environment and safety, procurement, corporate governance, and so on. The goal is often referred as an important aspect of development objectives, for example as Institutional development Impact. As borrowers from public and private sectors have to comply with multiple MDB safeguards, the latter constitute an important instrument of achieving the development mandate of an MDB. The safeguards are in process of coordination and harmonization among most MDBs.

SDG See ***Sustainable Development Goals***.

Self-Regulation MDBs are self-regulated institutions as they establish their own rules that function as extraterritorial legislation, outside the scope of central bank and other authorities.

Sound Banking Principles Same as ***hard loans***—all financing operations should be financially sustainable and priced in line with the market, as opposed to ***soft*** or ***concessional loans***.

Sub-Regional MDB MDB with a focus on a specific region that is smaller than a continent (this categorization is relative, as there are overlapping and border cases, see Global and Regional).

Subscribed Capital A portion of the authorized capital that is actually allocated (*subscribed*) to shareholders, based on their commitment to contribute it as ***paid-in*** and ***callable*** capital.

Sustainable Development Goals The United Nations 17 Sustainable Development Goals (***SDG***s), to be reached by 2030, as agreed worldwide in 2015. These set of goals aim to end poverty, protect the planet, and ensure prosperity for all as part of a new sustainable development agenda. Each goal has specific targets to be achieved over 15 years.

Tier 1 Capital BCBS defines Tier 1 capital as shareholders' equity and retained earnings. It measures a bank's financial strength and is used to absorb losses without ceasing bank's operations. Under the Basel III accord, the minimum Tier 1 capital ratio is 10.5%. It is calculated by dividing the bank's Tier 1 capital by its total risk-based assets.

Tier 2 Capital Includes revaluation reserves, hybrid capital instruments and subordinated term debt, general loan-loss reserves, and undisclosed reserves. Tier 2 capital is supplementary as it is less reliable than Tier 1 capital. In 2017 the Basel III accord set the minimum total capital ratio at 12.5%, which implies that the minimum Tier 2 capital ratio is 2%, as the Tier 1 minimum is 10.5%.

Treasury Function or department, as well as activity of a bank, focused on attracting external resources and financial liquidity management. As MDBs are neither profit-maximizing nor distributing shareholder dividends by definition and exist to fulfill their development mandates, their treasury is devoted to ensure success of the core activities, rather than be a stand-alone business line.

WADB The West African Development Bank, established in 1973. Its membership includes 17 shareholders, and its headquarters are in Lomé, Togo.

Washington Consensus A set of ten economic policy prescriptions considered to constitute the "standard" reform package promoted by the institutions based in Washington, DC, such as the IMF, the World Bank, and the US Treasury Department. The term was first used in 1989 by English economist John Williamson. The prescriptions include policies in such areas as macroeconomic stabilization, economic opening with respect to trade and investment, including privatization, and the expansion of market forces within the economy. The phrase Washington Consensus is used widely in a second, broader sense, to refer to a more general orientation toward a strongly market-based approach (often described as market fundamentalism or neoliberalism).

World Bank A family of five international financial institutions, including the International Bank for Reconstruction and Development (IBRD), the International Finance Corporation (IFC), the International Development Association (IDA), the Multilateral Investment Guarantee Agency (MIGA), and the International Center for Settlement of Investment Disputes (ICSID).

Index[1]

[1] Note: Page numbers followed by ‘n’ refer to notes.

I. U. Delikanli et al., *Multilateral Development Banks*,
https://doi.org/10.1007/978-3-319-91524-1

This book provides a comprehensive overview and insight of virtually all multilateral institutions involved in lending for international socio-economic development. The analysis covers twenty-five MDBs globally by classifying them in three groups based on geographical lending outreach. Unlike similar books and articles, which treat MDBs as banks, this book offers a novel perspective by addressing the specifics of multilateral lending institutions, revealing multiple aspects of their operations and going beyond the "bank" concept towards "knowledge bank," "change agent," and even "benchmark setter."

The book reflects on the key role of most MDBs in inspiring and advancing sustainable economic development through transfer of knowledge and funding towards addressing multiple global challenges for the benefit of practitioners, consultants, government officials, borrowers, and researchers interested in MDBs.

Ihsan Ugur Delikanli served as CEO and Chairman of the Board of Directors of the Black Sea Trade and Development Bank (BSTDB, a Multilateral Development Bank, based in Greece), from 2014-2018. His experience includes various senior banking positions, e.g. Executive Vice President at an investment bank, Vice Chairman and Head of Department at the Banking Regulation and Supervision Agency of Turkey, member of the Turkish Accounting Standards Board, and representative at the Basel Committee on Banking Supervision. He holds an MBA in Financial Management from University of Exeter, UK, and PhD in Accounting and Finance from Baskent University, Ankara, Turkey.

Todor Dimitrov has worked as Head of the Independent Evaluation Office of the Black Sea Trade and Development Bank, since 2000. He has 30 years of experience in international development and evaluation, covering a wide range of countries, sectors, and institutions including the European Commission, the World Bank, think tanks, etc. He holds an MA degree in Economics from the University of the State of New York, USA.

Roena Agolli completed a cooperation as a Guest Researcher with the Independent Evaluation Office of the Black Sea Trade and Development Bank. Previously, she has been a research scholarship holder at the University of Sheffield, UK, and has served as a research assistant at the International Faculty of the University of Sheffield-CITY College, Greece. She specializes in banking and finance.

palgrave
macmillan

The manufacturer's authorised representative in the EU is Springer Nature Customer Service Centre GmbH, Europaplatz 3, 69115 Heidelberg, Germany. If you have any concerns regarding our products, please contact ProductSafety@springernature.com

Printed and bound by CPI Group (UK) Ltd, Croydon, CR0 4YY
05/10/2026
02228128-0020